MAKING RACE IN THE COURTROOM

Making Race in the Courtroom

The Legal Construction of Three Races in Early New Orleans

Kenneth R. Aslakson

NEW YORK UNIVERSITY PRESS

New York and London

NEW YORK UNIVERSITY PRESS
New York and London
www.nyupress.org

References to Internet websites (URLs) were accurate at the time of writing.
Neither the author nor New York University Press is responsible for URLs that
may have expired or changed since the manuscript was prepared.

Library of Congress Cataloging-in-Publication Data
Aslakson, Kenneth R., author.
Making race in the courtroom : the legal construction of three races in early New Orleans /
Kenneth R. Aslakson.
pages cm Includes bibliographical references and index.
ISBN 978-0-8147-2431-6 (hardback)
1. Free African Americans—Legal status, laws, etc.—Louisiana—History—19th century.
2. Louisiana—History—1803-1865. 3. Louisiana Purchase—Social aspects. I. Title.
KFL411.5.A34A83   2014
342.763'350873—dc23   2014015123

New York University Press books are printed on acid-free paper,
and their binding materials are chosen for strength and durability.
We strive to use environmentally responsible suppliers and materials
to the greatest extent possible in publishing our books.

Manufactured in the United States of America

10 9 8 7 6 5 4 3 2 1

Also available as an ebook

For my parents

CONTENTS

ACKNOWLEDGMENTS

It is my great pleasure to be able to formally recognize and thank the many people who have not only helped me to write this book but also made possible my dream life as an academic.

First and foremost I would like to thank my family, without whose support and encouragement I would never have been able to complete this project. My mother, a high school English teacher, has read many versions of the manuscript over the years, correcting my grammar and helping me to clarify my prose. I consulted with her over and over again regarding how to best express the ideas and arguments of this book. From her influence, more than anyone else's, came my desire to be an educator and a student. My father was less involved in the writing of the manuscript but no less important to its completion. He, more than anybody, provided me the opportunity to pursue the life of the mind. My two sisters, Elizabeth Aslakson Mathis and Carla Aslakson-Yarnal, have supported, challenged, and inspired me, in different ways and at different times, throughout my life. Beth, my older sister, has a very logical mind and has helped me to grapple with some of the more difficult theoretical concepts challenging me. Carla, two years younger than I, serves as a model of courage and virtue by living according to the selfless principles she espouses.

A great many friends and mentors have also made it possible for me to complete this project. These include influential teachers such as Carolyn Huff, Diana Jernigan, Weldon Crowley, Leonard Giesecke, Ken Roberts, Winston Davis, David Sokolow, Michael Tiger, and David Silver. I am especially grateful to Dr. Jan Dawson, my favorite professor at Southwestern University. She is the reason I pursued a PhD in history. These friends also include former classmates Pete Kennedy, Sarah

Rushing, Doug Wipff, Russell Kirksey, Kerry Dunn, Scott Pass, Paul Nie-meyer, and Craig Donahue; mentors such as E. Eldridge Goins Jr., John Rosenberg, Jim Morris, Hance Burrow; and those who have encouraged me and shared parts of their lives with me while I struggled through this arduous process—the Thorne family, Lawrence, Reesa, and Logan, and the Gorsuch family, Rob, Gwynn, and Claire. And, of course, thank you Julia Hormes for being there at the book's completion.

Three long-time friends in particular, whom I respect and admire a great deal, deserve further mention. Rob Gorsuch has been my close friend for more than forty-five years, almost all of our lives. He also provided me a quiet space to think and write during critical times as the manuscript was coming together. Chris Albi has been a great friend since early on in graduate school when I discovered that he is also a former lawyer. Our common interest in the ways that legal institutions interact with the historical process allows us to justify a round of golf as an exercise of the mind. When I met Lawrence Thorne in Mrs. Gibson's class almost forty years ago, we immediately bonded and have been best friends ever since. Lawrence keeps me both grounded and excited about life's possibilities at the same time. I have a great deal of respect for these great friends and seek the same from them.

I would also like to thank another friend, the city of New Orleans, for being such an interesting place to study and having so many fas-cinating stories to tell. Many knowledgeable and helpful archivists, librarians, and curators make the telling of the history of New Orleans possible. The people at the Historic New Orleans Collection, the New Orleans Notarial Archives, the Louisiana Supreme Court, and the vari-ous libraries of Tulane University and the University of Texas have all been very helpful in my research efforts. I owe the most gratitude to the people at the New Orleans Public Library, especially Irene Wain-wright, Wayne Everard, and Greg Osborn. With few financial resources, the people of the NOPL have maintained one of the richest collections of archives on the history of New Orleans that any scholar could find. Their work and assistance have been invaluable to me.

Thanks to the seemingly endless inspiration the city provides and the work of these curators, there is plenty to share among the large and growing cadre of historians of New Orleans. These scholars include, but are not limited to, Hans Baade, Caryn Cosse Bell, Warren Billings,

Patricia Brady, Carl Brasseaux, Emily Clark, Craig Colton, Glenn Conrad, Thomas Dargo, Mark Fernandez, Virginia Gould, Gwendolyn Midlo Hall, Kimberly Hanger, Thomas Ingersoll, Ari Kelman, Paul F. Lachance, Alecia Long, Reid Mitchell, Judith Schafer, Mark Souther, and Daniel Usner. These women and men, some of whom I know personally and others whom I admire through their work, have broadened and deepened my understanding of the city so as to make the writing of this book much easier.

Four scholars of New Orleans in particular have been especially helpful. Nathalie Dessens's early work on the influence of the refugees of the Haitian Revolution on New Orleans shaped the topic of this book in the early stages of my research. Having only recently gotten to know Nathalie herself, I am happy to learn that she is just as good of a person as she is a scholar. I met Jennifer Spear in the archives when she was near completing her book and I was just beginning mine. She encouraged me to pursue publication and offered sound advice. A little later, Emily Landau, over the course of many conversations, helped me see race relations in New Orleans in a broader historical context. Finally, I owe a special debt of gratitude to Lawrence Powell, one of the distinguished scholars who reviewed my manuscript for the press. His comments and suggestions made this book much better than it otherwise would have been.

I have also received a great deal of assistance from other scholars who do not specialize in the history of the lower Mississippi valley but are just plain smart and thoughtful. From the University of Texas I want to especially thank Julie Hardwick, Neil Kamil, Bob Olwell, Willy Forbath, Judy Coffin, Jorge Canizares Esguerra, Kevin Roberts, Tim Buckner, Sara Fanning, Lissa Boletino, and Karl Brown. Thank you as well to all the faculty of Union College, especially those in the History Department, and more specifically to Melinda Lawson, Andy Foroughi, and Bob Wells for reading and commenting on various portions of my manuscript. Allison Games, Lauren Benton, and Laurent Dubois also read portions of the manuscript and/or discussed its basic arguments with me. Matt Childs and Carolyn Eastman not only read many different versions of the manuscript and helped me to build upon and structure my arguments but also have been great mentors.

Finally, my deepest gratitude goes to my adviser, Jim Sidbury. When he took me on as his student many years ago, I already had a good sense of how important he would be as an adviser. His knowledge of the field, his insightful comments in seminars, and his careful readings of his students' work made his attributes as an academic adviser obvious. But as he continues to read my work, offer constructive criticism and encouragement, and serve as a source of inspiration, I have come to regard him as not only a great mentor but also a close friend. I look forward to many more years of good times and great conversations.

All the people I have mentioned here have helped me to make the publication of this book possible. Yet, in the end, the people of NYU Press made that possibility a reality. Debbie Gershenowitz first introduced me to the press several years ago, and I became impressed with its attentiveness and honesty. Clara Platter has fostered this good relationship, and Constance Grady helped out more and more as we got closer to publication.

Thank you all.

Introduction

Men make their own history, but they do not make it as
they please; they do not make it under self-selected circumstances, but under circumstances existing already, given and
transmitted from the past.
—Karl Marx, "Eighteenth Brumaire of Louis Bonaparte"
(May 1852)

After they were found guilty of larceny by a New Orleans jury in 1849,
Henry Levy and Jacob Dreyfous appealed their conviction to the Louisiana Supreme Court, claiming that the trial court erred in allowing the
testimony of a free man of color. There was no rule of evidence that
explicitly stated free people of color were competent to testify against
whites in criminal matters, and, the appellants argued, the presumption should be that they were not. In support of this argument, the
lawyers for Levy and Dreyfous cited decisions in the supreme courts
of South Carolina and Maryland. The Louisiana Supreme Court, in an
opinion written by Justice George Rogers King, rejected the appellants'
argument, stating that the "legislation and jurisprudence" of Louisiana
"differ materially from those of the slave States generally, in which the
rule contended prevails. This difference of public policy has no doubt
arisen from the different condition of that class of persons in this State."
This was especially true in the city where the members of the jury and
the witness lived.[1] The people of color in New Orleans, Justice King
continued, "are respectable from their intelligence, industry and habits of good order. Many of them are enlightened by education, and the
instances are by no means rare in which they are large property holders.
So far from being in that degraded state which renders them unworthy
of belief, they are such persons as courts and juries would not hesitate

to believe under oath."[2] If the question in this case was whether Louisiana law recognized that a free man of color in New Orleans had the intellectual capacity to understand the significance of an oath and the integrity to abide by it, Justice King's answer was yes.

Free people of color had been interacting with the American court system in New Orleans since its origins during the territorial period (1804–11). They were not only witnesses in criminal cases, as in *State v. Levy*, but also litigants in private lawsuits seeking to distinguish themselves from enslaved people of African descent and claim their rights as free citizens. Acting individually in the courtroom, these free people of color created a collective representation of themselves as "respectable" people due to their "intelligence, industry, and habits of good order" that came to be seen in racial terms. Near the end of the territorial period, the 1811 Superior Court case of *Adele v. Beauregard* judicially recognized a *racial* distinction between *gens de couleur* (who were presumed to be free) and Negroes (who were presumed to be slaves).[3]

Making Race in the Courtroom is about the process by which free people of color living in New Orleans during the Age of Revolution made history under circumstances they did not choose. It argues that in the process of negotiating a legal system that supported and legitimized racially based slavery, free people of African descent in New Orleans, through their participation in the courts, caused the legal reshuffling of racial categories. New Orleans's legio-racial system was in flux during the transition from the colonial era, and a more thorough Anglo-Americanization of the system was deterred by the arrival of St. Domingan refugees (white, black, and of color), which helped to fix the fluidity in a direction that was more comparable with late eighteenth-century St. Domingue norms than with contemporary Anglo-American ones. The refugee *gens de couleur* and other members of New Orleans's free colored community did not necessarily intend to create a third race. Rather, acting within the context of political, cultural, and legal uncertainty, they were seeking to protect and gain privileges denied to free blacks elsewhere in the United States. One of the unintended consequences of their behavior, however, was a recognition in the laws of a racial distinction between "Negroes" and "people of color."

The courtroom was not the only venue in which free people of color sought to protect and expand their legal rights. Justice King acknowledged in his opinion that the "earliest legislation" of the Territory of Orleans protected the rights of free people of color. Free men of color also offered their military services to the territorial governor, William C. C. Claiborne, who recognized them as a "highly useful corps." Thus, free people of color also sought to influence the legislative and executive branches of the territorial government, with some success.

Nevertheless, the impact of free people of color was more far-reaching on the judiciary than it was on the other branches of the government. As local white planters gained control of the representative government in the region, they excluded free men of color, as a group, from political participation—voting, holding office, or even petitioning the legislature. Yet individual free people of color could still use the court system to protect their property rights, in part because they were an important part of New Orleans's expanding commercial economy. Consequently, the principle of Louisiana law that New Orleans's *gens de couleur* were qualitatively different from free people of African descent in "the slaves states generally," as expressed by Justice King, was established by judicial precedent rather than a legislative act or an executive decree.[4]

Moreover, the greater access to the judicial branch than to the legislative or executive branches of government had gendered implications. In the early American republic, voting, petitioning the government, and holding office were the exclusive province of men. Unmarried women, on the other hand, could sue and be sued in courts. As the chapters that follow show, women of color were involved in litigation in early American Louisiana at about the same rate as men of color and far more often than white women. Some of the most influential cases in the territorial courts of New Orleans, including *Adele v. Beauregard*, involved women of African descent. Thus, women of color were just as important as men of color, if not more so, in shaping the legal definitions of race in early New Orleans.

The last two decades have seen a veritable explosion of works about the history of New Orleans. Since the 1990s, no fewer than two dozen scholarly books and as many articles about the city's history have been published, most of them focusing on issues of race.[5] While a number of factors may have contributed to the surge in scholarly interest in historical New Orleans, it is largely a result of changes in the dialogue about race in this country, specifically with regard to transformations within America's "black community." An increasingly well-established, vocal, and self-conscious (if not significantly larger) black bourgeoisie has given rise to class divisions within this country's African American community. Moreover, the "voluntary" immigration of Africans to the United States that began in the late twentieth century and continues today has created distinctions between black Americans who are descendants of the transatlantic slave trade and those who are not. Although second-generation Americans of African descent still suffer from racial discrimination, their perceptions of America differ from those of Americans whose ancestors came as slaves more than 200 years ago.[6] Even black West Indian immigrants and their children, whose ancestors were slaves, often see the United States in a different light than native-born African Americans.[7] The election of Barack Obama, a black man who is the descendant of a white mother and a Kenyan father, serves to highlight the increasing diversity of the black American experience.[8] In short, pre–Civil War New Orleans has become a popular place to study in recent years because it, more than anywhere else in early America, was home to a complex and multivalent racial system similar to the one Americans live in today.

It is now commonplace to say that race is a social construction. Yet, while this tells us what race is *not* (i.e., genetically distinct groups of humans), it does little to define what race *is*. This book takes the position, as its title suggests, that race is best understood not as a category at all but as a process. It builds upon the work of Ian F. Haney-Lopez, who, in his influential essay "The Social Construction of Race," argues that race is "an ongoing, contradictory, self-reinforcing, plastic process subject to the macro forces of social and political struggle and the micro effects of daily decisions."[9] Under this definition, race is historically constructed by the choices that individuals make within structural boundaries. Recognizing that race is a process, continually made and remade, this book does not claim to demarcate an originary point at which "people of color" became a distinct race. Instead, it seeks to demonstrate the role of free people of African descent, interacting within the courts, in the process of race making.

Recent scholarship has demonstrated *what* race relations in pre–Civil War New Orleans looked like, especially with regard to the legal position, socioeconomic status, and culture of the city's free people of African descent. Many scholars have discussed the uncommon legal rights and privileges enjoyed by free colored people in antebellum Louisiana, who could own all types of property, including slave property, move about freely, enter into legal contracts, and, perhaps most important, sue and testify in court against whites. Of course free people of color did suffer certain legal restrictions; they could not vote or serve on juries, and they were not free to marry whites or slaves, for example. Still, the legal rights of free people of color were more expansive in Louisiana than in any other slave state.[10] Historians have also shown that, in addition to having greater legal rights, New Orleans's *gens de couleur* were wealthier and better educated than free blacks in most other parts of the United States. Many owned land and slaves and were educated in schools in the northern United States or France. Although they were precluded by custom from the medical and legal professions, many free people of color were accomplished artists, artisans, small-business owners, and landowners and built a unique and rich culture.[11] The scholarship has reached a general consensus that Louisiana's *gens de couleur* enjoyed an unusually privileged position compared with free people of African descent in the rest of the United States.[12]

Much has also been written, though there is less agreement, on *why* antebellum Louisiana's *gens de couleur* enjoyed rights and privileges denied to free blacks throughout most of the United States. The arguments usually hinge on the differences between Anglo-America, on the one hand, and French or Spanish America, on the other. Following the lead of Frank Tannenbaum and Stanley Elkins, several historians of race in Louisiana argue (some explicitly, others implicitly) that slavery in the English colonies of the New World was harsher than in the colonies of Spain and, to a lesser extent, France. One corollary of the Tannenbaum-Elkins thesis that seems especially relevant in the context of New Orleans is that the institutions in Latin America allowed former slaves to assimilate into free society much more easily than those in Anglo-America.[13] Thus, some historians argue that the French and Spanish colonial governments in Louisiana granted exceptional rights and privileges to free people of color that survived the Louisiana Purchase.[14] For other historians the relatively privileged position of free people of color in Louisiana was a product less of Louisiana's French and Spanish colonial heritage than of the influence of the French West Indies. This argument centers on the thousands of *gens de couleur* immigrants from St. Domingue and, to a lesser extent, Martinique and Guadeloupe, where many free people of color identified more closely with the property-holding free whites than with the masses of enslaved blacks, most of whom were African born.[15] Both sets of arguments are bolstered, in part, by evidence that in the late antebellum period the increasingly Anglo-American planter-controlled Louisiana government attempted, with limited success, to circumscribe the rights and privileges of Louisiana's community of free people of color. Such attempted circumscription is considered an important (and negative) aspect of the "Americanization" of Louisiana.[16]

In the end, a combination of factors (demographic, economic, cultural, and institutional) contributed to the unusually privileged status, within the United States, of Louisiana's free people of color. Throughout most of the eighteenth century, the white population was so overwhelmingly male as to encourage intimate relationships between white men and enslaved women of African descent.[17] This produced a significant community of people of mixed ancestry who were the offspring of white male slaveholders. Kimberly Hanger has shown that during the Spanish period masters were more likely to free their mixed-race children than other slaves they owned. Moreover, despite the plans of early French officials, slavery did not become central to the Louisiana economy until the 1790s. In eighteenth-century Louisiana's "frontier exchange economy," racial categories were much more fluid than they would become after the plantation revolution. Furthermore, the Spanish policy of *coartacion,* under which slaves had the legal right to purchase their freedom with or without their masters' consent, significantly contributed to further growth of the free colored community in the late eighteenth century.[18] Finally, the immigration from the French West Indies in the last decade of the eighteenth century and first decade of the nineteenth century added thousands of sophisticated and educated free people of mixed ancestry. All these factors help explain *why* Louisiana's free people of color enjoyed a privileged position relative to the rest of the American South.

This book, however, is less concerned with the *what* and *why* than with the *how* questions. It accepts the consensus view that the status of free people of color in Louisiana "differ[ed] materially from [that of free blacks in] the slave states generally." But instead of looking for the root cause of this difference in institutions, cultural traits, or material conditions, it shows *how* individual free people of color inserted themselves into the legal system to protect and enhance their rights as free people. As a result of their efforts, the "difference" between *gens de couleur* and other people of African descent came to be perceived as a racial difference that became embodied in the law, where it informed future courts and legislatures. This book is about how free people of color acting within institutions of power shaped those institutions in ways beyond their control.

While free people of color interacted within many different institutions in early New Orleans, this book focuses on the legal system. Legal institutions were important sites in which status and race were negotiated and defined. One important purpose of the laws of New World slave societies was to support a socioeconomic system that was built on racially based slavery. Thus, at various times throughout the early modern era, statutes, decrees, and/or court decisions in the New World slave societies created legal presumptions that people of African descent were enslaved and people of European descent were free.[19] Yet the prevalence, even very existence, of free people of African descent challenged these presumptions. Whereas in much of the southern United States these contradictions were dealt with by passing laws discriminating against free blacks (by making them slaves without masters), jurists and lawmakers in New Orleans took a different approach. They created a new legio-racial category: people of color.

The law is a useful lens through which to view the historical construction of race because, as Haney-Lopez states, "the law serves not only to reflect but to solidify social prejudice, making law a prime instrument in the construction and reinforcement of racial subordination."[20] Moreover, the letter of the law, which is designed, in part, to uphold certain principles, at times differs from the law as applied, which reflects on-the-ground social realities. But, *Making Race in the Courtroom* is less a legal history than a cultural history.[21] It focuses on the interaction of law and culture in New Orleans's courtrooms in the aftermath of the Louisiana Purchase, when the city's legio-racial order was particularly malleable. Furthermore, rather than looking at the law in the abstract, by focusing on the laws and policies handed down by the legislatures and the judicial decisions of the highest courts, this book examines the interactions of free people of color within the legal system.[22] Free people of color forged a distinct identity with their behavior outside the courtroom that was both reflected and reinforced within it.

While the chronological focus of this study is relatively short, roughly 1791 to 1815, the book grapples with important issues such as the intersections of law and culture, the impact of the American and Haitian Revolutions in the Atlantic world, the dialectic of agency within structure, and the contingent nature of historical development. Much of the evidence for this study comes from the records of the New Orleans City Court, a court that existed from 1806 until it was disbanded in 1813. The City Court heard a little more than 3,500 cases in its eight-year existence. All of them were private lawsuits (as opposed to criminal or administrative matters) involving individuals and/or corporations. Free people of African descent were litigants in around 350 of these cases,[23] and they were witnesses in dozens of others. They were involved in a wide variety of lawsuits on both sides of the docket. By examining every record of the New Orleans City Court involving free people of color, this study not only closely examines how the abstract laws became concrete when they were enforced within this community but also, more important, highlights inconsistencies in the application of these laws and shows how free people of color responded to them. Indeed, in some important instances, the actions of free people of color led to changes in the laws.

The court records are supplemented with multiple other primary sources, such as notarial records, probate records, census data, letters and diaries, and other sources, all of which reveal a great deal about the individuals involved in these lawsuits. Using details about the lives of hundreds of individual free people of color outside the courtroom, this book demonstrates their shared culture and how it shaped their behavior in the courtroom. This detailed research allows this study to move beyond generalizations about a three-caste system arising out of French or Spanish or Catholic culture. Instead, it shows that the system arose because free people of African descent were able to manipulate different aspects of the plural legal traditions of the city to maximize their fortunes in individual lawsuits. Free people of color were not always acting as conscious members of a free colored community or a middle caste.[24] But the sum of their individual actions had the unintended consequence of producing an enhanced body of legal rights for Louisiana's *gens de couleur* that was justified by those in power with the assertion, embodied in the law, that free people of color were racially distinct from enslaved blacks.

Free people of color in New Orleans were able to protect and enhance their rights in the courtroom in large part because judges, generally speaking, applied the law with an eye toward evenhandedness.[25] The 1812 case of *Massant v. Veda* serves as an example. On August 4, 1812, a free woman of color named Henriette Massant was passing in front of the house of a white man named François Veda when two young women from within the Veda home tossed the contents of a chamber pot onto her. Massant identified these women as Louise and Deloritte Couso—their status within the household is unclear, but they were likely servants or slaves. Believing that Veda's daughter, Félicité Veda, had ordered the disgusting act, Massant leveled a series of insults at the young Veda. François Veda then pursued Massant to her home and proceeded to hit her and throw objects at her, including a chair. Massant sued Veda for assault on August 6, 1812, and the judge of the New Orleans City Court awarded her a judgment for $500.[26]

The case of *Massant v. Veda* reveals a lot about the ways in which the social hierarchy was contested in New Orleans's courts. The events that gave rise to the lawsuit were, for the most part, undisputed. Massant had four witnesses testify on her behalf, and Veda had three testify for him. None of the witnesses contradicted each other. Yet the meaning of these events was hotly contested. Each side claimed that the other had been "insolent" and disrespectful. Veda claimed to be protecting the honor and dignity of his daughter. He implicitly argued that he and his daughter should not be held accountable for throwing bodily waste onto Massant, but that Massant should be held accountable for reacting strongly to getting bodily waste thrown onto her. Indeed, this case tested the meaning of section 40 of the newly passed Black Code, which admonished free people of color never to insult whites. Judging by his ruling in the case, the justice of the peace with whom Massant originally filed her complaint apparently interpreted section 40 to prohibit only *unprovoked* insults. On appeal, Veda claimed that the justice of the peace's decision had unjustifiably harmed his reputation. Yet the decision was upheld on appeal and provoked no social outrage. It was not unusual for women of color to win favorable judgments against white men in the territorial and early state courts of New Orleans.[27] The court was intent upon interpreting the law fairly, even if this, at times, upset the social dynamics of the parties involved in the lawsuits.

To say that courts, in general, ruled evenhandedly is not to suggest that the law treated all people, or even all free people, equally. The very existence of the Louisiana Black Code of 1807 is evidence of racial inequality. The great majority of the regulations in the code dealt with slaves rather than free people of color. But slavery was, of course, racially based, and race served to justify the institution, even in the letter of the law. The Black Code explicitly states that "free people of color shall not presume to be the equal of whites."[28] Still, this law was only necessary in a society in which racial subordination was contested.

At times the limits of racial subordination (as well as other elements of the social hierarchy) were negotiated even in cases in which none of the parties were people of color. In the 1811 case of *Brengle v. Williams and Colcock,* for example, two white men asked the court to deprive another white man of custody of the latter's two daughters on the basis of his alleged sexual relationship with a black woman.[29] The petitioner, Christian Brengle, claimed that defendants David Williams and William Colcock illegally took possession of his two daughters, Lucinda and Harriet, both minors. The defendants invoked a provision of the *Civil Digest of 1808* that stated that "persons of a conduct notoriously bad and of depraved morals" are to be "excluded from the tutorship and are even liable to be removed from it."[30] Colcock claimed to have taken possession of the children at the repeated requests of their mother and the children themselves because otherwise they would have been placed under the care of "a black woman of notorious ill fame."

The details of what gave rise to the lawsuit are unclear. Brengle's marriage was legally dissolved on September 14, 1808, owing, according to Brengle, "to his wife's unconscionable conduct for three or four years prior to separation, i.e. 'whoredom,'" after which Brengle struggled to get custody of his daughters. Eventually, the children's mother gave up custody of Lucinda and Harriet and permanently moved back to Kentucky, from which both she and Brengle had come to New Orleans. For around two years Brengle lived with one or both of his daughters in a boardinghouse operated by a black woman named Mrs. McCoy. It is unclear if Brengle had a sexual relationship with McCoy, but the defendants alleged that he lived "in open prostitution" with her, a "circumstance which . . . rendered him ineligible to the charge of curator and tutor." For his part, Brengle claimed that he "became displeased with [his] children's situation owing to a crowd of boarders" at Mrs. McCoy's house. He then "immediately turned [his] attention to endeavoring to procure more suitable lodgings for them." William Colcock, who was then in charge of the New Orleans port, was one of many applicants and "appeared anxious to have them on certain terms but for no certain time." Brengle would pay Colcock ten dollars a month for the care of his youngest child, but "the eldest was taken as a companion for [Colcock's] wife" free of charge. After several months, Brengle became dissatisfied with the arrangement. He was concerned about an apparent "neglect of dress and [lack of] cleanliness." His concern heightened when he "discovered that their treatment was not such as children of their age and sex should have had—[his] principle objection was that of a male child nearly about their own age and size bedding with them." When he tried to remove his children "to send them to [his] brother in Maryland or put them in some good families in this city," however, Colcock and Williams prevented him from doing so. Brengle then filed his lawsuit asking the court to order the defendants to return his children to their father. A few days later, after a hearing on the case, the court ordered the defendants to "deliver the children together with the wearing apparel belonging to them to [Brengle] on his giving security in the sum of two thousand dollars that he will place them in a respectable family to be there treated and maintained at his expense." Unfortunately, the judge in this case did not provide a rationale for his ruling.

In addition to the issues of whether or not Brengle had a sexual relationship with McCoy and whether, if so, this would have disqualified him from being the tutor and curator to his daughters, the ambiguous and contradictory testimony in this case raises several questions. Why was Colcock so intent on retaining custody of Brengle's children? Was he sexually exploiting them? Was he otherwise exploiting their labor? Why was Brengle seeking to obtain another home for his daughters in the first place? The documents of this case alone do not provide sufficient answers to these questions. But read in the context of hundreds of other cases in the New Orleans City Court involving inter-personal relationships in this particular time and place, one can make reasonable assumptions about the events leading up to *Brengle v. Williams and Colcock*. For example, several other cases in the same court involve vulnerable young children who were exploited for their labor, sexual or otherwise, shedding light on Colcock's possible motives. Similarly, it was not uncommon for a party to make allegations about the character and social position of a woman of color, as the defendants did with regard to Mrs. McCoy. Many inhabitants of the territory, especially recent Anglo-American immigrants like all three parties in the *Brengle* case, were perplexed by the financial independence of many women of African descent, assuming that their entrepreneurial success resulted from immoral pursuits. Finally, the resolution of the *Brengle* case is consistent with many other custody cases in the New Orleans City Court in which the judge's primary concern was with the ability of the father to provide for his children. All of these issues are dealt with in the chapters that follow.

The historical context that sheds light on cases such as *Massant v. Veda* and *Brengle v. Williams and Colcock* is New Orleans in the Age of Revolution.[31] Thus, *Making Race in the Courtroom* is a local history that addresses broad issues regarding historical change. Local histories serve several important purposes, but, most important, they allow for an in-depth analysis that can show when the on-the-ground reality does not comport with abstract ideals.[32] This book builds on the important work of Melvin Ely in his book *Israel on the Appomattox*.[33] Ely's findings show a significant disjuncture between the abstract ideology regarding free people of African descent, as reflected in the laws, treatises, and pre-scriptive literature, and the everyday interactions between free people of color and whites. *Making Race in the Courtroom* goes further to show not only the disjuncture between abstract ideology and human behavior but also the linkages between the two. It shows how individual interactions at the local and concrete level actually changed the abstract perceptions of free people of color in Louisiana.

New Orleans during the Age of Revolution is a great place in time to study these linkages because it was there and then that abstract cultural and legal constructions of race were ripe for change. *Making Race in the*

Courtroom views New Orleans in the context of the important global transformations associated with the Haitian Revolution, which established the second independent republic in the New World, created the first black nation in the world, and was the only successful slave revolution in history.[34] Historians have shown how this climactic event of the Age of Revolution had varied and, at times, competing influences on different parts of the New World. In some parts of the United States, for example, the economic, political, and ideological revolutions of the era led to the abolition of slavery, while in others they led to the entrenchment of slavery and the hardening of racial categories used to justify the institution.[35] The Haitian Revolution's impact on the city of New Orleans was monumental; it led to the Louisiana Purchase itself and contributed to national debates about slavery in the region. During and immediately after the Haitian Revolution, slavery became entrenched in New Orleans, but racial categories did not develop along the same lines as they did in other parts of the United States. This is, in part, due to the influence of the massive refugee immigration from St. Domingue to New Orleans during the era.

The refugee immigrants did not completely reshape New Orleans's social structure so much as they reinforced it and gave it new meaning. New Orleans's three-tiered social hierarchy of whites, free people of African descent, and enslaved people of African descent had taken a recognizable form during the Spanish colonial period. In many ways, the refugees to New Orleans were entering a society very familiar to them where complicated alliances were based on a variegated sense of differences based on color, ancestry, class, and status. Yet, as hundreds of free colored refugees sought to put together the pieces of their lives and maximize their rights in the courtroom, where the presiding judge, Louis Moreau-Lislet, was himself a refugee, these differences were explained using the language of race. The three-tiered social structure of Spanish colonial New Orleans became the three-race society of antebellum New Orleans.[36] Therefore, this book does not argue that the history of Louisiana in the French and Spanish period did not matter, only that it did not predetermine antebellum Louisiana's racial structure.

*   *   *

The first two chapters of *Making Race in the Courtroom* set the stage by examining the material and legal structure of New Orleans in the era of the Louisiana Purchase. Chapter 1 introduces the reader to the rising new industries, busy markets, crowded streets, and newly built suburbs of the burgeoning port city in the era. Unlike comparable cities such as New York, Boston, and Philadelphia, where the developing industrial and commercial economies were based on free labor, New Orleans was rapidly emerging as a slave society. In the era of this study, New Orleans was more closely tied to the Caribbean slave societies through the Gulf of Mexico than to the trans-Appalachian farms through the Mississippi River. Chapter 2 focuses on the malleable and uncertain legal situation created by the transfer of the Louisiana Territory from Spain to France to the United States. While Anglo-American and English-born lawyers trained in the common law clashed with those born in Louisiana, France, and St. Domingue who were trained in the civil law, white jurists from both traditions put aside their differences and compromised in order to focus their attention on preserving and expanding racially based slavery in Louisiana. At the same time, free people of color solidified their access to the courts and, in the process, helped to create for themselves a distinct racial identity.

The engagement of free people of color with various aspects of the law is the subject of the next four chapters of the book. Free men of color are the dominant subjects of chapter 3, which explores the attempts of free militiamen of African descent to stake a claim to citizenship and political participation in the early American republic by invoking the language of republicanism. Despite these efforts, the incoming American government denied these men some of the basic aspects of citizenship in a republic, such as the right to vote or hold political office. Free women of color then take a prominent role in the final three chapters of the book. Both men and women of color retained the right to own property, even slave property, and the legal rights necessary to secure their property. But women of color were parties to the cases that had the most significant impact on the racial order. Chapter 4 focuses on both the significance of domestic law in shaping racial identity and its limitations in regulating behavior. The laws of the Territory of Orleans and the state of Louisiana prohibited marriages across the color line, but they could not prevent extramarital relationships between free women of color and white men in early New Orleans. This chapter debunks the myth that beautiful and refined women of color were essentially concubines of young, wealthy, white gentlemen, showing, instead, that interracial relationships were much more complex and involved than simple exchanges of sex for financial security. Still, because unmarried women of color could not rely on financial support from a husband, they had to take care of themselves and, hence, developed a stronger sense of autonomy and independence than most white women in New Orleans. Chapter 5 analyzes the efforts of free people of African descent to acquire and accumulate property and to use the laws and court system to protect their property rights. While Louisiana's legal system, which was undergirded by racially based slavery, subordinated free people of African descent, it above all else elevated private property rights. In accumulating property, free people of color in New Orleans sought, among other things, to protect their free status. They took advantage of this system that viewed the protection of private property as a fundamental pillar of its private law to change perceptions of their community's character traits. Finally, chapter 6 examines how illegally enslaved people of color sued their enslavers and, in the process, helped to create a three-tiered racial caste system in antebellum New Orleans. The majority of freedom suits in territorial New Orleans involved refugees from the French West Indies who, though they may have appeared vulnerable, were more sophisticated and knowledgeable of their legal recourse than most American free black victims of kidnapping. The 1811 case of *Adele v. Beauregard*, involving a young, illegally enslaved woman of mixed ancestry, served as the basis for the legal distinction between "Negroes" and "people of color."

*   *   *

As Robin Blackburn insightfully posited more than twenty years ago, "New World slavery coded 'black' skin as a slave characteristic; free people of colour might be led to deny their blackness—or to deny slavery."[37]

For the most part, free people of color in early New Orleans did not deny slavery for it would have been economically irrational and politically risky to do so. And while they did not deny their African ancestry, they did, in many respects, seek to distinguish themselves from slaves. By bringing this perspective into the courtroom, free people of color in New Orleans helped to make New Orleans, and indeed most of Louisiana, a three-race society.

1

The Gulf and Its City

The flat-bottomed scow schooners carrying thousands of refugees fleeing the Caribbean for New Orleans during the two decades straddling the Louisiana Purchase followed a similar route to the Crescent City. They traveled westward along the coast of present-day Alabama and Mississippi before entering Lake Borgne. From there, the vessels passed through one of "several narrow channels called the *Rigolets* which lead into Lake Pontchartrain." They then entered Bayou St. Jean, "which communicate[d] with New Orleans by an artificial canal dug by the efforts of Baron Carondolet, the [former Spanish] governor of Louisiana." The canal led the schooners to the back of the city, near present-day Rampart Street and the public space that came to be known as Congo Square, where the passengers disembarked. From there it was a fifteen- to twenty-minute walk to the levee in the front of the city, where the refugees would have seen the expansive Mississippi River for the first time.

The Lake Pontchartrain route to New Orleans was "much shorter and safer than by way of the mouth of the Mississippi." The former was no more than fifty leagues (125 miles) in length and could have been made in two days. It was sheltered from both storms and enemy attacks. The river route, on the other hand, was much longer (eighty leagues or 200 miles) and much more dangerous. The storms are frequent along the Chandeleur Islands, and ships were vulnerable to enemy attack. Travelers to the city commented, moreover, that "the land at the river's mouth is so low that it can be seen only when one is very near and hence is very dangerous to approach." Once at the mouth of the Mississippi, furthermore, it sometimes took "twenty or thirty days to get up to New Orleans" due to the swift current of the river. "When the wind was from the north, ascent was impossible, because a sailing ship could only move against it by tacking back and forth across the river whose current would cause the ship to lose as much, or more, distance as it gained by tacking. Ships would therefore have to anchor below English Turn and wait for a favorable wind."[1] Most people in the eighteenth and early nineteenth centuries arrived in the city from the Gulf rather than from upriver, and since the river's current was a hindrance to access to the city from the Gulf, ships with little drag that could navigate the shallow waters of Lake Pontchartrain circumvented the Mississippi altogether.

While the importance of the Mississippi River to New Orleans can hardly be overstated, the Gulf of Mexico has also profoundly influenced the city's history. Jean Baptiste Le Moyne (Sieur de Bienville) chose the site for the city not only because there is no higher ground closer to the river's mouth but also because of its proximity to Bayou St. Jean, Lake Pontchartrain, and an alternate route to the Gulf. In the era of the Louisiana Purchase, moreover, New Orleans's ties to the West Indies through the Gulf of Mexico were much stronger than its ties to the North American heartland through the Mississippi River as reflected in the city's economy, demography, and culture. This chapter provides the socioeconomic framework of New Orleans in this Age of Revolution and locates the city's free people of color within this framework, identifying where they resided, what they did for a living, and how they spent their leisure time. It also introduces the reader to both the West Indian influence on the Crescent City and the material conditions that would help shape the city's developing legal structure, which is the subject of chapter 2.

The "Inevitable City on an Impossible Site": The Geography

About 100 miles (as the crow flies) from the mouth of the Mississippi, New Orleans's French Quarter sits on soil deposited by the river as it twists and turns its way through its expansive delta into the Gulf of

Mexico. The lakes, marshlands, and bayous that surround this natural levee give New Orleans the feel of an island city as much as a river city. Its humid, semitropical climate is kept from extreme temperatures by surrounding waters, and rainfall occurs throughout the year. The elevation ranges from five feet below sea level to fifteen feet above, with the highest ground bordering the river.[2] New Orleans geographer Pierce Lewis described the Crescent City as an "inevitable city on an impossible site."[3] Bienville's 1718 decision for the siting of New Orleans was based on geographic reasons of accessibility and defendability, as well as a lack of better alternatives. According to Bienville:

> The capital city ... is advantageously situated in the center of the French plantations, near enough to receive [their] assistance ... and ... reciprocally to furnish the settlers with the things they need ... from its warehouses. Bayou St. John which is behind the city is of such great convenience because of the communication which it affords with Lake Pontchartrain and consequently with the sea that it cannot be esteemed too highly.[4]

From its founding New Orleans's commercially and strategically advantageous situation had to be balanced against its precarious site. After visiting New Orleans in 1722, Jesuit priest Pierre François Xavier de Charlevoix shared his ambivalent feelings about the city. On first arriving he praised the fertility of its soil, the mildness of its climate, and its proximity to "Mexico, the Havana, the finest islands of America, and lastly, to the English colonies." With these observations he asked, "Can there be any thing more requisite to render a city flourishing?" Within just a couple of weeks, however, Charlevoix had changed his tune about New Orleans. Claiming that there was "nothing very remarkable" about the country around New Orleans, Charlevoix asked his readers to imagine "two hundred persons . . . sent out to build a city . . . who have settled on the banks of a great river, thinking upon nothing but upon putting themselves under cover from the injuries of the weather, and in the mean time waiting till a plan is laid out for them, and till they have built houses according to it." Charlevoix complained about the marshy soils downriver from the city, whose "depth continues to diminish all the way to the sea." "I have nothing to add," he wrote dismissively, "about the present state of New Orleans."[5] The same ambivalence remained around the time of the Louisiana Purchase, as reflected in the comments of French-born traveler François Marie Perrin du Lac: "New Orleans, at which I arrived in six weeks, does not merit a favorable description. All that can be said in defense of its founder is that there is not for a great distance a finer, more elevated, or healthier position. If higher, it would be too distant from the sea; if lower, subject to inundations."[6]

Despite New Orleans's problems with regard to climate and terrain, it had all the potential to be a great port city due to its location at the terminus of North America's largest river system. Americans moving west of the Appalachians after the colonists' victory in the American Revolution coveted access to the Mississippi River and its port city of New Orleans because it assured them of greater access to markets for their agricultural products and raw materials. Echoing the sentiments of many American travelers to the city in the years leading up to the Louisiana Purchase, New York merchant John Pintard predicted in 1801 that New Orleans would "very shortly become a vast commercial emporium." Thomas Jefferson summed up the city's importance to the West in 1802 when he said "there is on the globe one single spot, the possessor of which is our natural and habitual enemy. It is New Orleans, through which the produce of three-eighths of our territory must pass to market."[7] The expansiveness of the Mississippi River seemed to predetermine the importance of New Orleans.

In fact, by the time of the Louisiana Purchase in 1803, New Orleans was emerging as one of the most important cities in North America, but it was not because of the western river trade. As the pages that follow demonstrate, during the Age of Revolution New Orleans was a Gulf city more than a river city. French and Spanish colonists had forged ties with the Caribbean that were reinforced by immigration and remained strong for decades after the Louisiana Purchase. The West Indian influence is reflected in the demography, the economy, and even the architecture of the period.

Migrants and Refugees: The Demography

Between the American Revolution and the Civil War, New Orleans experienced urbanization much more intensely than any other city in the Deep South. In general, as Douglass North has shown, "As the South shifted out of a diversified agriculture into cotton and its income increased, the effect was quite different from that generated in the Northeast by rising incomes from the re-export and carrying trade. Urbanization did not increase."[8] To be sure, Mobile, Savannah, and Charleston all grew along with the cotton trade. But Charleston's growth from 16,000 residents in 1790 to 24,000 in 1810, for example, "was less than the rate of population growth for the country as a whole" and well behind that of other urban centers. New Orleans was the exception to the rule for cities in the South. The population of New Orleans grew rapidly and steadily, from 5,028 in 1785 to 27,176 in 1820, at which time it was the fifth most populous city in the United States.[9] By the time Louisiana became a state in 1812, New Orleans had surpassed Charleston as the largest city in the Deep South, and this was just the beginning. By 1840 it was virtually tied with Baltimore as the second-largest city in the country with 102,000 residents.[10]

There were two main reasons for New Orleans's rapid population growth in the late eighteenth and early nineteenth centuries. The first was directly related to the upheaval caused by the Haitian Revolution. In three main waves during the course of that revolution, tens of thousands of refugees fled St. Domingue (and smaller numbers fled Guadeloupe) for safer ground in Europe, North America, and the British and Spanish Caribbean. The first wave was set in motion by the burning of Cap Français in 1793, sending thousands of refugees to, among other places, the East Coast cities of the United States such as Boston, New York, Philadelphia, Baltimore, Richmond, and Charleston. The second wave occurred in 1798, when defeated British forces withdrawing from the war-torn island took shiploads of refugees with them to Jamaica. The final and largest wave came in 1803–4, after the insurgent forces led by Jean Jacques Dessalines defeated the French army. The great majority of these refugees fled to Cuba.[11]

The influx of immigrants from the French West Indies into New Orleans eventually dwarfed that of Anglo-Americans, but only a small percentage of these refugees followed a direct route to the city due to the restrictive immigration policies of the Spanish government in Louisiana. Although the first refugee immigrants arrived in New Orleans as early as 1791, only about a thousand refugees came to New Orleans prior to the Louisiana Purchase, usually after spending some time in other American port cities or in the English or Spanish Caribbean. Among the early arrivers was Antonio Morin, the man who was greatly influential in the birth of Louisiana's sugar industry.[12]

A thousand more refugees came to New Orleans during the first year of American rule, more than the total number of West Indian immigrants in the previous eleven years, because American policies toward the refugees were much more liberal than the Spanish policies had been.[13] Many of these men, women, and children came from Jamaica, but others came from Eastern Seaboard cities in the United States. Several of these refugees, who were welcomed by the native French-speaking inhabitants, proved to be very influential on New Orleans's society and culture. Louis Moreau-Lislet, for example, a refugee immigrant from St. Domingue in 1804, made an immediate impact on the legal system. He was appointed the first judge of the New Orleans City Court in 1806 and was the principal author of the 1808 Louisiana *Civil Digest*.[14]

By far the largest wave of refugee immigration into New Orleans came five years after the American takeover. Napoleon invaded Spain in 1809, and the French-speaking refugees in Spanish Cuba were forced to either take an oath of loyalty to the Spanish crown or leave the island. Between May 1809 and February 1810, nearly 10,000 St. Domingan refugees fled Cuba for New Orleans on dozens of vessels. These schooners, sloops, ships, brigs, and chebecks had telling names such as *L'Esperance, Triumph, Republican,* and *Le Sauveur.* The vessels carried as many as 417 passengers (the ship *Beaver*) and as few as 17 (the schooner *Fanny*).[15] The captains of smaller vessels, such as the chebecks, sloops, and some of the schooners, had the option of taking either the Mississippi River or the Lake Pontchartrain route. The larger ships and brigs, on the other hand, had too deep of a drag to navigate Lake Pontchartrain and were thus required to sail up the river, at times a difficult task.

The 1809–10 refugee immigration increased the population of New Orleans and surrounding areas by close to 60 percent, creating housing dilemmas, food shortages, and general chaos.[16] In the midst of the nine-month-long influx of refugees, Governor Claiborne expressed concern about the ability of the city to accommodate them. In an effort to put a halt to the immigration, he wrote to William Savage, the consulate to Jamaica, that "New Orleans and its vicinity are crowded with strangers;

House Rent and Provisions are extravagantly high, families of limited resources find them soon exhausted, and the number of the poor and distressed are daily augmenting." He asked Savage to inform any refugees who "should pass by the way of Jamaica, that it is advisable for them, to seek an asylum elsewhere, than in the Territory of Orleans, for the Refugees from Cuba, who have arrived here, are so numerous as to be embarrassing to our own citizens."[17] While Claiborne had encouraged Anglo-American immigration during the territorial period, he was worried about the influx of refugees. Clearly, Claiborne's concerns had to do with more than just logistics. The "strangers" arriving from the West Indies daily were making it very difficult for the governor to comply with his charge to Americanize the city.

The second main reason for New Orleans's population growth in the era was expansion of slavery in the lower Mississippi valley, which both produced a great demand for enslaved labor and encouraged immigration of whites seeking to benefit from the expanding economy. Between 1796 and 1810, nearly 10,000 African slaves passed through the port of New Orleans. This was the first major wave of Africans since 1743, when just under 2,200 slaves arrived in the Louisiana colony.[18] Some of the trade in the later period was illegal, as the Spanish government, out of fears concerning the "contagion of revolution," had prohibited the introduction of slaves on several occasions during the 1790s, and Congress briefly forbade the transatlantic slave trade in Louisiana almost immediately after the Louisiana Purchase. Between 1805 and 1808, a legal slave trade also developed that brought African slaves to New Orleans via other U.S. port cities, mostly Charleston, South Carolina.[19] Most of these African slaves were purchased for labor on cotton, sugar, and indigo plantations in the region and did not remain in New Orleans. Nevertheless, the slave population in the city itself almost tripled from 1,631 in 1785 to 4,618 in 1810.

Anglo-American migration, primarily from the Mid-Atlantic and Chesapeake states, accounted for a modest increase in New Orleans's white population in the era. In 1790 most of New Orleans's white residents were of French descent. The small Spanish population consisted of mostly officials and their families, and there were only a few American merchants and German farmers. The plantation revolution that began in the middle of the decade brought in scores of Anglo-American merchants from East Coast cities such as Baltimore, Philadelphia, and New York, as well as professionals from the Chesapeake and Mid-Atlantic seeking to profit from New Orleans's booming economy. Staple merchant Richard Relf came to New Orleans from Philadelphia in the 1790s where he partnered with Beverly Chew. After the Louisiana Purchase, a new wave of Anglo-Americans flocked to the city, seeking political, as well as economic, power. Among the Anglo-American immigrants to New Orleans in the immediate aftermath of the purchase was Edward Livingston, a lawyer and politician from New York who would make an important, if controversial, impact on early New Orleans politics and law. President Jefferson and Governor William Claiborne, himself a recent arrival to the city, encouraged this migration, as they sought to bring Louisiana's political and legal system in line with the rest of the United States.[20] Yet the president and governor were powerless to prevent the upheaval in the French West Indies and its subsequent demographic impact on New Orleans.

At the time of the Louisiana Purchase there was a great variety of people living in New Orleans and the surrounding area. Among the whites there were individuals of French, Spanish, American, English, and German descent. The francophone population could be further broken down into those born in Louisiana, France, and the French Caribbean. The slaves consisted of Louisiana Creoles and "saltwater" slaves.[21] The free people of African descent, most of whom were born in either Louisiana or the French Caribbean, were descended from a variety of European and African ethnicities and spoke French, Spanish, and English. Finally, many Native Americans still lived in the area, though they had already been marginalized to the point of not being recognized in the censuses.[22]

The heterogeneity of the population made an impression on dozens of travelers to the city in the early nineteenth century who contributed to racial and gender stereotypes in their accounts of their visits. Irish traveler Thomas Ashe, for example, made distinctions among the white men. The Americans, according to Ashe, were "so occupied by politics and legislation, that their minds have never been sufficiently unbent to form a course of pleasures for themselves." The "French gentlemen" were a more culturally refined group. "Their pleasures are forever varied, and of a nature to be participated by the most delicate of the female sex. This casts over them a considerable degree of refinement, and the concert, dance, promenade, and *petit souper*, are conducted with as much attention as at Paris or Rome." In reference to Spanish men, Ashe claimed that he had "more than once heard the guitar under the windows of a sleeping beauty or the harp delicately touched under a corridor over which some charming girl attentively reclined." Ashe's portrayal of the differences between English-, French-, and Spanish-speaking men in New Orleans both fed off of and contributed to common stereotypes.[23]

In describing the women living in New Orleans when he visited the city, Ashe claimed that "in point of manners and character [they had] a very marked superiority over the men." Yet, instead of discussing differences between the American, French, and Spanish women, as he had done with regard to white men, Ashe categorized the women of New Orleans into "two ranks—the white and the brown." According to Ashe, "Those [women] called the whites are principally brunettes with deep black eyes; dark hair and good teeth. Their persons are eminently lovely, and their movements indescribably graceful, far superior to anything I ever witnessed in Europe." The women of color were "very beautiful, of a light copper colour, and tall and elegant persons. Their dress is widely different in general from that of the White Ladies; their petticoats are ornamented at the bottom with gold lace or fringe richly tasseled; their slippers are composed of gold-embroidery, and their stockings interwoven with the same metal, in so fanciful a manner, as to display the shape of the leg to the best advantage."[24] While Ashe claimed to have divided the women into two ranks, he then described two more:

Negresses and female Mestizes next follow: the first are principally employed as servants, of which every family has a considerable number; the second perform all kinds of laborious work, such as washing, and retailing fruit throughout the city in the hottest weather; and being considered as a cast too degraded to enter into the marriage state, they follow a legal kind of prostitution without deeming it any disparagement to their virtue or to their honor.[25]

Ashe's description reveals the complex interactions of race, sex, and power in the heterogeneous society of post-Purchase New Orleans. He discusses white men in terms of the political, commercial, and cultural tendencies of the various ethnic groups, while neglecting to even mention enslaved men or free men of color. On the other hand, he describes white women and women of color almost exclusively in terms of their appearance, and black and mestizo women in terms of the labor they performed, sexual and otherwise. Several other travelers adopted this practice of dividing the (white) men into categories based on nationality or language while discussing women in terms of race.[26]

Other travelers during the period wrote explicitly and more extensively about the city's population of African descent. French traveler Perrin du Lac spoke of the "badly fed" Negro slaves who were "naturally crafty, idle, cruel, and thieves; I need not add, that in their hearts they are all enemies to the Whites. The serpent endeavors to bite him that tramples him under his feet; the slave must hate his master."[27] Du Lac divided free people of African descent into several categories based upon their perceived degree of African blood. In reference to the attitudes that free blacks had about enslaved blacks, du Lac wrote, "It is difficult to account for the brutality and aversion of the free Blacks to those of their own species. They [the slaves] are treated by them [the free blacks] worse than by the Whites." Yet, according to the Frenchman, free blacks were "far from being as dangerous as the Mulattoes. These seem to participate as much in the vices of both species as of their color; they are vindictive, traitors, and equal enemies to the Blacks and Whites." The "men of color" (by which term Du Lac probably meant "quadroon" or "octoroon" men) were "still more dangerous" and responsible, in part, for the "intemperate conduct of the whites towards their slaves."[28] Du Lac, like several other European travelers to New Orleans at the time, supported slavery but opposed its excesses, and believed in the superiority of the European "race" while opposing, in theory, intimate relations across the color line.

While travelers to the city commented on the many distinctions within New Orleans's heterogeneous population in the early nineteenth century, the census makers and government officials divided the people into three main groups: whites, slaves, and free people of color, reflecting a tripartite society that had developed during the Spanish colonial period. This method of categorization acknowledged the dominating influence of racial slavery in the region, but it did not reflect a three-race society. The distinction in the census between whites and free people of color was one of race, while the distinction between free and enslaved people of African descent was one of status. Whites were presumed to be free (and did not require a status descriptor), while slaves were presumed to be black (and did not require a racial descriptor). The term "free person of color," which identifies both status and race, conveys the seemingly exceptional nature of this group of people.[29]

The refugee immigration bolstered this tripartite social hierarchy while also altering it. Following the lead of the census, city officials categorized the refugees into three groups based on status and race, something that was familiar to both the then-existing population in Louisiana and the refugees themselves. Official records produced at the time show the immigrants to have been roughly evenly divided between whites, slaves, and free people of color, as illustrated in table 1.1. But these numbers invite criticism and deserve deeper analysis. First of all, as Rebecca Scott has astutely observed, depending on when and the circumstances under which those classified as slaves left the island of Hispaniola, many had been freed by colonial officials, the French National Convention, invading armies, and/or their own martial efforts. Thus, potentially thousands of men, women, and children who had been freed in St. Domingue were reenslaved in Cuba and/or Louisiana.[30] In the four decades following the immigration, the various courts of New Orleans heard dozens of lawsuits in which the status of refugees of African descent, as enslaved or free, was disputed.[31] Therefore, the numbers assigned to each "category" of people coming from the West Indies to New Orleans were both dubious and temporary.

One of the most noticeable aspects of the refugee immigration from Cuba is the imbalance of the sexes. As shown in table 1.1, among whites there were far more men than women, while among both slaves and, especially, free people of color, there were far more women than men. This is not surprising, however, when viewed in the context of the sex demographics of colonial St. Domingue and the results of the Haitian Revolution. Due to the harsh environment of the French colony, relatively few white women ever settled in colonial St. Domingue. The male-to-female ratio of the white refugee immigrants, therefore, reflected the ratio of the colony before the revolution.[32] On the other hand, due to the gendered dimensions of warfare, formerly enslaved men and free men of color were much more likely to stay behind and fight rather than flee.

Table 1.1. Refugee Immigration from Cuba through August 1809

	Men	Women	Children	Total
Whites	1,373	703	655	2,731
Free persons of color	428	1,377	1,297	3,102
Slaves	962	1,330	934	3,226
Total	2,763	3,410	2,886	9,059

Many of the white refugees had aspirations to be sugar planters, so few of them stayed in the city for long. Anglo-American city and state officials, most of whom were slaveholders themselves, sympathized with their plight but worried that the "preponderance of French influence" would make it much more difficult to Americanize the city.[33] Yet none of the white refugees from 1809–10 made as notable an impact on New Orleans as some of the white refugees who had arrived earlier, such as Moreau-Lislet.

Of the three groups, the free colored refugees had the most significant impact on the demography of the city. First of all, free people of color saw the largest percentage increase in New Orleans during the Age of Revolution, primarily as a result of the refugee immigration. Free people of color accounted for 11 percent of the population in 1785, rising to 16.5 percent in 1803, and then to 27 percent in 1810. Refugees accounted for the great majority of New Orleans's free colored community in 1810. Moreover, the immigration greatly exaggerated the preexisting numerical dominance of women and children over adult men within the free colored community.[34] As table 1.1 illustrates, adult men made up less than 14 percent of the 3,102 free colored refugees arriving through July 1809. Because more than 40 percent of the free colored refugees were children under the age of fifteen, the immigration ensured a strong presence of refugees throughout most of the antebellum period.[35]

The demographics of the immigration had two other important consequences for New Orleans society throughout the antebellum period. First, it further skewed the already imbalanced sex ratios among both whites and free people of color in New Orleans. As late as 1820, men made up almost 60 percent of the white population in New Orleans, while women constituted more than 60 percent of the free colored population.[36] These skewed sex ratios among the two groups contributed, in part, to the large number of intimate relationships between white men and women of color in the first two decades of the nineteenth century, a subject that chapter 4 covers in greater depth. Second, as shown in chapter 6, women and, especially, children of African descent were more vulnerable than men of African descent to illegal enslavement. In response to the unusual number of female and minor refugees who brought suits against their enslavers, the courts developed the *Adele* rule. In making "people of color" a racial category separate from "Negroes" with different presumptions as to status, the courts did something the census makers did not—they made race.

Before the *Adele* decision, however, anxious white officials in New Orleans had mixed feelings and sent mixed messages about the free colored refugees. In 1806, the territorial legislature passed a law creating a presumption of enslavement for all "free people of color from Hispaniola [then] residing" in New Orleans. While the legislature repealed this act less than a year later, it replaced it with a law that prohibited "the emigration of free Negroes and Mulattoes into the Territory of Orleans." This act imposed a penalty on free colored violators "in the amount of $20 a day for every day past two weeks" that they remained in the territory and stated that "failure to pay such fine will result in commission to jail and [the violator] may be sold for a time sufficient to pay the fine."[37] During the 1809–10 immigration, however, the government in New Orleans appeared powerless to enforce the law. Claiborne first attempted to selectively enforce it against men of color above the age of fifteen, but even this proved unsuccessful. He then resorted to pleading with American diplomats in Jamaica and Cuba for assistance. In separate letters to Maurice Rogers, in St. Iago, and William Savage, in Kingston, he asked the consulates to "discourage free people of color of every description from emigrating to the Territory of Orleans" because New Orleans already had "as much proportion of that population, than comports with the general Interest."[38]

Mayor James Mather defended the free colored immigrants in a letter to the governor, writing that "few characters among the free People of Colour have been represented to me as dangerous for the peace of this Territory." Mather's opinion was shaped by his understanding that "these very men possess property, and have useful trades to live upon." With regard to the territorial law, Mather wrote, "In the application of the Territorial law relative to free people of color, I have been particular in causing such of them as had been informed against, to give bond for their leaving the Territory within the time allowed in such cases—in the mean time there has not been one single complaint that I know of, against any of them concerning their conduct since their coming to this place."[39] Mather appears to have been trying to justify his inability to enforce the territorial law.

The refugees labeled as slaves presented a more pressing legal issue for American officials because Congress had prohibited the importation of slaves from areas outside the United States as of January 1, 1808.[40] In 1809, the legislature for the Territory of Orleans passed a law excepting slaves coming from Cuba and Jamaica from the congressional prohibition. After the constitutionality of the act was called into question, Claiborne and other Louisiana officials asked the national government to make an exception in the case of the refugee immigrants. American officials in Orleans tried to convince the national leaders (and, perhaps, themselves) that these slaves from "Santo Domingo" did not pose a threat to security in the territory. Mayor Mather wrote to Governor Claiborne that they were "trained up to the habits of strict discipline, and consist wholly of Affricans bought up from Guineamen in the Island of Cuba, [and] of faithful slaves who have fled with their masters from St. Domingo as early as the year 1803." Congress passed a law on June 28, 1809, that gave the president the power to suspend enforcement of the law of Congress with regard to these slaves coming from Cuba and Jamaica.[41] Like the forced migrants from Africa, the majority of the slaves arriving in New Orleans during the first few years of the nineteenth century were destined for the sugar plantations in the parishes upriver from New Orleans. While the special exception to the slave trade ban was billed as a humanitarian act allowing refugees to keep their property, it effectively deprived thousands of people of their liberty—indeed, in many senses, the act deprived them of their humanity.

Cotton and Sugar: The Economy

Although New Orleans was established as a planned slave society to compete with the English colonies that were producing wealth from staple crop production, its economy floundered for the better part of a century. When Bienville founded New Orleans in 1718, the French monarchy had planned that Louisiana would both grow tobacco, relieving French dependence on the British colonies, and supply the French sugar colonies in the West Indies with lumber and foodstuffs. But Louisiana-grown tobacco could not compete with that grown in Virginia, and the French monarchy had trouble finding would-be planters and farmers to settle the region. At the end of the Seven Years' War, therefore, France had few reservations about ceding the Louisiana Territory to Spain. During the first two decades of the Spanish period, moreover, Louisiana was little more than a frontier territory serving as a buffer between the expansionist Anglo-Americans and the riches of New Spain.[42] The government of the United States was less interested in the Territory of Louisiana itself than it was in open access to the Mississippi River. The 1795 Pinckney Treaty with Spain secured American westerners free use of the river as well as the "American deposit," a place in New Orleans to dock their vessels and load and unload their goods. Spain then closed New Orleans to American trade in 1802, prompting Jefferson, then president, to step up his efforts to acquire the city for the United States.[43]

Despite the talk of the city's importance to the western river trade, however, New Orleans's rise to economic prominence began with the revolutionary events of the 1790s and was intimately tied to plantation slavery in the lower Mississippi valley. The invention of the cotton gin in 1793 allowed for the profitable production of short staple cotton, and the Haitian Revolution, which began in 1791, created a void in the worldwide supply of sugar that was partially filled by sugar production in lower Louisiana. Sugar was grown profitably in Louisiana for the first time in 1794 after St. Domingue refugee Antonio Morin, who had granulated small quantities of sugar in 1792 on the plantation of Don Antonio Mendez, took his process to the plantation of Étienne Boré two years later.[44] The rise of sugar and cotton plantations in the lower Mississippi valley dramatically increased the importance of New Orleans as a port city. By 1799, the port received $1 million worth of goods, and in 1802 the amount was $2,634,564. After the Louisiana Purchase, the trade continued to grow, reaching $5,370,555 in 1807 and $13,064,540 in 1816.[45] While some of this was wheat, corn, lard, pork, furs and hides, whiskey, hemp, and lead from the upper reaches of the Mississippi River system, the vast majority of the products were cotton, sugar, molasses, and tobacco from the lower Mississippi valley.[46]

As demand for slave-grown products, especially cotton and sugar, increased worldwide and large, efficient plantations rose to meet it, commission merchants who acted as agents for planters in the region quickly emerged as the most influential, powerful, and prosperous businessmen in New Orleans. These staple merchants, also known as factors, "sold goods for planters; made remittances from such sales in cash, bills, or goods; shipped goods on consignment; provided storage, drayage, and additional packaging services; and procured shipping for staples." Factors traded all sorts of agricultural products, but those that specialized in cotton and sugar were the wealthiest. A few prominent staple merchants controlled most corporate enterprises in early New Orleans.[47] One of the most successful American merchants in early Louisiana, the partnership of Beverly Chew and Richard Relf, also engaged in the slave trade, at times circumventing the law. After Congress forbade the importation of Africans as slaves in 1808, Chew and Relf "used their business contacts with Spanish officials in West Florida to facilitate the landing of slave ships and the distribution of their cargos at the port of Mobile."[48] They acted as middlemen for other firms, many in Charleston, South Carolina, that wished to import Africans into North America.

The new wealth from commerce in slaves and slave-grown products contributed to New Orleans's development as a banking and financial center in the era of the Purchase. The city's bankers, lawyers, and insurance agents provided services that helped make planters' and merchants' commercial dealings more profitable and less risky. New Orleans's law firms tried to keep their clients' business affairs operating within the limits of the law. The New Orleans Insurance Company, chartered in 1805, insured vessels, cargoes, and money in port and in transit, assuming some of the risks (and profits) associated with shipping large quantities of slaves, agricultural products, and manufactured goods. Between 1804 and 1812, four banks in the Crescent City received their charters, the New Orleans branch of the First Bank of the United States (1804), the Bank of Louisiana (1804), the Bank of New Orleans (1811), and the Louisiana Planters Bank (1811). These banking companies loaned money for the expansion of plantations, the purchase of goods, and many other enterprises.[49]

In addition to banking and commerce, New Orleans also saw an increase in manufacturing interests in the two decades straddling the Louisiana Purchase. New businesses, such as cotton mills, sugar refineries, rice mills, tobacconists, sawmills, distilleries, and cordage factories, converted the raw materials being shipped down the Mississippi River into finished products. New Orleans also developed a small shipbuilding industry. The port required stevedores, dockworkers, and carters, while a growing and increasingly sophisticated population demanded clothiers, shoemakers, furniture makers, silversmiths, lithographers, daguerreotypists, printers, and bookbinders. The expanding plantations helped produce a variety of jobs in the city.

Nevertheless, New Orleans remained primarily a commercial, rather than a commercial-industrial, metropolis with an economy closely tied to plantation slavery. The biggest employer outside the government was the port. The manufacturing interests were "directly connected with the processing and movement of staple crops," and the port's main business was shipping these products. The top four exports in 1801 were raw sugar, cotton, tobacco, and indigo. By 1812, cotton accounted for more than half the value of the city's exports, followed in value by sugar, foodstuffs, and then tobacco. The economy based on commerce in staple crops did not stimulate the development of an urban center as diversified as the emerging metropolises of the Northeast at this time or the cities that rose in the Northwest in the middle of the nineteenth century.[50] New Orleans's economy resembled that of the port cities of the Caribbean more than the port cities of the young United States.

Working mostly from their homes or in the homes of others in all parts of this urban center, free people of color made a living primarily in the manufacturing, commercial, and service sectors. Very few free people of color worked the land at the time of the Louisiana Purchase. Out of more than 150 free black heads of household who listed their occupations in the last census of the Spanish period, only 2 listed farmer as his or her primary occupation. Instead, free people of African descent in New Orleans worked as skilled laborers, small-business owners, and, to a lesser extent, domestic servants. All in all, free people of color played an important role in the New Orleans economy, where labor was often in short supply. Many owned successful businesses or engaged in the professions and amassed substantial estates that included real, personal, and slave property.[51]

The important role that free people of color played in New Orleans's economy was augmented by the refugee immigration. On the eve of the Haitian Revolution, the *gens de couleur* of St. Domingue were the wealthiest, most educated, and most privileged community of people of African descent in the New World. Some free colored refugees had the capital to invest in coffeehouses, inns, or taverns. Some brought with them "slaves" whom they sold or rented to planters in the region to provide capital or income to help them adjust to their new setting.[52] Others, who had lost all of their wealth during the revolution itself or when they hastily fled the island, still brought with them skills and cultural capital that allowed them to succeed. For the most part, these refugees took the same positions in the economy as the free people of color born in Louisiana.

With very few exceptions, free men of color and free women of color performed separate tasks, with men's work concentrated in the manufacturing sector and women's jobs concentrated in the service or commercial sector. Many free men of color were artisans of some sort, as demand for skilled labor was high (as were wages) and few white artisans lived in the city at the time. Less than a third of the free men of color at the time of the Purchase worked outside of the manufacturing sector. They dominated such skilled trades as carpentry, masonry, shoemaking, and barrel making.[53] The great majority of the adult male refugees of color were skilled artisans, and the young men among them were apprenticed in a variety of trades, too numerous to list.[54] The militiamen in St. Domingue were, generally speaking, artisans, and many of them found their way to New Orleans in the 1809–10 immigration. Recall that in the midst of this immigration, Mayor James Mather informed Governor Claiborne that the men among the colored immigrants "had useful trades to live upon." The wealthiest and most successful artisans of color in the territorial period, however, were Louisiana Creoles as opposed to immigrants. Among them was Rafael Bernabee, who accumulated several thousand dollars in savings while working as a carpenter in the city and its environs in the last decade of the Spanish period.[55] He invested his money in real estate in the Vieux Carré and newly emerging suburbs, making close to 100 percent profit on three lots that he held for less than ten years. In each real estate purchase, Bernabee secured his mortgage with one or all of his three slaves, Henriette, Marie, and Jean Pierre.[56] In addition to Bernabee, some other prominent free black artisans in the period were Carlos Brulet (carpenter) and Marcellin Gilleau (mason).

Free men of color worked in the trades, in part, because they were excluded from the professions. James Durham was an exception to the rule. A report given in August 1801 gave the names of six unlicensed physicians in New Orleans, one of them a free black man named Santiago Derum (James Durham). Born a slave in Philadelphia in 1762, Durham learned to read and write as a young boy. As a young adult, he was the enslaved assistant of three different doctors, John A. Kearsey, a Philadelphia physician and loyalist during the American Revolution; George West, a surgeon in the British army; and Robert Dow, a New Orleans physician.[57] After the Revolutionary War, Dow brought Durham to New Orleans, where he sold him his freedom a few weeks before his twenty-first birthday for the sum of 500 pesos. By the late 1790s, Durham was a practicing (if not licensed) throat specialist. In an 1801 law that specifically mentioned Durham by name, the Spanish government in New Orleans prohibited any person without a medical degree from practicing medicine in New Orleans. In the United States, however, only 5 percent of practicing physicians had medical degrees, and after the Louisiana Purchase, Durham became the first known licensed African American physician in the United States.[58]

Free women of color were just as, if not more, important to the early American New Orleans economy, if for no other reason than they greatly outnumbered free men of color. At the time of the Louisiana Purchase, 60 percent of free black heads of household were women, and most of them worked in the service or commercial sector. Free colored refugee women fit right in, working as "hairdressers, washerwomen, seamstresses, milliners, and needlewomen." They also took jobs as wet nurses.[59] No free women of color were listed in the official records as artisans, since women were barred by custom from the trades. But the labels can be misleading. The Negress Marie Louise Dupre, for example, is listed as a domestic servant even though she worked in the blacksmith shop of Nicholas Duquery from the late 1790s until Duquery died in 1812. More than half of the colored female heads of household in the territorial period were either seamstresses or laundresses. The fact that seamstressing was considered a part of the service sector, and not a skilled trade, further reveals the gendered assumptions of the government officials who created the categories.[60] Almost a fourth of the colored female heads of household were either shopkeepers or retail dealers. Mrs. McCoy, the woman who provided lodging for Christian Brengle and his daughters, for example, was one of several women of African descent who owned and operated a boardinghouse. Hers was on Canal Street and catered to newcomers to the town, of all races. Many of New Orleans's free colored businesswomen in the territorial period were refugee immigrants. The mythical image of women of color in New Orleans is that they were set up in business by wealthy white "gentlemen" as a type of compensation for sexual services. There is little evidence to support this position. While dozens and possibly hundreds of women of color formed long-term relationships with white men in New Orleans during the Age of Revolution, they usually contributed to the household income. Many refugee free women of color had been the mistresses of planters in St. Domingue. Yet these *ménagères,* as they were called, performed valuable services for the plantation. These multifaceted relationships are discussed more fully in chapters 4 and 5.[61]

While precious few free people of color were as wealthy as elite white merchants and planters in New Orleans and the surrounding area, they were, as a community, far more prosperous than in any other region of the United States. In terms of property holdings, only the Charleston District in South Carolina, another place influenced by Caribbean social and economic patterns, was remotely close. Perhaps most tellingly, there were far more free colored slaveholders in Louisiana than in any other state, and most of these resided in Orleans Parish.[62] Out of 565 free colored heads of household in the 1810 census, 248 (44 percent) owned slaves. These households owned, on average, two and a half slaves each. Most of these slaves were likely either house servants or shop workers. In the Spanish period, free people of color often owned relatives as slaves, but this became less and less common after the Louisiana Purchase.[63] Dozens of immigrants of color entered the port of New Orleans with people they claimed as their slaves. Many others, no doubt, had owned slaves back in St. Domingue but had lost them in the revolution. As shown in chapters 5 and 6, for free people of African descent, especially refugees, slave ownership was an effective way of securing their own freedom.

The Vieux Carré and Beyond:
The Layout and Expansion of the City

Throughout the period of this study, most of New Orleans's population lived in the confines of what is today called the French Quarter and was then called the Vieux Carré, or old quarter. The Vieux Carré "was spread out in the form of a parallelogram extending, roughly speaking, some 1300 yards along the river front with a depth of 700 yards, or thereabouts."[64] Its borders were the Mississippi River, Le Chemin Derrière de la Ville (present-day Rampart Street), the plantation of Madame Delachaise (Esplanade Avenue), and the commons (Canal Street). Perched atop a natural levee created by centuries of the river's flooding over its banks, the Vieux Carré was (and still is) some of the highest ground in the area, though still only twelve to fifteen feet above sea level.[65] The Place d'Armes, now known as Jackson Square, occupied a strategic location front and center at the peak of the natural levee in New Orleans's Vieux Carré. As the name suggests, this piece of land is where the militia and the regular army drilled. The St. Louis Cathedral and the Cabildo building, both constructed in the 1790s, face the square, symbolizing the three prongs of Spanish monarchical authority over its subjects, laws, church discipline, and military might.[66]

By the time of the Louisiana Purchase, the cost of real estate in the old city was rising due to the city's population and economic booms, and "lots of ground in the principal streets [were] very high for so new a city."[67] Houses facing the river on Levee Street ranged from 4,000 to 6,000 pesos (a peso roughly equaled a dollar in value), those on the second and third streets (Chartres/Conde and Royal) cost 3,000 to 4,000 pesos, and lots in the back of the city sold for 1,200 to 2,000 pesos.

These prices represented a three- to fivefold increase over the period of a decade. Most of the buildings were new, even in the established part of town, because the city had twice within a few years suffered severely by fire. In March 1788, fire destroyed more than 850 houses, leaving only about 200 remaining. Then, in December 1794, an additional 212 buildings were burned to the ground, mostly warehouses, government structures, stores, and barracks. Most of the new buildings were built of brick with tile roofs pursuant to regulations enacted after the second fire.[68]

Whites, slaves, and free people of color lived side by side and in some of the same households on every occupied street in the old city. According to the 1805 city directory, the most populated streets were Bourbon, with 697 residents, and Royal, with 645. Rue Dauphine du Nord, with 51 whites, 115 free people of color, and 83 slaves, had the highest percentage of free people of color of any street. By contrast, Rue Dauphine du Sud had 122 whites, 59 free people of color, and 76 slaves. As a commercial rather than an industrial city, New Orleans had few districts where only one ethnic or economic group lived and worked. Although some neighborhoods had distinguishing characteristics, in general, blacks and whites, natives and foreigners mingled in the city's shops, streets, and residential areas.[69]

As the metropolitan area grew in the late eighteenth and early nineteenth centuries, the city of New Orleans developed distinct suburbs. In 1778, Bertrand Gravier and Charles Trudeau laid out the plan for what would become New Orleans's first suburb on part of the land Gravier owned just upriver from the city. This land on the other side of the commons (Canal Street) became Faubourg St. Marie. In 1796, Trudeau expanded it back from Nayades (St. Charles Avenue) to Phillipa St. (Dryades). This part of Faubourg St. Marie is what is today the Central Business District. After Bertrand Gravier died in 1797, his brother Jean expanded the survey back to Circus Street (now Rampart). Americans began moving into the suburb as soon as it was developed and came in droves after the Louisiana Purchase. There were around a thousand residents of Faubourg St. Marie in 1805, most of them Anglo-Americans.[70]

Less than two years after the Louisiana Purchase, Bernard Marigny subdivided his plantation to create New Orleans's first suburb downriver from the Vieux Carré, the Faubourg Marigny. At twenty years of age, Marigny was a minor according to Louisiana law and thus had to first get permission from the government. In April 1805, the territorial legislature authorized Marigny "jointly with Solomon Prevost, his guardian, . . . to lay out his said plantation into such lots, streets, and squares as they with the consent of the city council of the city of New Orleans may deem proper." It further authorized Marigny, "notwithstanding his minority status," to sell or lease any of the lots so created.[71] Marigny then commissioned two men who had been architects and engineers under the Spanish administration, Nicolas de Finiels and Barthelemy Lafon, to draw up plans and design the streets for the new suburb. Marigny created hundreds of lots from his former plantation. The lots varied in size, but typically they were 60 feet in width and 120 feet in depth. The price of the lots depended, in part, on whether or not they had been improved with buildings. Unimproved lots could go for as little as $450, while lots with buildings on them could go for as much as $900.

Whether it was Marigny's intent or not, the vast majority of people who bought land in Faubourg Marigny were francophone. Contemporaries referred to Faubourg Marigny as the "Creole quarter" because few Anglo-Americans lived there.[72] Dozens of free people of color purchased lots in the faubourg. Because the development and rapid expansion of Faubourg Marigny coincided with the arrival of the refugees from Cuba in 1809–10, one might assume that the suburb was populated by refugees. A comparison of the names on deeds to lots in the Marigny with the names of known refugees, however, produced few matches, suggesting that the refugees were not themselves an important group of early purchasers of property in the Faubourg Marigny.[73] Nevertheless, the presence of dozens of "Creole cottages" represent a West Indian influence on the architecture in the quarter. These small houses with high slate rooftops built close to the banquettes (sidewalks) resemble houses built in the cities of the French West Indies. Perhaps some of the builders in Faubourg Marigny were refugees even if few of the purchasers were. In any event, a rivalry developed between the Anglo-American quarter located upriver in Faubourg St. Marie and the French "Creole" quarter located downriver in Faubourg Marigny. The antagonism between the sections lasted for several decades and got so heated that in 1831 the legislature amended the city charter to divide the city into three municipalities, the Vieux Carré, St. Marie, and Marigny.[74]

While Faubourgs St. Marie and Marigny developed on high ground along the river, other suburbs emerged in the territorial period as a result of New Orleans's relationship with Lake Ponchartrain. For decades, hundreds of people, mostly slaves working the land, had lived along Bayou St. Jean leading into the lake. In 1785, there were 91 whites, 14 free people of color, and 573 slaves living either along the road leading from the Vieux Carré to the bayou or along the bayou itself. After the Louisiana Purchase, however, this plantation land was slowly but surely subdivided and urbanized. In 1804 and 1805, Daniel Clark bought plantation land that bordered Bayou St. Jean and hired Barthelemy Lafon to draw up a plan for Faubourg St. Jean. The suburb had a fan-like formation with a focus at Place Bretonne (where today Bayou Road meets Dorgenois Street, just below Broad) resulting in thirty-five irregularly shaped blocks. Then, in 1810, the city purchased the plantation of Claude Tremé, partly out of the necessity to provide housing for refugee immigrants. The plantation was subdivided by Jacques Tanesse with a plan similar to that of the Vieux Carré. Faubourg Tremé bordered both the back of the Vieux Carré and, on its upriver side, the newly formed Faubourg St. Jean. It also bordered, on its downriver side, the Carondolet Canal, providing water access to the bayou, Lake Pontchartrain, and, eventually, the Gulf of Mexico.[75] While St. Jean and Tremé did not develop as early or as rapidly as St. Marie or Marigny, they did, within a few years, provide an irregularly shaped but continuous urban area connecting the river to the lake.

New Orleans in the Age of Revolution was a very cosmopolitan and active city. In the daytime, the levee was "lined with its forests of masts and sooty cylinders, - the products of a foreign and domestic world crawling with warehouses and shops."[76] At night, the city was teeming with activity. Whites, enslaved blacks, and free people of color gathered in homes, in taverns, and on the streets to dance, drink, and gamble. By the late 1790s, Spanish officials and some planters had become concerned about the "dens of vice" operating in the Crescent City, prompting Louisiana's governor, the Baron de Carondolet, and Attorney General Don Pedro Dulcido Barran to shut down numerous gambling halls and taverns. By 1797, only ten out of a previous several dozen taverns were still operating, and potential tavern owners required a license from the *mayordomo de proprios* to operate a bar. After Carondolet left Louisiana in 1798, the number of drinking and gambling establishments began to increase again. Beginning in the 1790s, residents of New Orleans also had an opportunity to experience "high culture." The first public ballrooms began operating in 1792, the same year New Orleans's first theater (known as the Coliseo) was built. New Orleans was also home to the first opera house in what is now the United States, which opened its doors in 1796.[77]

By the time Louisiana became a state in 1812, New Orleans was home to several dance halls. Two blocks upriver from the cathedral, at the corner of Rue Conde (today Chartres Street) and Rue Dumaine, stood the Conde Street Ballroom, a "whites only" ballroom that opened in October 1792. One more block upriver and one block closer to the river, Bernard Coquet offered dances for free people of color in his home at 27 Rue St. Phillipe. The dances at "la Maison Coquet" began in 1799 and immediately attracted both whites and enslaved blacks as well as the intended patrons. The house also hosted the first quadroon ball in 1805, when August Tessier rented Coquet's home for this purpose and renamed it La Salle de Chinoise. In 1808, Coquet opened La Salle de Spectacle, a "magnificent building of Philadelphia brick," located several more blocks away from the river at 721 Rue St. Phillipe. This building, later renamed the Washington Ballroom, hosted free colored balls and quadroon balls throughout most of the antebellum period. The Anglo-American perceptions of all these interracial gatherings and the government's attempts to regulate intimate relations across the color line are discussed in greater detail in chapter 4.

One block back from the Conde Street Ballroom, at the corner of Royal and Dumaine, stood a small building that operated as a courthouse in the early years of American rule. According to an early historian of New Orleans, Andrew Jackson was tried here for contempt of court in 1815.[78] This may have been the building that housed the New Orleans City Court for part or all of its eight-year tenure (1806–13). The City Court was probably the most influential site at which free people of color asserted and protected their status and rights. In eight years, this court heard around 350 cases involving free colored litigants (about

10 percent of the total number of cases it heard), including the cases that begin chapters 2, 4, 5, and 6.

Another site that was equally if not more influential in shaping New Orleans's society in this period was the slave market.[79] It stood where the French Market is today, just on the other side of the levee from the Mississippi River on the downriver end of the Vieux Carré. Adjoining the levee at the lower end of town, "the flesh market [was] entirely enclosed, each separate stall, of which there [were] about 7 or 8—being a distinct apartment with a door & window." According to John Pintard in 1801, the New Orleans slave market was "the most filthy" of its kind he had ever seen, and he could not say "whether it be ever hoed out or not."[80] Yet, by the time Louisiana became a state in 1812, the slave market in New Orleans was on its way to becoming North America's largest. The slave market showed that whatever its similarities to the great port cities of New England and the Mid-Atlantic states, and whatever its economic ties to the grain- and livestock-producing Northwest, New Orleans remained a slave society and, in fact, the main supplier of enslaved labor to the cotton South. The slave market served as an ominous symbol for free people of color as well. It reminded them that because of their African ancestry, partial or not, they always risked enslavement themselves, whether this be actual (if illegal) enslavement through kidnapping or fraud, or virtual enslavement through restrictive black codes.

* * *

As the St. Domingan refugees disembarked in New Orleans, whether at the port of New Orleans on the Mississippi River, the depot at Bayou St. Jean, or the Carondolet Canal basin, they were entering a world that was both different and familiar. On the one hand, the region was the territory of an English-speaking republic rather than a colony of a French- or Spanish-speaking empire. If St. Domingue had been the "jewel of the Antilles" due to its unprecedented production of cash crops, the lower Mississippi valley was still on the American frontier. And New Orleans, though seemingly destined for commercial greatness, was much less refined than the well-established port cities of the Caribbean such as Le Cap, Port-au-Prince, Havana, or even St. Iago de

Cuba. On the other hand, these differences were small compared with the similarities. Although officially inhabitants of the United States, most of the residents in New Orleans spoke French as their primary language—there was no language barrier for the refugees. Indeed, because the refugees themselves made up a significant portion of the population in the late territorial period, many of the sights and sounds would have been familiar. Most important, however, the refugees' new home in New Orleans, like their previous homes in St. Domingue, Jamaica, and Cuba, was a slave society. Once they had been in the city for a few days, possibly even a few hours, they would have likely encountered both the slave market and the courthouse. The slave market was symbolic of the material structure that dominated the lower Mississippi valley— the commerce in slaves and slave-grown products. The courthouse was symbolic of the legal structure that supported this material structure. The legal structure is the subject of the next chapter.

2

A Legal System in Flux

When Jean Baptiste sued for his freedom in the New Orleans City Court in 1811, he was invoking Spanish law before a francophone judge in an American court. The petitioner, a thirty-year-old black man, admitted to being a slave but claimed a legal right to purchase his own freedom based on a contract formed when Louisiana was still a Spanish colony. His petition alleges that on July 4, 1789, Andres Almonaster, his master, contracted with Coffi, his father, to grant liberty to all four of Coffi's children for a total sum of 2,400 pesos.[1] Coffi had paid a total of 316 pesos before he died in the late 1790s. Shortly thereafter, Almonaster also died. In 1811, Jean Baptiste asked the City Court to order Almonaster's widow, Louise Laronde Castillon, to accept the sum of 284 piastres and grant him his freedom.[2] Thus, the case involved complex issues of not only contract law but also slave law, estate law, and conflict of laws from different jurisdictions. More important for Jean Baptiste, it would determine whether or not he would legally gain his freedom.[3]

The judge in the case, a white refugee of the Haitian Revolution named Louis Moreau-Lislet, denied Jean Baptiste's claim. Although he did not provide a written rationale for his decision, Moreau-Lislet could have based his judgment on any number of factors. Jean Baptiste did not provide the original contract or proof of the payments made by Coffi but instead had the agreement's terms and the payment schedule transcribed in the petition. He also did not offer a reason as to why he deserved the entire credit of 316 piastres—he never explained what happened to his three siblings who also stood to gain their freedom. The defendant's lawyer, a former congressman from the Orleans Territory and future justice of the Louisiana Supreme Court named Pierre Derbigny, answered the petition by claiming that Louise Laronde Castillon did not inherit the obligation of her late husband. Perhaps most important, Jean Baptiste claimed his right to freedom by virtue of the Spanish policy of *coartacion*, which had been expressly overturned by the territorial legislature. Whatever his reasoning, the judge was well equipped to deal with all the complicated issues in Jean Baptiste's case. Since he arrived in New Orleans from revolutionary St. Domingue after the Louisiana Purchase, Moreau-Lislet had spent a good part of his time familiarizing himself with both the laws of Spanish Louisiana and the legal system of Anglo-America.

This chapter examines the legal structure of New Orleans in the years following the Louisiana Purchase. It explores the interrelated juridical contests between civil law and common law jurists, between proponents and opponents of slavery, and between national and local rule of the lower Mississippi valley. It further illustrates the influence of West Indian refugees on the territory's legal system and the way its laws treated free people of African descent. The legal system that emerged from these struggles was a reflection of the ideals of the Age of Revolution converging with the material conditions of plantation slavery. While the laws supported slavery, racism, and patriarchy, they also, above all else, protected property rights. The legal structure, therefore, allowed those free people of color with property to undercut some of the power structures created by slavery and racism.

The Many Legalities of the Louisiana Purchase

Jean Baptiste's pursuit of his freedom was interrupted by the Louisiana Purchase, which raised a plethora of juridical questions. In this treaty, signed on April 30, 1803, the Republic of France agreed to transfer the "Province of Louisiana" to the United States of America for a total sum of 78 million francs (the equivalent of $15 million), thereby doubling the size of the United States. While the Louisiana Purchase was later seen as a coup for President Jefferson, in part because it secured westerners unfettered access to the Mississippi River and, through it, the Gulf of Mexico, it met strong opposition at the time. Federalists opposed the treaty out of fear that it would strain relations with Great Britain, while some members of Jefferson's own party feared that it set a dangerous precedent for expansive powers of the national government. Many believed that the treaty was unconstitutional. Jefferson himself, who had previously favored limitations on the power of the central government, temporarily set aside his idealism to tell his supporters in Congress that "what is practicable must often control what is pure theory." The majority of Congress agreed, and the treaty narrowly passed a House vote, 59 to 57.[4]

In addition to the issue of its constitutionality, the treaty raised questions regarding how the newly acquired territory would be organized, who would govern, and under what law.[5] The U.S. Congress addressed some of these questions on March 26, 1804, when it passed "An Act Erecting Louisiana into Two Territories and Providing for the Temporary Government Thereof." Under this act, all of the Louisiana Purchase territory south of the thirty-third parallel (roughly all of the present-day state of Louisiana on the right bank of the river plus New Orleans) became the Orleans Territory. The law gave the president of the United States the power to appoint, among others, the governor, secretary, judges, and legislators of the territory. The legislative council was to be composed of "thirteen of the most fit and discreet persons of the territory . . . from among those holding real estate therein, and who shall have resided one year at least, in the said territory." Together, the governor and legislative council had the "power to alter, modify, or repeal the laws which may be in force at the commencement of this act . . . but no law shall be valid which is inconsistent with the constitution and laws of the United States." Finally, the March 26 law incorporated a total of twenty-one other laws of Congress so as to apply to the Territory of Orleans, among them, the Fugitive Slave Law and "An Act to Prohibit the Carrying On of the Slave Trade from the United States to Any Foreign Place or Country." With this act, therefore, the central government assumed a great deal of control of the Territory of Orleans.[6]

Once Orleans had been established as a separate territory from the rest of the land acquired in the Louisiana Purchase, the question turned to what type of legal system would prevail in the territory. Namely, would it be subject to common law or civil law? While a struggle ensued after the Louisiana Purchase between proponents of each tradition, it never posed a serious threat to disunion, as some at the time claimed it would. Both sides proved willing to compromise. Many elements of Spain's civil law tradition survived the Louisiana Purchase, other elements were imported from the French West Indies, and common law principles from the United States also made their way into Louisiana's legal system, some immediately after the Louisiana Purchase. Yet the legal contests of territorial Louisiana were more complex than simply cultural and legal battles between Anglo-American supporters of common law and French and Spanish supporters of civil law. Rather, they were also intimately tied to the desire to preserve and protect the Union, assertions of local rule, and, ultimately, the future of slavery in the region.[7]

Common Law, Civil Law, and Local Rule

In order to understand the common law versus civil law debates in the Territory of Orleans, it is necessary to understand the basic differences between the two.[8] Common law and civil law are not legal *systems* so much as legal *traditions*. A legal system is "an operating set of legal institutions, procedures, and rules," while a legal tradition is "a set of deeply rooted, historically conditioned attitudes about the nature of law, about the role of law in society and the polity, about the proper organization and operation of a legal system, and about the way law is or should be made, applied, studied, perfected, and taught."[9] Louisiana's legal system is the product of both traditions.

The differences in the two traditions center on their different visions of the source of law and are illustrated by their different visions for the role of legislators, legal scholars, and judges. The civil law tradition adheres to "legislative positivism," which holds that only statutes enacted by a legislature have the power of law. In the common law tradition, on the other hand, law finds its source in judicial precedent and custom, as well as statutes.[10] Civilian law is premised on the view that lawmakers are able to anticipate conflicts and, based on reasoning from basic premises, enact laws that will resolve these conflicts. When civil law countries go through codification, it is all-encompassing. Any principles of prior law that are not included are no longer binding. Common law countries also have statutes, but these are not exclusive and are often codifications of customary or judge-made law stemming from previous disputes rather than anticipations of future conflicts.[11] A common law advocate might argue that the civil law has a utopian view of codification.

Legal scholars play significantly different roles in the two traditions. In civil law countries, they serve as advisers to lawmakers, providing their expertise on the function and impact of laws. While law professorships in common law countries are often prestigious positions, the scholar plays no real part in the lawmaking process. Students of civilian law read legal scholars and learn about the historical development of ideas about the function of law. Students of common law, on the other hand, pay little attention to legal scholars but instead read great cases and learn about the historical circumstances giving rise to them. In other words, legal history in civil law tradition is intellectual history, while in the common law tradition it is most often social or economic history.[12]

Finally, and perhaps most important, judges in the two traditions serve different functions. In the common law world, the decisions of judges can become precedent, which, in itself, becomes a form of binding law. This has led to criticism from proponents of the civil law on the basis that common law countries do not strictly adhere to separation of powers. The civil law countries created administrative courts and limited or prohibited judicial review of legislation in order to prevent the judge from taking on the role of a lawmaker. In the civil law world, judges are seen as civil servants or functionaries.[13]

While the civil law tradition claims roots in classical Greece and Rome, if not before, it was reinvigorated during the Age of Revolution. Prior to the Enlightenment, it was not uncommon for judges in jurisdictions based on Roman law to act like common law judges. But as the revolutionaries on the European continent saw it, this was a problem. Thus, in the late eighteenth and early nineteenth centuries, many emerging states on the European continent went through processes of radical and extensive codification. The most notable and most influential of these was the enactment of the French Civil Code of 1804. The main author of the Code Napoleon, as it came to be called, was Jean Étienne Marie Portalis, who worked on his compilation from 1800 until its completion four years later. Law in England was transformed much more slowly. Nevertheless, by the eighteenth century, it had transformed a great deal from its medieval state.[14]

At the same time Portalis was working on the Code Napoleon, President Thomas Jefferson was working on acquiring the Louisiana Territory from France. After successfully doing so, he insisted on Americanizing the new territory's legal system. When Jefferson first took office in 1801, he expressed his desire for a nation of "people speaking the same language, governed in similar forms, and by similar laws."[15] Thus, two years later, he was convinced that the loyalty of Louisianans to the United States was dependent upon their acceptance of its common law traditions. Jefferson had been trained in the common law at the same time he was participating in the birth of the United States. In his view, this legal tradition was an essential component of the American political system, and if Louisianans failed to adopt it, they would never be fully integrated into the Union. But the president feared that the civil law tradition was so well entrenched in the lower Mississippi valley that its inhabitants would resist attempts to impose common law. In 1803, therefore, he pushed for the annexation of New Orleans and the surrounding countryside into the Mississippi Territory. As he explained to Horatio Gates, "We shall endeavor to introduce the American laws there, and that cannot be done but by amalgamating the people with such a body of Americans as may take the lead in legislation and government."[16] But this plan had little support, and Jefferson soon abandoned it.

Once the plan to integrate New Orleans into the Mississippi Territory was abandoned, the hopes for instilling the common law in the lower Mississippi valley rested on Anglo-American immigrants to the region. In fact, several influential Anglo-American jurists trained in the common law tradition immigrated to New Orleans immediately after the Purchase. Among them was William Charles Cole Claiborne, the man Jefferson appointed to be the Orleans Territory's first governor. Although Claiborne was born in Jefferson's home state of Virginia and studied at the College of William and Mary, he lived in many different parts of the United States before coming to Louisiana. At the age of sixteen, he moved to New York, where he worked under John Beckley, the clerk of the House of Representatives. When the nation's capital moved to Philadelphia in 1790, he went there with it and began to study law. In 1794, he moved to Tennessee to start his legal practice. He later served as justice of the Tennessee Supreme Court and then governor of the Mississippi Territory before Jefferson made him governor of Orleans in 1804. Jefferson charged Claiborne with overseeing the territory's adoption of common law principles.[17]

Several other common law lawyers made an early impact on the territory. James Brown, another Virginia-born lawyer, arrived in New Orleans in November 1804 after practicing law for many years in Frankfurt, Kentucky. He served as secretary and district attorney for the Orleans Territory but turned down an appointment to the Superior Court, apparently because it did not pay well enough. He purchased a sugar plantation on the German Coast and became one of the largest slaveholders in the territory.[18] Another Brown, Jeremiah Brown, wrote a pamphlet in 1806 defending the common law tradition in which he accused refugee lawyers "from the bloodletting on the island of Santo Domingo" of seeking to undermine the American legal system.[19] John Prevost, the stepson of Aaron Burr, was born in New Jersey and studied law in New York. He came to New Orleans in October 1804 and accepted a position as justice on the Orleans Superior Court. Supporters of common law hoped that Prevost would use his position to help Americanize the territory's legal system.

The most influential and probably most controversial Anglo-American jurist to come to New Orleans was Edward Livingston, brother of Robert Livingston, one of the signers of the Louisiana Purchase treaty. Edward Livingston studied at Princeton and then apprenticed himself to noted lawyer and legal scholar John Lansing.[20] While studying under Lansing, Livingston developed an appreciation for Roman law, which he thought to be much more efficient than the "judge-made" law of England. Still, he was admitted to the New York bar and became a successful common law attorney and lawmaker. He was a congressman from New York State, the U.S. attorney for the state, and the mayor of New York City before coming to New Orleans in 1804. He left New York in the wake of a financial scandal that both left him deeply in debt and soured his relationship with Thomas Jefferson. Most important,

Livingston was a brilliant legal mind who was constantly working to make Louisiana's laws clearer and its legal system more efficient.[21]

While Jefferson and Claiborne encouraged these common law jurists to immigrate to the Orleans Territory, local supporters of the civil law tradition resisted the efforts of the central government to Americanize the region's legal system. Among the civil law–trained jurists living in New Orleans at the time of the Purchase, Pierre Derbigny, the lawyer for Louise Laronde Castillon in the case that begins this chapter, was the most accomplished.[22] Derbigny opposed Anglo-American common law in Louisiana and defended the retention of civil law practices established during the French and Spanish colonial periods. Yet some of the most vocal supporters of civil law were not lawyers at all but wealthy French-speaking planters such as Joseph Dubreuil and Julien Poydras. Dubreuil was very critical of Claiborne's appointment of both American and French judges to the territorial courts and the "awful cacophony which was bound to result from such an arrangement."[23] Poydras proclaimed "of all the evils to which lower Louisiana was exposed by American rule, nothing was more nefarious than the threat to its ancient laws and legal institutions."[24] Poydras's assertion raises a central contradiction to the Jefferson administration's attempts to transform Louisiana's legal system from civil law to common law. As Louisiana legal historian Mark Fernandez has observed, since common law "rests on the notion that, over the centuries, the law will evolve and eventually approach the ideal of justice . . . , how could the common law replace the civilian legal heritage of Louisiana?"[25]

Some francophone planters put their words into actions. In November 1805, a group of rural planters published a set of "Instructions" for their delegates in the House of Representatives complaining of the newly imposed county court system, which they saw as both oppressive and inconvenient.[26] Then, in June 1806, ten non-English-speaking members of the legislative council resolved to immediately dissolve the newly formed General Assembly. Their main reason for doing so, as explained in a manifesto they had published in a local newspaper, was to protest the attempts of the governor, acting on behalf of the national government, to impose a foreign and unfamiliar legal system on the residents of Orleans: "The most inestimable benefit for a people is the preservation of its laws, usages, and habits. It is only such preservation that can soften the sudden transition from one government to another and it is by having consideration for that natural attachment that even the heaviest yoke becomes endurable."[27] It seems that many elites who had lived in Louisiana prior to the Louisiana Purchase feared that an American legal system threatened the vitality of their culture.

The most influential civil law jurist in Louisiana during the territorial period, however, was not one of Louisiana's own but a post-Purchase immigrant from St. Domingue, and the judge in the case that opens this chapter, Louis Moreau-Lislet. Born in Cap Français, St. Domingue, in 1766, Moreau-Lislet studied law in Paris, becoming an *avocat* just before the outbreak of the French Revolution. He returned to Le Cap prior to its burning by slave insurgents in 1793. In 1794, he served as agent and attorney for several emigrants who expected to return to the island after the hoped-for defeat of the insurrection, but by 1800 he held an official position in the revolutionary government. In 1801–2, he sat as interim judge on a court in Port Republicain (Port-au-Prince), and as late as February 1803 he was a public defender and a trial judge in Le Cap. In August 1803, after the French army had surrendered to Jean Jacques Dessalines's forces, Moreau-Lislet left St. Domingue. He went first to Cuba, but then sometime between August 1804 and February 1805, he arrived in New Orleans. Because Moreau-Lislet was fluent in French, Spanish, and English, Governor Claiborne made him official interpreter in the colony almost as soon as he arrived. The governor then appointed the refugee to be the first judge of the newly formed New Orleans City Court in 1806. He remained on the City Court's bench until early 1813, less than a year before a restructuring of the court system ended its existence. In addition to his service on the City Court, Moreau-Lislet was a practicing lawyer and, like Edward Livingston, an active participant in clarifying the region's laws.[28]

One of the most controversial cases in New Orleans during the territorial period pitted Louis Moreau-Lislet against Edward Livingston as lawyers on opposite sides of the docket. The case was officially called *Gravier v. City of New Orleans,* but it is remembered simply as the "batture case" after the piece of land that was the subject of the suit. In lower Louisiana, a batture is an area of land between the river and the levee that remains dry for most of the year but is covered by the river in its annual swells.[29] The batture in question in the *Gravier* case was upriver from the Vieux Carré in Faubourg St. Marie. In the late eighteenth century the land was part of Bertrand Gravier's plantation, but in 1788 he subdivided much of the land in establishing New Orleans's first suburb and sold parcels of this estate throughout the 1790s. When Bertrand died in 1797, his brother, Jean Gravier, inherited the land that had not been sold. The batture land bordering Faubourg St. Marie had been neither sold nor improved but was being used by the public. In 1803–4, Jean Gravier attempted to move the levee on this batture closer to the river in order to claim more land, a practice that had developed throughout New Orleans's history because the batture was constantly widening due to the buildup of soil. This time, however, the public protested because Gravier did not own any of the land bordering the batture. Gravier then sued the city in the Orleans Superior Court to establish his title to the St. Marie batture. Livingston agreed to represent Jean Gravier on a contingency fee. If he won, Gravier would grant Livingston a part of the batture on which Livingston planned to construct a commercial dock. In answering the lawsuit, the city of New Orleans, represented by Pierre Derbigny and Louis Moreau-Lislet, claimed that the St. Marie batture was public land. On May 23, 1807, a unanimous court granted a decision in favor of Gravier. Yet, while Livingston won the case for his client, he was never allowed to build on the land. President Jefferson claimed the land as federal government property and ordered the eviction of Gravier and Livingston pursuant to a law of Congress of March 3, 1807, that allowed the government to evict squatters on public lands. The order was executed, and Gravier and Livingston were evicted, in January 1808.[30]

While the batture case pitted New Orleans's most accomplished common law–trained lawyer against two of the civil law's best, the issues of the case had little to do with disputes over the Americanization of the legal system.[31] Livingston's client, Jean Gravier, was Louisiana born and tended to favor the civil law tradition, while Claiborne and Jefferson, avid proponents of the common law tradition, both supported the city's position. In fact, Moreau-Lislet and Livingston came to admire and respect each other even though they were opponents in the case and were trained in different legal traditions. Each showed an appreciation of the other's legal tradition. In his time on the City Court bench, Moreau-Lislet acted like a common law judge in his liberal interpretations of existing law and willingness to make decisions based on custom and precedent. For his part, Livingston was a proponent of civilian law even before coming to Louisiana. Once he got there, he became one of its most articulate defenders against common law encroachment. Moreau-Lislet and Livingston were both ambitious men seeking power and influence, but both also seemed genuinely interested in improving the territory's legal system. Under the influence of these two men, the heated debates between proponents of civilian law and proponents of common law subsided by the end of the territorial period.

Indeed, the respective careers in New Orleans of both Moreau-Lislet and Livingston suggest that each was more concerned with creating certainty in the territory's laws than in pushing for one tradition over the other. As a result, they were willing and active participants in the drafting and clarification of the substantive laws and legal procedures of early American Louisiana. In 1804, having recently arrived in New Orleans from New York, Livingston wrote that the governor's "ordinances in English mixed with those of his predecessors in Spanish and French, the laws of Castile, the Customs of Paris, the Leyes de Partidas, les Edits du Roi, the Statutes of the United States and the omnipresent common law of England make a confusion worse than that of Babel."[32] He helped clarify the territory's laws by drafting a code of civil procedure in 1805. Moreau-Lislet also played a big role in providing certainty and clarity to the territory's laws. In June 1806, the legislature assigned him and James Brown the task of compiling the region's laws into a written digest. Moreau-Lislet was the dominant partner in this joint effort. Two years later the two submitted their work for legislative approval, and the legislature quickly adopted a bill to make it the law of the land in Louisiana. Despite some concerns that he would, Claiborne did not veto the bill.[33] The 1808 compilation of laws was a digest rather than a code. Moreau-Lislet did not create a set of laws by reasoning from basic principles (as Portalis had done in drafting the Napoleonic Code); rather, he studied existing laws in Louisiana and organized and categorized them in written form. This is important because it means that the *Civil Digest of 1808* did not break from past law; it merely organized and summarized it, and it was not the exclusive law of the land.[34] Finally, in 1822, the state legislature commissioned Livingston, Moreau-Lislet, and

Derbigny to prepare a full revision of the civil code, a commercial code, and a comprehensive code of civil procedure. The new Civil Code of Louisiana was completed, was accepted by the legislature, and became law in 1824.[35]

The legal system that emerged in Louisiana from all these efforts was, not surprisingly, a compromise influenced by both the civil law and common law traditions. The U.S. Constitution guaranteed the rights of trial by jury and habeas corpus, both elements of the English common law and strangers to Roman civil law. And the March 26, 1804, act of Congress created a common law (or adversarial) court system in the territory.[36] The law of civil procedure, while unique, adopted many of the basic components of the American system, including some of the common law forms of action, the adversary process itself, and the controlling importance of the judicial interpretation of the written law. The Civil Digest of 1808 did nothing to alter the American court system to which the local population had adjusted with surprising speed, and it did nothing to prevent the introduction of American criminal law and criminal procedure, again drawing little protest from the locals. Furthermore, Louisiana rejected a commercial code that might have alienated it from the national economy that was increasingly becoming the key to its prosperity. The only area of the Civil Digest that was truly civil law in nature was that of private substantive law, such as the laws governing contracts, marriage and family obligations, and inheritance.[37] Finally, the 1824 Civil Code incorporated common law principles of property and contract into the basic framework of the Napoleonic Code.[38]

Anglo-Americans and Franco-Louisianans also fought over what should be the official language of the Orleans Territory. English speakers argued that it should be English only so as to conform to the rest of the country. They claimed that requiring publication in both French and English would be too costly and cumbersome. French speakers, on the other hand, feared that an English-only requirement would put them at a grave disadvantage in legal proceedings. The French speakers, with the support of Livingston and Superior Court justice John Prevost, won the day, at least officially. The Civil Digest of 1808 was printed in both French and English, and Livingston's rule of civil procedure required all court documents to be drawn up in both languages. In the

City Court, however, this requirement was ignored more often than it was followed. Out of all the cases in the court involving free people of color, about a third of the court documents were filed in English, about a third in French, and about a third in both. Only a handful of parties objected when the rule was not followed.[39]

The battles over the future of Louisiana's legal system and clash of legal cultures were intertwined with concerns about preserving a fragile Union and assertions of local control. At the time of the Purchase, Jefferson was convinced that the best way of ensuring the loyalty of Louisiana's *ancienne habitants* to the United States was by indoctrinating them into Anglo-American culture, especially its legal culture. He appointed Claiborne as governor with instructions to oversee the overhaul of the legal system. After many local elites resisted attempts at a complete overhaul, however, Claiborne let up in his campaign against the civil law. He had come to accept that he could best win the loyalty of the old inhabitants by allowing some of their customs, including the civil law, to continue. In an October 1808 letter to James Madison regarding the legal system in Louisiana, the governor made establishing the common law his third priority. His first goal was "to render the laws certain; [his] next . . . to render them just, and [finally] to assimilate [Louisiana's] system of jurisprudence *as much as possible,* to that of the several states of the union [emphasis added]." By the fall of 1808, therefore, Claiborne had compromised his loyalty to the common law with his sensitivity to the sentiments and wishes of the "Ancient Louisianans."[40] As a result, Claiborne's once strained relationship with the French-speaking population of Orleans improved considerably. In 1812, he defeated Jacques Villère in the state of Louisiana's first gubernatorial election, an election he could not have won without support from some francophone elites who preferred the civil law.

In the end, local elites in New Orleans from both legal traditions were more concerned with maintaining local rule than with which tradition ultimately prevailed in the region. As one of the representatives of the new Americans in Washington, Pierre Derbigny led the charge for self-government in the Orleans Territory, but he was joined by Anglo-Americans as well, including Daniel Clark and Edward Livingston. Their collective call for the national government to stop interfering with their domestic institutions is a familiar theme throughout

American history—and resembles the cries coming from the seceding states half a century later. Their similarities with the secessionists of the mid-nineteenth century do not end there. Most local elites in the Orleans Territory were willing and able to compromise on the type of legal system in the region, but none of them, whether *ancienne habitants*, West Indian refugees, or Anglo-American newcomers, could accept national government restrictions on slavery.[41]

The Legal Battles over Slavery

Whatever differences existed between civil law and common law with regard to the issue of slavery, they paled in comparison to their similarities. Both traditions developed in the early modern era to support bourgeois values by naturalizing the individual's right to private property. Indeed, both common law and civil law supported property rights above all else.[42] And in lower Louisiana, as in the Caribbean and the southern states of America, both traditions supported New World slavery. Livingston, Moreau-Lislet, and Derbigny, all slaveholders themselves, were key participants in establishing a legal system that legitimated the treatment of human beings of African descent as chattels.[43]

Slavery and a legal system that supported it were well entrenched in the lower Mississippi valley at the time of the Louisiana Purchase. France founded New Orleans as a planned slave society in 1718, by which time the colonial power already had a codified law of slavery: the 1685 Code Noir, which was enacted to govern African slavery in the French Caribbean. The Code Noir was supposedly modeled on Roman slave law, but its name, which translates as the "Black Code," expressly acknowledged the racial element of New World slavery. Some aspects of the Code Noir recognized the humanity of slaves. It stated that slaves should be instructed in the Catholic faith, and it promoted slave families. It further allowed masters to free their slaves at their own discretion, and once freed, the former slaves had "les mêmes droits" as all free people.[44] However, other aspects of the code were more severe. Slaves could not own property and, therefore, were legally incapable of purchasing their own freedom. They could not be a party to a lawsuit or testify against free people except in cases in which the defendant was accused of inciting rebellion. Louisiana enacted its own slave code in

1724. Although it adopted most of the 1685 law, the Louisiana Code Noir made it more difficult for masters to free their slaves. Under the 1724 code, manumission required the approval of the Superior Council, French Louisiana's governing body, and masters had to show good cause for manumission, such as a special service to the colony.[45]

The Louisiana Code Noir, adapted from a set of laws designed for the prosperous West Indian sugar colonies, was ill suited for the conditions of Louisiana. Staple crop production floundered in the lower Mississippi valley for most of the eighteenth century. The quality of tobacco could not compete with that grown in Virginia, and while indigo was successfully grown in the region, this crop alone could not support a slave society. As a result, the Louisiana Code Noir was honored in the breach. Most notably, masters did not take seriously the restrictions placed on their ability to emancipate their slaves. At the end of French rule, there were close to 200 free people of African descent living in or around New Orleans.[46]

The laws and policies of the Spanish government in Louisiana with regard to slavery were more in tune with the economic reality. The slave laws were taken from the law of Castile (the Siete Partidas) and the Spanish Indies rather than France.[47] Like the Code Noir, the slave law of the Siete Partidas was modeled after Roman slave law, but it also evolved under the influence of Enlightenment principles and looked to those aspects of Roman law that were supportive of liberty rather than slavery. Title 21 of the Fourth Partida, taken directly from Roman slave law yet in tune with one strand of Enlightenment ideology, declared slavery to be contrary to natural reason. The new Spanish government seems to have taken this seriously because its policies were much more conducive to manumission. The Cabildo, which replaced the Superior Council as Louisiana's governing body, did not require masters to show "legitimate cause" to free their slaves. Moreover, under Spanish laws in Louisiana, a slave could own property without the consent of his or her master. Finally, Governor Alejandro O'Reilly's "Instructions" of 1769 allowed slaves to petition the Cabildo for transfer or freedom if they were being treated cruelly by their masters.[48]

The most significant change to Louisiana's law of slavery resulting from Spanish rule, however, was the introduction of *coartacion*, the legal right of any slave to purchase his or her freedom with or without the master's consent at an agreed-upon price or the administratively determined market value. *Coartacion* was not a part of the Siete Partidas. Rather, it was a customary practice that first developed in Cuba and then spread to some of the other Spanish colonial possessions, including the lower Mississippi valley. There was nothing comparable to *coartacion* in French Louisiana, where there is a total lack of freedom purchase cases before the French Superior Council. The first contested case of *coartacion* was in 1771. In total, the Spanish tribunals freed more than 150 slaves under this policy. However, *coartacion* never existed in Spanish Santo Domingo, whose slave law more closely resembled that of French St. Domingue than that of Cuba.[49]

The impact of *coartacion* was much more significant than the number of cases before Spanish tribunals suggests. It likely contributed to a huge increase in the numbers of "voluntary" free purchase agreements. While freedom purchases did exist in the French era, they were mostly contracted between already free husbands and their wives' consenting owners, and they were small in number, fewer than a hundred in almost fifty years. During the forty years of Spanish rule, however, almost 1,000 slaves purchased their freedom from willing owners. The legal right of slaves to their administrative hearing almost certainly encouraged these "voluntary" agreements. These numbers clearly indicate that people of African descent were knowledgeable about and took advantage of legal avenues to freedom prior to the Louisiana Purchase.[50]

Nevertheless, *coartacion* proceedings are more accurately labeled as administrative proceedings before colonial officials rather than legal proceedings in an adversarial court system, which was unique to Anglo and Anglo-American legal systems. To say that *coartacion* cases were not "adversarial" proceedings is not to say that they were friendly or uncontested. See, for example, *Catherina v. Estate of Juan Bautista Destrehan,* in which Étienne Boré, one of the executors of the estate of Destrehan, unsuccessfully argued that due to her "bad conduct" as a slave, Catherina had forfeited her right to *coartacion.*[51] *Coartacion* proceedings were not "adversarial trials" in the sense that they were not subject to the rules of procedure and evidence that governed trials in England and Anglo-America, including rules of burden of proof. The distinction between *coartacion* as an administrative proceeding and lawsuits for freedom is addressed in chapter 6. The implications of these differences, especially with regard to issues of burden of proof, are also discussed in detail in that chapter.

Jean Baptiste, the son of Coffi and the former slave of Andres Almonaster, was not one of the slaves freed by a Spanish tribunal, but he still claimed rights under the policy of *coartacion*. In his 1811 lawsuit before the New Orleans City Court, Jean Baptiste claimed to be a *cuartado*, someone who had contractual rights to purchase his freedom but had not yet done so. In most cases, a slave became a *cuartado* when he or she agreed to make payments to his or her master in installments. Freedom was never granted until the final installment was made, but the master was contractually bound to accept the payments and grant freedom upon the final one. Jean Baptiste's case was complicated by many factors, including the fact that his father, rather than he, was the party to the contract with Andres Almonaster.

Coartacion is particularly representative of Spanish slave policy in New Orleans during the Age of Revolution. As Sue Peabody and Keila Grinberg argue in their excellent comparative study of the law of slavery, "*Coartacion* reinforced the values of urban, merchant culture (hard work, thrift, delayed gratification) over the paternalistic, authoritarian regimes of the rural plantocracy." Moreover, the institution of self-purchase reflected the Spanish view that "slavery was not the natural condition of man [and] that slaves had the right to aspire to freedom."[52] Still, some slaveholders also stood to gain economically from the policy of *coartacion*. As slavery became more entrenched in the region, the price of slaves, and the cost of self-purchase, increased substantially. To be sure, as Jennifer Spear has shown in her recent work, "The cost of *coartacion* became increasingly cheaper in relation to the cost of a creole slave."[53] Yet some masters sold freedom to their slaves at prices well above their market values, as in the case of the agreement between Coffi and Andres Almonaster. Coffi agreed to pay 2,400 pesos for his four children in 1789, even though the average price for manumission of an *adult male* slave at that time was around 500 pesos. Coffi may have been unaware that he was being overcharged, or he may have agreed to the price simply to avoid an administrative hearing. Thus, while *coartacion* certainly provided exceptional rights to slaves in Spanish Louisiana, it did not threaten the long-term viability of slavery as an institution.[54]

After the Louisiana Purchase, the lower Mississippi valley became an early battleground regarding the future of slavery in America. Congress dealt with several bills designed to eventually eliminate slavery in all of the Louisiana Purchase lands, including the Orleans Territory. First, the Louisiana Ordinance of March 26, 1804, prohibited the introduction of any slaves into the territory except by U.S. citizens who were "bona fide" settlers. In other words, the act forbade the transatlantic and domestic slave trades in Orleans upon the penalty of such slaves being freed. The House introduced and passed a bill that would have prohibited the introduction of slaves altogether, but this bill failed to pass the Senate. The national government was divided on the issue. But local elites were united in opposition to any national government restrictions on slavery in the area. In the face of strong protests, the law prohibiting the slave trade in Orleans, which expired by its own terms a year after it was enacted, was never renewed.[55]

Both the attempts to prohibit slavery in Orleans and the ultimate decision to allow it were wrapped up in fears of revolution and disunion. Some members of Congress from states that had already abolished slavery saw the immediate post-Purchase period as an ideal time to set the entire nation on a course toward the peaceful abolition of slavery. Yet, for most northern politicians, preventing slavery took a backseat to preserving the Union west of the Appalachian Mountains. Some believed that slaveholders in the West needed to be appeased in order to assure their loyalty to the Union. Indeed, many westerners had threatened to leave the Union if slavery were abolished there. Thomas Pickering, for example, an antislavery Federalist and opponent of Jefferson, favored allowing slavery in the Louisiana territories because he feared the erosion of American authority in the region otherwise. On the other hand, Senator John Breckinridge from the slave state of Kentucky favored prohibiting the slave trade to the territories altogether. Breckinridge was motivated by fears of rebellious slaves inspired by the events in St. Domingue.[56] These fears, as well as fears of disunion, only increased as more and more West Indians of various statuses and complexions arrived in Louisiana. In the end, Congress as a whole put preserving the Union ahead of any antislavery views.[57]

Local elites, from both civil law and common law backgrounds, stood united in the name of local control on the issue of slave law in Louisiana. Pierre Derbigny's 1804 address to Congress in favor of self-government for the Orleans territory also argued for the reopening of the slave trade. A little more than a year later, after Congress had failed to renew the slave trade prohibition, James Brown tied local rule in Orleans to "the right of importing . . . Slaves."[58] Even as jurists were debating whether the civil law or common law tradition best suited the lower Mississippi valley, slaveholders there were fighting their own legal battles with the national government about the future of slavery in the region. As these elite white men were engaged in a form of unofficial nullification, Congress learned that any laws it passed restricting slavery in the Orleans Territory were useless without the willingness of white Louisianans to enforce and abide by them. The battle for local control was a battle to preserve slavery.[59]

On March 2, 1805, Congress enacted a second statute dealing with the Orleans Territory. This law created a bicameral legislature in the territory and gave local elites much more autonomy. The territorial assembly was to be elected by the territory's qualified voters. The assembly was then to nominate ten candidates for five positions on the new legislative council (roughly equivalent to a senate). President Jefferson was then to submit five of these ten for approval from the U.S. Senate. The election took place in October 1805, with the *ancienne habitants* gaining most of the seats. Further, eight of the ten candidates nominated for the council and all five selected by the president and approved by the Senate were French speaking.[60]

Once in control, the local legislature took measures to legitimate the power of the slaveholding class. In its first session in June 1806, the legislature passed a Black Code that reshaped the law of slavery in the region. The laws of the code, among other things, deprived slaves of the ability to own property without the consent of their masters and ended the right of a slave to sue and demand to be sold to a new master for cruel treatment. Then, in March 1807, the legislature amended the Black Code to make it much more difficult for a slave to obtain freedom. The amendment prohibited a master from emancipating his or her slave unless the slave was at least thirty years old and had not tried to run away or committed any other crime in the four years prior to emancipation. It also officially ended *coartacion*.[61] When Jean Baptiste sued for his freedom in 1811, therefore, he was invoking a policy that had been expressly abolished by the new territorial legislature. The road to freedom had become much more difficult to travel.

Codes, Courts, and Free People of Color

The local legislature not only made it more difficult for slaves to become free but also placed new restrictions on the lives of those people of African descent who were already free.[62] For example, despite their efforts to gain full rights as citizens, as discussed in the following chapter, free men of color were denied the franchise. Also, section 40 of the 1806 Black Code admonished free people of color "never to insult or strike white people, nor presume to conceive themselves equal to whites: but on the contrary that they ought to yield to them in every occasion." Moreover, new laws required all notaries or other public officers to insert the words "free man of color" or "free woman of color" when applicable on public documents. The laws of the *Civil Digest* prevented free people of color from marrying either whites or slaves. Another law specified that only white women or girls could be the victim of capital rape. Women of color, therefore, were left more vulnerable to sexual abuse.[63] Finally, the abolition of *coartacion,* while technically applying to slaves, had an important impact on free people of color. While the lines between slaves and *gens de couleur* remained blurred after the Louisiana Purchase, the abolition of *coartacion* in 1806 made it much more difficult for slaves to attain their freedom. As Louisiana moved deeper and deeper into the antebellum period, therefore, an increasing number of free people of color had never been enslaved.

It would be an oversimplification to attribute the post–Louisiana Purchase restrictions placed on free people of color entirely to the incoming American government. The French passed similar laws in St. Domingue in the aftermath of the Seven Years' War. In 1764, the king's law barred free people of color from the medical profession. A 1773 law prohibited free people of color from using the same surnames as their white relatives, and a 1779 law prohibited their affecting the style of or imitating whites.[64] The laws concerning free people of color enacted by the territorial legislature of Orleans resemble those laws passed in post-1763 St. Domingue. The Spanish had passed similar regulations in their colonial possessions in the late eighteenth century. Indeed, restrictions on free people of African descent emerged throughout the circum-Caribbean as their numbers and their wealth increased.

Elite whites were divided on how the law should deal with lower Louisiana's free colored population, and these divisions crossed linguistic lines. Some Anglo-Americans believed that placing too many legal restrictions on the free colored community would be counterproductive, while some white *ancienne habitants,* who had favored cracking down on slaves and free people of color before the Louisiana Purchase, feared that the United States would be too lenient. The events of the Haitian Revolution informed all debates about how the law should deal with free people of African descent, but it pulled elite whites in different directions. On the one hand, some whites saw free people of color as the "natural allies" of enslaved blacks and felt like they needed to legally restrict the former in order to curtail the possibility of another "Santo Domingo." On the other hand, other white officials saw the free colored community as a buffer between whites and potentially rebellious enslaved blacks. It would be misguided, therefore, to assume that the relatively privileged position of free people of color under Louisiana law (compared with the laws of other states in the U.S. South) was the inevitable product of Louisiana's colonial heritage or West Indian influence.

Nevertheless, the legal restrictions on free people of color created by the Orleans territorial legislature rarely matched the severity of those passed in the U.S. South. Unlike laws in most southern states, the Black Code of 1806–7 did nothing to limit the ability of free people of color to own property, even slave property, to move about freely, to freely assemble, or to carry weapons. Perhaps most important, unlike in most southern states and some northern states, free people of color retained the right to sue and testify in court proceedings against white people, a right that greatly enhanced their ability to protect their property.[65] Indeed, one of the consequences of the new government's policies toward free people of African descent was to close the road to *political* participation while at the same time leaving open the avenue of *judicial* participation.

This is not to suggest, of course, that in practical terms people of color had the same access to the courts as whites, or even that all people of color had equal access. There were (and are) many costs associated with filing or defending a lawsuit, including filing fees, attorneys' fees, and the costs associated with procuring witnesses and other sources of evidence. Moreover, many people of color, just like many whites, may not have been able to devote the time that lawsuits required. Therefore, even though all free people of color had the right to access the courts, many, presumably, lacked the knowledge or the resources to protect themselves and their property through the judicial system.

Nevertheless, those free people of color who did go to court, either as petitioner or as defendant, generally received a fair trial. This has much to do with what Eugene Genovese calls the hegemonic function of the law. "In modern societies," Genovese writes, "the theoretical and moral foundations of the legal order and the actual, specific history of its ideas and institutions influence, step by step, the wider social order and system of class rule, for no class in the modern Western world could rule for long without some ability to present itself as the guardian of the interests and sentiments of those being ruled."[66] Slaveholders had an interest in both legal certainty and the appearance of neutrality. They were willing to allow small victories for people of African descent in order to legitimize the system of racially based slavery.

The general impartiality of the City Court's judicial decisions applied to both jury trials and trials before a judge. The Bill of Rights, which applied to Louisiana after the Purchase, guaranteed the right to a trial by jury in all criminal prosecutions and in most private lawsuits.[67] In such cases, juries decided questions of fact while judges ruled on questions of law. Yet, while a trial by jury is a right in private lawsuits, it is not a requirement; it must be requested by one of the parties. In the absence of a jury, the presiding judge decided both questions of fact and issues of law. Most trials in the New Orleans City Court were jury trials. Still, in territorial New Orleans, as was true everywhere in the United States at the time, only white men could serve on juries. In certain cases, juries might be inclined to make different decisions than judges, especially cases involving the alleged insubordination of women of color. In property disputes, domestic law cases, and suits determining the status of a person as enslaved or free, however, judges and juries tended to reach similar conclusions. Judges and juries came from the same segment of society. They were elite white men intimately tied to an economic system dependent upon the enslaved labor of Africans and their descendants. But in order to legitimize this system in the eye of the law, they needed to at least present the appearance of neutrality. Thus, the men who sat both on the bench and in the jury box were intent upon a fair application of the law.

*   *   *

After the Louisiana Purchase, as the local government took steps to control the growing population of free people of color, these same free men and women of color took steps to deal with the law. The next four chapters examine their negotiations with New Orleans lawmakers and courts. Free men of color fought to retain their right to bear arms, and in doing so they staked their claim to citizenship. Their efforts went largely unrewarded, however. Free women of color found positions within the economy from which to accumulate property, having been denied the opportunity to marry by virtue of skewed demographics and laws prohibiting marriage across the color line. Both men and women used the courts to protect their status and property. The courtroom was not the only site for their negotiations with those in power, but it was one of the most important. By taking advantage of their right to sue and testify in court, free men and women of African descent became actors in precedent-setting cases that both secured their rights and shaped the racial structure of antebellum Louisiana.

3

"We Shall Serve with Fidelity and Zeal"

On the morning of December 20, 1803, 300 armed free militiamen of color mustered in the Place d'Armes, along with the rest of the Louisiana militia and several hundred soldiers of the French army, while incoming American governor William Claiborne and French prefect Pierre Laussat met above them on the second floor of the Cabildo to finalize the Louisiana Purchase.[1] Later that day, in his first official act as American governor of the Orleans Territory, Claiborne promised that the "natives of Louisiana" would be "incorporated into the United States, and admitted as soon as possible according to Principles of the Federal Constitution to the enjoyment of all the rights, advantages and immunities of citizens of the United States." In the meantime, Claiborne continued, Louisiana's *ancienne population* would be "maintained and protected in the free enjoyment of their Liberty, Property and the Religion which they profess."[2] No doubt the men of the free colored battalions wondered if Claiborne's promise extended to them.

Two weeks later, fifty-five members of the free colored militia, claiming to act on behalf of "the Free People of Color of New Orleans," inquired as to the impact of the Louisiana Purchase on their status in a letter they delivered to Governor Claiborne. Calling themselves "free Citizens of Louisiana," the letter writers claimed to feel a "lively joy" that Louisiana was "at length united with that of the American

Republic," because it meant that their "personal and political freedom [was] thereby assured to [them] for ever." They then "respectfully" offered their military service to their new government "as a Corps of Volunteers," promising to "serve with fidelity and zeal." The militiamen ended the letter by congratulating Claiborne "on the happy event" that had united Louisiana with the United States and promised "so much real prosperity" to both.[3]

This chapter examines the struggles of New Orleans's militiamen of African descent to stake a claim to political participation in republican New Orleans after the Louisiana Purchase. Their claims need to be understood in the context of both the system of colonial slavery in the New World and the revolutionary challenges to that system in the late eighteenth and early nineteenth centuries. In Spanish colonial New Orleans, militia service was a way for free men of African descent to achieve status and secure at least some form of political inclusion. Militiamen of color enjoyed rights and privileges as a result of the sacrifices they made for their "country" of Louisiana. They saw service to the government, participation in the government, and protection from the government as inextricably intertwined. The ideology of the American, French, and Haitian Revolutions presented both opportunities and challenges to members of the Louisiana free colored militia. On the one hand, it gave them the language to stake their claim to citizenship based on their independence as property holders and their martial sacrifices for the common good as militia members. On the other hand, because the American Revolution had fallen short of abolishing slavery and, indeed, enhanced the need for a racial justification of the institution, the Louisiana Purchase subjected free colored militiamen to continued oppression based on their ancestry.[4] As it became apparent that the incoming American regime would not grant free men of color the same civic rights as white men, militia service became less appealing to New Orleans's men of color. This attitude was reinforced by both the experience of many St. Domingan free men of color arriving from Cuba and the treatment of free soldiers of color after the Battle of New Orleans. By the middle of the second decade of the nineteenth century, the focus of New Orleans's community of color had shifted from the martial and political to the commercial and legal.

Free Colored Militias in New World Slave Societies

The Louisiana free colored militia was not unusual in the Atlantic world. Armed men of African descent (free and enslaved) served vital functions in supporting slavery in many New World colonies, especially where the racial demographics were such that few white men were able or willing to serve in militias or police forces. As early as the beginning of the sixteenth century, the Spanish crown turned to volunteer civilian companies made up of white, free black, and free "mulatto" men. As its defense needs grew, so did its reliance on free soldiers of African descent; in 1770, Cuba alone was home to 3,413 free colored militiamen, or about one-third of the colony's soldiers. Moreover, the Spanish New World was not alone in its reliance on free men of African descent for its defense needs. Locally organized militia companies of free men of color were important elements to defense forces throughout the Caribbean. In the late eighteenth century, free blacks and coloreds constituted about one-third of Jamaica's militia, and on the eve of the Haitian Revolution free people of African descent made up more than two-thirds of St. Domingue's defense forces.[5]

Free men of African descent in many Caribbean slave societies used militia service as a way of proving loyalty to the government and gaining rights and privileges otherwise unavailable to them. The militia corps allowed for an unusually open and democratic military pattern, "especially so in this age before the creation of mass conscript citizen armies." In the Spanish New World, free black militiamen were on theoretical equal footing with white militia members. In St. Domingue, the colonial militia was one of the key French institutions "employed by free families of color . . . to maintain and reinforce their status in local society." The British Caribbean, however, was less hospitable to free militiamen of African descent. In Barbados and Jamaica, freedmen were required to serve in the militia even as they were denied important rights.[6]

Throughout the Caribbean, black militiamen performed some of the most dangerous, unhealthy, and at times humiliating tasks. They served on slave patrols and police forces, provided the first line of defense in battle, and acted as scouts and diversionary forces. Free men of color fought rebelling slaves, maroons, privateers, insurgents, and veteran

European soldiers. They repaired levees, roads, and bridges, dredged swamps, put out fires, dug trenches, and took on many other public works projects.[7] In short, free colored militiamen performed tasks that few white men were willing to do.

The colonies of British North America were much less reliant on free black militias. To be sure, men of African descent fought on the continent in the French and Indian War, for both the French and the British, and in the American Revolution, for both the Patriots and the Loyalists. But these were exceptional circumstances. British militias on the continent were initially inclusive, but as the seventeenth century neared its end, they became more selective. Indentured servants, free blacks, and slaves were the first to be purged. Virginia led the way among the colonies in excluding blacks from militia service. In January 1639, the House of Burgesses passed a law requiring that only white Virginians arm themselves. By the eighteenth century, no British North American colony fielded an organized colored militia corps in times of peace. The demographics of the British North American continent in the late colonial period, unlike those of the British islands in the Caribbean, simply did not require it.[8]

In colonial Louisiana, on the other hand, both the French and the Spanish allowed—indeed, encouraged—the organization of free black militias. The French turned to armed black men early on to help them fight Louisiana's native Chickasaw, Choctaw, and Natchez populations. Dozens of African and African American slaves won their freedom by risking their lives for the French crown in the 1720s and 1730s. French colonial leaders first organized formal free colored militia units in 1735 when Governor Jean Baptiste Le Moyne, Sieur de Bienville, organized "a company of forty-five free blacks and slaves with free black officers" and led them into battle against the Chickasaw.[9]

The Spanish acquisition of Louisiana in 1763 created cultural tensions that are often associated with political transfers, giving rise to a new role for New Orleans's free colored militia as a buffer between the city's Spanish government officials and its French inhabitants.[10] In 1769, French planters revolted against the Spanish officials, prompting the Spanish crown to send General Alejandro O'Reilly, then stationed in Cuba, to quell the uprising. O'Reilly took with him from Cuba 1,847 royal troops and 240 militiamen, two-thirds of whom were free blacks.[11]

Few Spanish settled in Louisiana, even after O'Reilly's arrival, and the predominantly French-speaking population remained hostile to the Spanish government. Hence, the government relied on the free black militia to not only supplement but also balance out the potentially rebellious white militia.

The New Orleans free colored militia rose in importance as a result of Spain's policy in the last quarter of the eighteenth century of placing the burden of defense on its colonies, turning increasingly to civilian militia corps. If militias were more economical than standing armies, then free colored militias were still less expensive. And if civilian corps were more adept at traversing local terrain than were veteran troops, free men of color were just as, if not more, knowledgeable of the local lay of the land. After he became governor of Louisiana in 1791, the Baron de Carondolet vowed to increase military potential *and* decrease expenses by reorganizing and expanding the militias, including those of local free blacks. On July 3, 1791, the governor created a second company of free *pardos*, to go with the existing one *pardo* and one *moreno* militia companies, and he added to the number of corporals in each company.[12] Under the Spanish, the corps membership rose in numbers from 89 in 1779 to 469 in 1801.[13]

Free men of color gained advantages through militia service in Spanish New Orleans but were never accepted as equals by the mass of white society. The greatest advantage was the *feuro militar*, a set of coveted military privileges, including "exemption from paying tribute, opportunities to receive retirement and death benefits, and the right to bear arms and wear uniforms." The *feuro militar* also ensured that militia members would be tried in a military court in all criminal and civil matters in which they were the defendant, which was especially important given the notorious cruelty and corruption of the colonial Spanish judicial system in Louisiana.[14] As the free colored militia became more established in New Orleans, one's rank in the militia increasingly came to reflect one's relative wealth and power within the community of free people of African descent.[15] Free colored militiamen prominently placed their rank on public documents, often instead of their occupation. Members of the militia used the corporate body to achieve social advancement as well as to wield its organizational strength on behalf of all free people of African descent in the city. Militiamen (usually militia officers) petitioned the governor for relief and filed grievances on behalf of the city's people of color. In short, by the 1790s, the officers of the free colored militia had become the undisputed leaders of New Orleans's free black community. Yet their role as a "buffer," which gave them the ear of the governor, also placed them as outsiders to the larger free community of predominantly French-speaking whites.

The Impact of Revolution

The revolutions in France and St. Domingue intensified the conflict between the Spanish government in Louisiana and the majority franco-phone population while also increasing fears of slave insurrection and contributing to racial tension. The free colored militia took advantage of this opportunity to prove their loyalty. Spain feared that revolution-ary France might try to retake Louisiana along with Spain's other colo-nial possessions in the Caribbean, especially after Spain declared war on France on January 21, 1793, in response to the execution of Louis XVI. In preparation to defend against land operations in the region, Caron-dolet stationed free colored troops at recently erected fortifications sur-rounding New Orleans. Late in 1793 he also dispatched members of the free *pardo* and *moreno* militias downriver to reinforce Fort San Felipe de Placaminas, where they guarded the colony against an anticipated French invasion from the Gulf of Mexico. The expected invasions never came, but the free colored militiamen stood ready for them anyway.

The Spanish governor also worried that the revolutions' ideals about "liberty" and "equality" would incite rebellion from francophone whites, enslaved blacks, free people of color, or all of the above. The French revolutionary government's abolition of slavery in its colonies and the continued success of slave insurgents in St. Domingue contributed to these fears. The fears seemed to have been realized in April 1795, when dozens of slaves were arrested at Pointe Coupee, 150 miles upriver from New Orleans, for conspiring to kill their masters, incite a slave revolt, and abolish slavery in Louisiana.[16] After uncovering the plan, whites retaliated with typical brutality. On May 4, a governor's court convicted fifty-seven slaves and three local whites. Within a month, authorities had hanged twenty-three slaves, deported several others, and lined the river from New Orleans to Pointe Coupee with the severed heads of the executed. Spanish officials concluded that the slaves had been inspired to revolt by events in France and St. Domingue. While there were other potential reasons for the aborted revolt, including recent Spanish legislation on slaves and free coloreds, the trial summary suggests that there was some basis for this conclusion. Several witnesses testified that the leaders of the revolt were trying to induce a transfer of Louisiana from the Spanish to the French, which, they believed, would then lead to emancipation.[17]

While the slaves in Pointe Coupee may have been inspired to try to overthrow slavery in the colony by events in St. Domingue, there is little evidence that Louisiana's free colored population adhered to the most radical ideals of the age. The revolutionary fervor created fears among Spanish officials and planters about armed men of African descent, but for the most part the free colored militia soothed these fears with its collective behavior during the era. The corps helped to quell two minor slave disturbances in the 1790s. As a result, throughout the decade, Carondolet promoted members of the corps rapidly, further entrenching the loyalty of most free black militiamen to the Spanish government.[18]

For some members of the corps, however, promotions and praise were not enough; they wanted respect and treatment equal to that given the white militia members. The revolutionary ideals of the age inspired at least one prominent member to speak out against both monarchy and racial prejudice, though not against slavery. Between 1779 (when he first appears on the militia roles) and 1791, Pierre Bailly was a model member of the free colored militia, advancing from corporal second class to first lieutenant and accumulating a long record of loyal service.[19] In the 1790s, however, Bailly was tried by a military tribunal twice for conspiracy and treason, with both trials arising from comments he allegedly made about living up to the ideals of the French and Haitian Revolutions.[20] His first trial occurred in October 1791 after a group of men led by a white merchant named Don Louis de Lalande Dapremont accused him of inciting a rebellion "just like that breaking out in St. Domingue." Dapremont testified that Bailly had tried to recruit his fellow militiamen to join him in leading a rebellion against the Spanish government, expecting the French populace to join him. He was allegedly awaiting instructions and reinforcements from St.

Domingue. Bailly was tried for sedition a second time in February 1794. According to the second indictment, while stationed at Fort San Felipe de Placaminas in 1793, Bailly "denounced Spain's social hierarchy and discrimination based on color and praised the equality he perceived in the new French constitution."[21] Bailly allegedly had a conversation with a white militia commander, Don Louis Declouet, in which he expressed reluctance to fight the French should they invade. He had also allegedly conspired to murder his superior officer, Francisco Dorville, and place himself in command of the battalion. Furthermore, when a white superior officer, François Bernoudy, approached Bailly and called him "mi mulatto," Bailly reportedly replied insubordinately, "When was I ever your mulatto." According to the indictment, he also openly complained about a Señor Maxent, who refused to receive black officers at his breakfast table.

Bailly was acquitted in the first trial and convicted in the second, even though the evidence against him in both trials was flimsy, and other factors suggest that his accusers were motivated more by self-interest than by the security interests of Louisiana. In the first trial, two key witnesses, Charles Lalande and Carlos Brulet, both fellow officers in the free *pardo* militia, modified their testimony, claiming that the accusations against Bailly were hearsay. Moreover, Bailly had twice successfully sued Dapremont, Bailly's accuser, for breach of contract and unpaid rent in 1791 based on debts incurred beginning in 1787. Thus, Dapremont had incentive to see Bailly convicted, calling into question the credibility of his testimony. Without sufficient evidence to support a conviction, Governor Miro acquitted Bailly. The main witness against Bailly in the second trial, Francisco Dorville, was also indebted to Bailly, suggesting his testimony was not reliable. Yet the new governor, the Baron de Carondolet, determined that Bailly had expressed ideas suggestive of revolution and found him guilty. Bailly spent two years in a Cuban prison before returning to New Orleans in 1796. By this time he had apologized to the governor and his fellow militia officers and had resumed business dealings with whites. Apparently, he had come to terms with his world as a free man of color in a racially based slave society.

Throughout the course of the two trials, other leaders of the free colored militia tried to distance themselves from Bailly and his plans.

Dorville and Carlos Simon, who had brought the charges against Bailly in his second trial, claimed that Bailly was not a dedicated member, that he shirked his responsibilities when he could, and that he refused to parade through the city with his company. He substituted his slaves to do the menial tasks of militiamen, including repairing cracks in the levee. He feigned illness to avoid manual labor and supposedly encouraged such insubordination from others as well. In the view of these other militia officers, Bailly did not have the sense of duty, community, and corporate identity that a militia soldier should have had. In short, Bailly was in the militia not to serve his country but for personal advancement. The militiamen who testified in Bailly's two trials wanted to convey to the Spanish court that to the extent the rabble-rouser was plotting against white officials, he was acting alone. In the first trial, militia officers Charles Lalande and Carlos Brulet took the opportunity to assuage the fears whites may have had about their intentions. Brulet promised to support whites in case of any slave insurgency, while Lalande testified that "he could never resolve to take up arms against the whites and that, on the contrary, he would sacrifice his life to defend them." Thus, Bailly's rejection of the importance of the militia in gaining social status was not representative of his fellow militia officers in the Spanish period.

Bailly may have acted alone in "expressing ideals suggestive of revolution," but he was not the only member of the free colored militia to resist racial discrimination in the late Spanish colonial period. On October 24, 1800, four members of the free black militia, recently returned from an expedition in West Florida (present-day eastern Louisiana), petitioned the Cabildo for the right to have regular dances for free people of color.[22] The four-paragraph petition is noteworthy for several reasons. The petitioners were critical of whites, protective of women of color, and adherent to an ethic of martial virtue. The third paragraph of the petition asks the Cabildo to provide the city's guards to oversee the dances in order to prevent disorders:

> When we were on expedition, we were informed that *some people* came to the dances that were given there, determined to disrupt the peaceful diversions—some by provoking fights, others by chewing vanilla seeds and spitting them out for the purpose of producing an intolerable

stench, others by putting chewed tobacco on the seats so that the women would stain their garments—in short, doing and causing as much havoc as they could. This example of maliciousness was never experienced in the innumerable dances that were given in the chosen house while the guards were present. The guards, once you give them orders to attend, will be anxious to come, owing to the special privileges we shall offer them on the nights the dance is given. (emphasis added)

Who were these people about whom the militiamen complained? In all likelihood they were white men. Ninety percent of the city's free men of color were in the militia, and most would have been away at the time of the previous disorders. Furthermore, if the disturbances had been caused by free people of color or slaves, the petitioners probably would not have felt they needed guards to prevent them. They were not likely to expressly identify the troublemakers as whites because this would have risked raising the ire of the Cabildo and causing the subsequent rejection of their petition. Indeed, the petitioners were appealing to the prominent members of New Orleans's white society, the members of the Cabildo, asking for assistance in preventing disturbances caused by those who were acting in a manner unbefitting of refined society. They were not claiming equality with whites, but they were sending a message that they did not condone such inappropriate behavior and should not themselves be considered as the "low orders" of New Orleans's society.

In their petition the free colored militiamen reasserted their masculinity in the language of civic virtue. Classical republicanism identified a virtuous citizen as a tough-minded individual who made personal sacrifices for the common good. The militiamen embodied this masculine ideal of citizen-soldiers who took up arms when needed to defend their and their fellow citizens' freedom, as they had done in their "recent expedition," but laid them down again when the threat had subsided. In the revolutionary era, furthermore, an emerging middle class had begun to develop a feminine definition of virtue, rooted in evangelical Christianity, which identified female virtue with sexual propriety.[23] By identifying white men at the free colored dances as the persons who were behaving inappropriately while the free colored militia was away, the militiamen were defending the "virtue" of free women of color. Therefore, rather than comparing themselves to the colony's whites, as Bailly had done, these militia leaders contrasted their loyalty and attentiveness to duty against the debauchery of the local white men. Indeed, the petitioners contrasted themselves against local white men to present themselves and their community as the most virtuous and loyal citizens of Louisiana.

The various views of New Orleans's free men of color in the last decade of the nineteenth century parallel those of prerevolutionary St. Domingue's *gens de couleur*. First of all, some prominent free colored men in each colony openly sought racial equality for all free men. Soon after the fall of the Bastille in Paris, a group of St. Domingue's "free citizens and landowners of color" appealed to the French National Assembly for equal rights. They informed the Assembly "that there still exists in one of the lands of the empire a species of men scorned and degraded, a class of citizens doomed to rejection, to all the humiliations of slavery: in a word, Frenchmen who groan under the yoke of oppression. Such is the fate of the unfortunate American colonists known in the islands under the name of mulattos, quadroons, etc." They then argued that the "Call for Liberty" in Europe "should certainly have erased these prejudices," but instead "it has brought forth even more appalling ones." The appellants claimed that they were "clearly as qualified as the whites to demand this representation" in government. The language that got Bailly in trouble sounds very similar. "All of us being men," Bailly proclaimed, "there should be no difference. Only their method of thinking—not color—should differentiate men." Thus, both the "free citizens and landowners of color" in St. Domingue and Pierre Bailly believed in social hierarchies, just not ones based on complexion.[24] Advocates of a republican society, they sought to abolish the aristocracy of the skin.

Yet, in both prerevolutionary St. Domingue and late colonial Louisiana, even the most radical and outspoken free men of color fell short of calling for an end to slavery. In St. Domingue, Vincent Ogé, who was executed in February 1791 for leading an uprising against the French colonial government, made his stance on slavery clear in a letter to the Provincial Assembly of the North while under attack from the white militia: "My claims included nothing about the fate of the *nègres* who live in slavery. You and all our adversaries have distorted my efforts so that respectable landowners will have no regard for me. No, no,

Monsieur, we have only made claims on behalf of the class of free men who have been oppressed for two centuries." Julien Raimond, a wealthy free colored indigo planter from the South Province, claimed that white planters had "deliberately confused the free colored cause with that of the slaves."[25] The situation was similar in Louisiana. Lalande and Brulet declared it unlikely that Bailly would support the slave revolt in St. Domingue because he and his family owned slaves. Clearly, being a slaveholder himself, Bailly considered his "method of thinking" to differentiate him from enslaved men of African descent. The 1800 petitioners do not mention slavery, but they disassociated themselves from Africa and Africans, claiming that "the season for such diversion [dancing] in America and Europe" was upon them.

Leading free men of color in colonial St. Domingue and Louisiana distinguished themselves not only from slaves but also from the "lower orders" among the whites. In the French island colony Julien Raimond claimed that the "talent, character, sophistication, and knowledge" of the free colored class "only drew attention to the vices and ignorance of the island's whites, who therefore scorned them. Just as tyrants cannot forgive virtue, the dim-witted resent intelligence." The 1800 petitioners express an elitism similar to Raimond's. They opened their petition by identifying themselves each as officers in the Quadroon and Octoroon Battalions, an identity that carries connotations of class and denotations of race.[26] Generally, only wealthy free men of color became high-level officers in the militia, and while the petitioners were not white, more than half of their blood was European. Throughout most of the 1800 petition, the militia officers distinguished themselves from white men. They recited the sacrifices they made on behalf of Louisiana and Spain during their West Florida expedition, implying that white militia members had not made these sacrifices. According to the petitioners, "The men experienced bad times such as irregularity of weather and nourishment, blistering heat due to the harsh season in which the expedition was undertaken, mosquitos, night air, humidity, and other nuisances harmful to human nature, and, finally, shelling from the cannons which they expected to receive at any moment." They felt unappreciated for their efforts. Rather than thanking them, the white militiamen "compared them to irrational animals who are only led and take shelter under the hot sun which bakes their brains." The petitioners criticize, by implication, the lower orders of whites who had been disruptive at the dances for free people of color. They argued that they needed a regular dance "to recompense them in some manner, to cheer up their spirit, so that they could forget the hardships of the expedition," hardships that whites had not suffered.[27]

Free men of color in both St. Domingue and Louisiana claimed that they were the most devoted class of people to their respective colonies. In their appeal to the National Assembly, St. Domingue's "free citizens and landowners of color" claimed that they had "shed their blood and [were] prepared to spill it again for the defense of the fatherland."[28] Many white landowners in the French island colony were absentee, and most white residents of the colony saw their time there as temporary. Free people of color, on the other hand, aspired to be *habitants*, gentleman farmers, and in transforming peasant households into commercialized farms, they clearly transacted business with a time horizon that was much longer than that of their white neighbors. Free people of color, more resistant to the disease environment than whites, lived longer than they did. They had more equal sex ratios and higher fertility rates.[29] Similarly, free men of color in New Orleans expressed loyalty and devotion to their "country" of Louisiana. The 1800 petitioners, for example, identified themselves as Louisianans, giving "infinite thanks to the Most High for granting them their wish to come back to their homeland." Their identification with the "Province of Louisiana," rather than France, Spain, or anywhere in Africa, provided continuity after the Louisiana Purchase and was a key element in the free colored militia's attempts to claim political rights in republican New Orleans.

Finally, in both St. Domingue, before the slaves rose up on the northern plains, and Louisiana, before the Purchase, the great majority of men of color fell short of calling for armed revolt against the government. Men like Ogé and Bailly were the exceptions. In St. Domingue, the free colored leaders of the West rejected Ogé's appeal to join him in open revolt. While assuring Ogé that they admired his "patriotic zeal" and were "more committed than ever" to the pursuit of equal rights with whites, they could not join Ogé in "the steps [he] want[ed] to take with the governor."[30] In New Orleans, free colored militia officer Charles Lalande represents the pragmatic position taken by most members of the corps. He concisely summed up the very reasonable position of the free colored militia when he testified in Bailly's second trial that it would be futile to attempt an uprising against whites in Louisiana.

Although the statuses of free men of color in late colonial St. Domingue and late colonial Louisiana were not identical, the similarity of their arguments is not mere coincidence. Both groups served as "buffers" within their respective societies. In St. Domingue they were buffers between white planters and slaves, while in Louisiana they were also buffers between the francophone population and the Spanish government. Moreover, in both colonies, the majority of free people of color were of mixed ancestry and had never been enslaved.[31] Finally, both groups of people were property holders, owning both land and slaves—though, to be sure, St. Domingue's elite free coloreds were much wealthier than Louisiana's. Thus, while in the late eighteenth century St. Domingue was a colony of France and Louisiana was a colony of Spain, free people of color in both regions had, for similar—though not identical—reasons, developed a distinct corporate identity.

Moreover, several men of color living in Louisiana in the late colonial period had previously lived in colonial St. Domingue. At least two of the four subscribers to the 1800 petition had lived in St. Domingue before coming to Louisiana sometime in the 1790s. Juan Bautista Saraza (Scarasse), who identified himself as an octoroon, left St. Domingue sometime in 1791, eventually making his way to Louisiana, where he joined the Spanish military service. He is listed as sergeant first class in the New Orleans *pardo* militia for 1792 and soon rose to the rank of captain in command of the Battalion of Octoroons. Later he went to Cuba with the *pardo* militia to be incorporated into the Havana regiment. When he returned to New Orleans, he established his residence at 89 Dauphine Street and opened an upholstery shop. Juan Bautista Bacusa (Bacuse) was born in Gonaives, St. Domingue, in 1738. It is unclear when he arrived in New Orleans, but by 1793, he was a sublieutenant of the New Orleans free black militia. Eventually he became a captain and commanded the Battalion of Quadroons. By 1800, Bacusa had established his residence at 7 Levee North in New Orleans.[32]

Ultimately, Pierre Bailly, Juan Bautista Saraza, and other men of color sought the same thing in Louisiana that Vincent Ogé, Julien Raimond, and other men of color sought in St. Domingue—political inclusion. In Spanish colonial New Orleans, free militiamen of African descent may not have had the right to vote, but they did have the ability to voice their concerns through petitions. They would employ this same method in the early years of American rule. Thus, even though they lived as colonial subjects of a monarchy, the idea and practice of participatory government was not completely foreign to them. Still, the prospect of joining a republic offered the potential for an even greater voice in government. While the language of liberty and equality stemming from the French and Haitian Revolutions inspired some free men of color to seek equal rights with whites, it led none of them to seek the abolition of slavery. Yet many whites did not understand the distinction, and this misunderstanding became readily apparent after the Louisiana Purchase.

The Impact of the Louisiana Purchase

The men of the Louisiana free colored militia had ambivalent feelings about the Louisiana Purchase. On the one hand, America was a republic that, at least in theory, adhered to the ideals of liberty and equality. Article 3 of the Louisiana Purchase treaty states, "The inhabitants of the ceded territory shall be incorporated in the Union of the United States and admitted as soon as possible according to the principles of the federal Constitution to the enjoyment of all these rights, advantages and immunities of citizens of the United States, and in the mean time they shall be maintained and protected in the free enjoyment of their liberty, property and the Religion which they profess."[33] As militiamen, these men of color could plausibly claim to feel "a lively joy" to be united with the American government, which idealized the citizen-soldier. The free colored militiamen may have hoped and believed that the democratic ideals of the new republic promised them an opportunity for political participation as citizens. On the other hand, a republican form of government did not necessarily translate into more freedom for all people. In colonial Louisiana under the Spanish monarchy, planters had little formal political authority, while democratic governments in the American South had given a group of united white planters the ability not only to exclude free people of color from political life but also to restrict or nullify other rights, such as the right to bear arms. Precedent from the U.S. South indicated that local planters would indeed try to restrict the freedom of free people of African descent.[34] Among other restrictions, no state or territory in the United States fielded a free black militia at the time of the Purchase.

The free colored militia corps took an active role in determining their fate almost immediately after the Louisiana Purchase. On January 16, 1804, fifty-five members of the corps delivered to Claiborne the following written "Address of the Free People of Color of New Orleans" that is referenced at the beginning of this chapter:

> We the Subscribers, free Citizens of Louisiana beg leave to approach your Excellency with the Sentiments of respect & Esteem and sincere attachment to the Government of the United States.
>
> We are Natives of this Province and our dearest Interests are connected with its welfare. We therefore feel a lively Joy that the Sovereignty of the Country is at length united with that of the American Republic. We are duly sensible that our personal and political freedom is thereby assured to us for ever, and we are also impressed with the fullest confidence in the Justice and Liberality of the Government towards every Class of Citizens which they have here taken under their Protection.
>
> We were employed in the military service of the late Government, and we hope we may be permitted to say, that our Conduct in that Service has ever been distinguished by a ready attention to the duties required of us. Should we be in like manner honored by the American Government, to which every principle of Interest as well as affection attaches us, permit us to assure your Excellency that we shall serve with fidelity and Zeal. We therefore respectfully offer our Services to the Government as a Corps of Volunteers agreeable to any arrangement which may be thought expedient.
>
> We request your Excellency to accept our congratulations on the happy event which has placed you at the Head of this Government, and promises so much real prosperity to the Country.[35]

The address appeals to new opportunities for "personal and political freedom" under the American republic while at the same time revealing important continuities with the Spanish period. While the subscribers admit to, indeed boast about, their "military service [to] the late Government," they do so claiming to be "Natives of the Province." Similar to the 1800 petitioners, these men identify themselves as "free citizens of Louisiana," making it clear that their national loyalties lay, first and foremost, with the region itself rather than with whatever distant government controlled it.[36] Their country had become united with, but not subsumed by, the American republic. While this sentiment was likely genuine to a certain degree, it may also have been a strategic self-representation designed to encourage Americans both to accept their claims to loyalty and to question the loyalty of native whites.

The 1804 address also resembles the 1800 petition in the way it both chronicles sacrifices made and appeals for rights.[37] These militiamen, like their predecessors, invoked the republican ideal of civic virtue, offering their services as soldiers and claiming their rights as citizens. They claimed that their conduct in the service of the militia had "been distinguished by a ready attention to the duties required of [them]" and conveyed a willingness and ability to make individual sacrifices for the public good. By offering their services to the government as a "Corps of Volunteers," these men wanted to convey to the incoming governor that they would not need to be controlled or subdued; rather, they would help him in controlling and subduing others more dangerous than themselves.

Yet, if the address resembles the 1800 petition in some ways, it also represents a pragmatic scaling down of the most ambitious claims of Pierre Bailly in the early 1790s or of St. Domingue's free men of color. These "free citizens" were careful not to claim equality with whites. The treaty between the United States and France granted to all inhabitants of Louisiana who professed loyalty to the United States all the rights, advantages, and immunities of U.S. citizens. By expressing "confidence in the Justice and Liberality of the Government towards every *Class* of Citizens (emphasis added)," the authors of the address implicitly recognized a hierarchy within the citizenry. As *free* blacks they were citizens, but as free *blacks* they were a different class of citizen. The 1800 petition had been critical of certain whites (though not explicitly) by suggesting that they had behaved inappropriately at the dances for free people of color. The 1804 address took a slightly different tone. It politely and directly made clear what its drafters hoped and expected: that they would be assured of their personal and political freedom despite their inferior social position within the citizenry.

The "Address of the Free People of Color of New Orleans," however, was not as inclusive as the title suggests. The names of several prominent free militiamen of color from the Spanish period are conspicuously absent from the document's signature page, most notably Charles Lalande, Carlos Brulet, and Francisco Dorville. These officers in Spanish Louisiana's free colored militia corps were likely less enthusiastic about their prospects under the American republic and more attached to the Spanish government.

When William Claiborne assumed governorship of the Orleans Territory, he inherited a diverse land wrought with conflict and seemingly ripe for turmoil. The governor and other newly arriving American officials and planters were charged with defending the newly acquired territory against potential Spanish military action, French Jacobism, and slave rebellion. In the two years following the Louisiana Purchase, there were rumors of each. New Orleans's existing population of armed men of African descent occupied a curious position within this matrix of conflicting loyalties. The militia's strongest devotion seemed to be to their homeland, Louisiana, and as Louisianans they offered their services as soldiers and requested their rights as citizens. Nevertheless, rumors of Spanish attack in 1804 had aroused distrust among American officials of all Louisiana Creoles, but especially Creoles of color.[38] In a letter to James Madison, Claiborne claimed to have "no doubt, but that the free people of color have been tamper'd with, and that some of them are devoted to the Spanish Interest."[39] The French and Haitian Revolutions presented far greater concerns, and American officials were unsure about and disagreed upon the extent to and ways in which the contagion of liberty from these two events had affected free men of African descent. American attitudes toward New Orleans's free men of color were ambivalent and varied, at times suspecting them of loyalty to the Spanish, at others accusing them of tampering with slaves, while sometimes trusting their devotion to the United States. In the end, white planters and officials, free from the restrictive hold of a royal governor and the Spanish colonial system, excluded men of color from politics and refused to formally recognize their militia corps.

Only six months after the Louisiana Purchase, it became apparent that local whites would try to exclude free men of color from republican politics. In June 1804, Edward Livingston organized a public meeting to adopt a written testimonial to be forwarded to the U.S. Congress expressing the disappointments of local planters with the new territorial government. Specifically, planters objected to the territorial division of Louisiana, to a governor who could not speak French or Spanish, to the structure of the territorial government, and, most important, to the prohibition of the slave trade. The meeting, held on July 1, 1804, was open to all white men in the city but closed to free men of color. About 140 white men signed the petition.[40]

Members of the free colored militia, angry at being excluded from the Livingston petition, tried to organize their own "citizens assembly," so that "they might consider their rights" and draft their own petition to Congress.[41] A "mulatto man" brought the announcement of the meeting to a local press, but the printer refused to set the type for the letter. Some white planters, disturbed by the insolence of this "mulatto man," demanded that he be punished and that the letter writer, when his identity was determined, be expelled from the territory. After hearing of the incident, Claiborne appropriated the letter, read it, and then destroyed it so that it would never be published, fearing that it would only inflame prejudices that existed in a population "composed of so heterogeneous a mass." He did not pursue charges against either the letter writer or the courier, believing that the less said of the matter the better in a territory "where the Negro population was so great." In the presence of New Orleans's mayor, Étienne Boré, Claiborne interviewed "nine of the most discreet and influential men of colour." After the meeting, Claiborne assured Secretary of State James Madison that the free men of color with whom he met "seemed convinced of their error" and "gave the most unqualified assurances of their friendly pacific disposition." However, Claiborne seems to have either wrongly assessed the situation or intentionally misrepresented it. In later correspondence, he reveals that he could not appease the free colored population, which continued to protest its exclusion. White citizens responded by discontinuing their public assemblies directed toward the U.S. government.[42]

The controversy over the "citizens assembly" and the unpublished letter reveals the pitfalls of republican government for free people of color. Under the Spanish monarchy, free men of color had always been allowed to petition the crown's colonial representatives and frequently took advantage of this privilege. After the American takeover, however, white men excluded free men of color from this fundamental aspect of participatory government. Under the Spanish, free people of African descent had been able to prove their loyalty to the government against the suspect loyalty of the French population. They tried to do the same with Claiborne by directing their displeasure toward the local white citizenry rather than the American government. However, Louisiana was a territory, not a colony, and the American territorial governor, who was checked by the legislature, did not have the same power as a Spanish colonial governor.

Nevertheless, the free men of color were not rendered powerless. While they were prevented from petitioning Congress, they were still able to express their concerns to the local government. They appealed to Governor Claiborne just as they had appealed to Spanish colonial officials. Nine of the most influential men of color gained an audience with both the governor of the territory and the mayor of the city. Moreover, because the free men of color were not satisfied with the results of the meeting, they continued to protest their exclusion from national politics. Instead of petitioning *with* white slaveholders to Congress, they were appealing *against* white slaveholders to the local government. The free black men had asserted themselves and had gotten the attention of two important government officials.

American officials in Louisiana disagreed on how to deal with New Orleans's formidable free colored population, but for the most part they agreed that the most pressing issue in this regard was what to do about the free colored militia. In the city of New Orleans and surrounding area, three out of every eight citizen-soldiers were men of African descent. General James Wilkinson confessed to Secretary of War Henry Dearborn that "the formidable aspect of the armed Blacks and Mulattos, officered and organized, is painful and perplexing." Claiborne, on the other hand, feared that "too rigid treatment" of the free colored class might lead them "to seek support and assistance of the Negro slaves."[43] Within days after taking office, Claiborne called upon President Jefferson and his cabinet for advice regarding the free colored militia. In a letter dated December 27, 1803, the governor told Secretary of State Madison that the free colored militia in New Orleans "were esteemed a very serviceable corps under the Spanish government." Yet he believed that to recognize them under his rule would likely create tension. To recommission them might be "considered as an outrage on the feelings of a part of the Union and as opposed to those principles of policy which the safety of the Southern States has necessarily established." On the other hand, refusing to recognize the corps also carried potential unsettling ramifications. To disband the organization, Claiborne claimed, "would be to raise an armed enemy in the very heart of the country, and to disarm them would savour too strongly of that desperate system of government which seldom succeeds." By seeking the "opinions and instructions" of the federal government, Claiborne washed his hands of direct responsibility for the decisions made on the matter.[44]

After considering the delicate situation, Secretary of War Dearborn offered instructions on how to appease both free men of color and local whites. He suggested that it would be "expedient either to continue or renew the organization" but with an eye toward ultimately disbanding it. He told Claiborne that it would "be prudent not to increase the Corps, but diminish, if it can be done without giving offense, the principal officers should be selected with caution, having regard to respectability and integrity of character, as well as their popularity and influence among their associates." The secretary advised the governor to "present them a standard or a flag as a token of confidence."[45] With this advice, Dearborn offered a temporary solution that would buy time until the territorial legislature could address the issue. Claiborne, who "was unwilling to take upon [him]self the responsibility of reorganizing this Battalion, . . . was therefore relieved by the instructions which were given." On June 21, 1804, he presented the corps a "stand of colours" made of white silk and "ornamented with fifteen stripes," which, the governor claimed, was received "with great excitement." Before doing this, however, he found it "indispensable" to present the Orleans Volunteers and the City Regiment (both white militia corps) each with a standard "in order to prevent jealousy."[46] He sensed that some of the "old inhabitants of Louisiana" would have liked to have seen the free colored corps neglected, but he felt secure in the support of the U.S. government. Claiborne instructed Major Michel Fortier, the white commander of the free colored corps, to diminish the corps over time "if it can be done without giving offense." Fortier was not to muster any free man of color who resided outside of the city and was to avoid enrolling any new recruit. If he were questioned on this, he was to state that such was the order of the governor, and, though he was not certain of the reason, he presumed that the existing free colored battalions were already sufficient in numbers and that "the freemen of color not now attached thereto, may hereafter be formed into separate corps."[47] Again, in his letter to Fortier, he claimed only to be the messenger, passing on the orders of Dearborn. Governor Claiborne was trying to disassociate himself from the matter, fearing repercussions from both sides.

As Claiborne had predicted, many prominent white Louisianans disapproved of his ceremonial recognition of the free colored corps. An anonymous white man, claiming to be a Creole and writing as a "Louisianan," published a letter in the *Louisiana Gazette* chastising the governor for presenting the free colored militia with a "standard similar to that of the white militia."[48] American immigrant Daniel Clark argued that the reason the white militia was in such disarray had nothing to do with the existing militia law but was because "they had seen the black Corps preferred to them and a Standard publicly given it, whilst their own repeated offers and wishes to be employed in their country's servic [sic] has been rejected."[49] Thus, white Louisiana Creoles and white Americans alike argued publicly that Claiborne was encouraging insolence and excessive pride among the free colored corps and in the process crippling white militia morale.

While many white leaders disapproved of the ceremonial recognition of the free colored militia, several members of this corps were upset at the lack of substance behind the ceremony. They refused to accept the white officers whom Claiborne had appointed for them. Then, in April 1805, the first territorial legislature of Orleans failed to mention the free colored militia in the general militia law, thereby officially disbanding the free colored militia.[50] Many former militia members were highly offended. Had they not expressed their loyalty to the United States? Had they not shown their willingness to perform their duties as citizen-soldiers? How were they supposed to show that they meant what they said if they could not serve in the militia? James Brown claimed, "The free people of color have lost their consequence by being stripped of their Arms and are anxious to regain it."[51] Brown's comment gets to the heart of the matter for free men of color. For more than a generation, the militia had been the main vehicle by which these men of color gained status and rights in Louisiana. Without such a vehicle, they would need to find a different route.

In early 1806, Claiborne received more news of possible discontent among the free men of color in New Orleans. A free black man identified only as Stephen informed the governor that "with the exceptions of John Laduff and Vallefrois Trudeau, and a few others," every free man of color in the city was conspiring against the American government. Stephen mentioned several men in particular as the leaders of the conspiracy, including militia officers Francisco Dorville and Carlos Brulet. He claimed that a "mulatto man" named Landau "carries about the paper to ascertain those who are friendly to the Spaniards." Stephen cautioned Claiborne that if the Americans "should hear the cry of Fire, not to go out, but to stand upon their guard." According to Stephen, "These people expect the [Spanish] Marquis [Casa Calvo] to arrive shortly with three or four thousand troops, and that he is to bring one or two nations of Indians with him, or that they are to follow him: they offer to set all the Black People free who will join them."[52] Thus, the conspiracy that Stephen had allegedly uncovered involved displaced Spaniards, disgruntled free militiamen of color, and the underclass of Indians and slaves.

While there was no direct evidence supporting Stephen's accusations, they suggest potential divisions within the ranks of the free colored militia between those who welcomed the Americans and those who supported the Spanish. None of the seven free colored conspirators who Stephen mentioned by name had signed the 1804 address. Two of the specifically accused, Brulet and Dorville, had been key witnesses on behalf of the Spanish government in the trials of Pierre Bailly. Even if Stephen's allegations were false, Dorville had shown signs of discontent after losing his commission in the militia law of 1804 in the way he signed his name to notarized documents. He followed his signature with "comandante de mulatos, que en tiempo de la Dominacion Espanola" (commander of the mulattoes, in the time of Spanish domination).[53] On the other hand, several of the subscribers to the 1804 address had taken pro-republican stances in the Spanish period, including Pierre Bailly, his son, and Valfroy Trudeau, one of the two men whom Stephen specifically named as exceptions to the conspiracy against the American government.

Despite this circumstantial evidence of divisions within the free colored militia, Claiborne was skeptical of Stephen's claims, stating in a letter to James Madison, "I do not suppose it true thro'out."[54] The governor
likely had reasons to distrust Stephen. First of all, the alleged conspiracy was too exaggerated. It involved all of the potential enemies of the
United States: the Spanish, free people of color, Indians, and slaves. Second, the informant may have had an ax to grind with some of the city's
free people of color. As a "Negro" and likely a former slave, Stephen
may have been discriminated against by the city's elite men of mixed
ancestry, few of whom had lived as slaves.

A year after the Stephen affair, in January 1807, Claiborne renewed
his efforts to obtain recognition for the free colored militia. He first
ordered a census taken of all free colored men in New Orleans and
surrounding area who had previously served in the militia, preparing
for the militia's reactivation "in the event that the Legislature should
by law declare them a permanent Militia Corps."[55] Then, in a speech
to the Orleans territorial assembly, the governor lobbied for the formal recognition of the free colored corps. After criticizing the existing militia as undisciplined, disobedient, and defective, he suggested
"the expediency of recognizing the Free men of Colour, who reside
in New Orleans and its vicinity as a part of the regular Militia." These
men, Claiborne argued, had formed "a highly useful Corps" under
the Spanish, and after the Louisiana Purchase, "their conduct was
such as to convince, that the measure [of formal recognition] was
a proper one." Claiborne concluded by reading to the Assembly the
"Address of the Free People of Color of New Orleans" that he had
received shortly after taking office. It is not clear what motivated the
governor to lobby the Assembly for a formal recognition of the free
colored militia. Perhaps he was persuaded by the address. Perhaps
the Stephen affair had convinced him to court the loyalty of the free
men of color to prevent the radicalizing of a potentially dangerous
group. Or maybe he needed allies against the white Louisiana Creoles who had opposed him as governor because he did not speak
French or Spanish. Whatever his motivation, however, Claiborne did
not persuade the legislature, which refused to amend the militia law
in 1807.[56] Perhaps Claiborne's support of the free colored militia had
been counterproductive.

For their part, free men of color were becoming increasingly disillusioned with militia service because it had not been accompanied with the rights and privileges of citizenship. Not only had they been excluded from petitions and denied access to the press, but also, as outlined in chapter 2, the territorial legislature had taken other steps to exclude free men of color from participation in Louisiana's new government, including denying them the right to vote. Being deprived of these rights, Louisiana's free men of color had less incentive to serve in the militia corps.

The Impact of Immigration, Rebellion, and War

The massive immigration of St. Domingans from Cuba in 1809–10 changed the complexion of the militia debate because it more than doubled the number of potential free militiamen of color.[57] In a January 1810 letter to General Wade Hampton, the governor wrote, "The free men of color, in or near New Orleans (including those recently arrived from Cuba), capable of bearing arms cannot be less than eight hundred. Their conduct has hitherto been correct, but in a country like this, where the Negro population is so considerable, they should be carefully watched."[58] Moreover, most of these men had lived through, and likely participated in, the wars in St. Domingue.

The free colored refugees arriving from Cuba, however, were not necessarily eager to join the militia. Many *hommes de couleur* in St. Domingue had come to see militia service as degrading and exploitative. Throughout most of the eighteenth century, free men of color in St. Domingue had "served in the military in order to increase their standing as a group in the eyes of whites." As the colony's export economy became more and more lucrative for planters and merchants alike, however, white colonial discourse "redefined patriotism as commercial, not martial."[59] While metropolitan government figures may have been impressed with the free coloreds' martial virtue, white planters were just as likely to look down upon these militiamen. Whites themselves increasingly resisted militia service, leading to widespread use of free coloreds in a military role. As the colonial government relied more and more on free men of African descent and their service became less and less appreciated by the planters, free men of color in St. Domingue became disillusioned with and resistant to militia service. In short, most of the free colored refugees who fled Haiti for Cuba and then came to New Orleans in 1809–10 aspired to be planters, artisans, and/or businessmen more than soldiers.

The loyalties of free men of color, both "natives" and refugees, would be tested twice within five years of the last of the immigration from Cuba. First, in January 1811, Louisiana experienced the largest slave revolt in U.S. history.[60] The rebellion began on the morning of January 8, on the plantation of Mañuel Andry about forty miles upriver from New Orleans. This area, known as the German Coast, was home to the largest sugar plantations in Louisiana and some of the largest plantations in all of the United States. At its height, the rebellion involved more than 200 slaves marching toward New Orleans. On the morning of January 10, as the rebel force dug in at the sugar works of Michel Fortier to defend against the U.S. Army approaching from Baton Rouge, a group of about eighty white planters, who had fled to the west bank of the river and hastily formed a militia, surprised the rebel force on its flank. The result was a massacre. Between forty and fifty slaves died in or immediately after the battle, and most of the rest were taken prisoner. No white man lost his life in the battle, and only two white people, one of them a child, died in the entire revolt.[61]

It is unclear how, if at all, the German Coast rebellion affected relations between immigrants and the *ancienne population,* but one can see potential for tension. All the scholarly literature on the rebellion agrees that it was inspired, at least in part, by the Haitian Revolution. White Louisiana Creoles and Americans had expressed fears of a repetition of the "horrors of Santo Domingo" throughout the territorial period. The 1809–10 immigration had recently emphasized just how close Louisiana's ties with the French island colony were. Some of the slaves in the rebellion may have, indeed, been from St. Domingue.[62] But the planters and white officials who wrote about the rebellion did not emphatically blame the immigration, and there were no reports of violence between immigrants and natives—of any class or color.

The evidence of the actions of Louisiana's free men of color during the rebellion is also vague, as few primary sources speak to the matter.[63] In a letter to James Madison sent shortly after the rebellion, Claiborne told the secretary of state that the free men of color "manifested the greatest zeal for the public safety." According to the governor, "Their services were tendered and one company placed by my orders under the command of a respectable citizen, Major Dubourg, performed with great exactitude and propriety a Tour of duty."[64] While this letter suggests that a company of free colored militiamen helped to put down the rebellion, one must be skeptical of Claiborne's claims. The letter is clearly intended to soothe the fears of the national government about both the uprising itself and any underlying conflicts that it may have brought to the surface. In his letter to Madison, Claiborne refers to the "prompt and judicious movement" of General Hampton and the "ardour and firmness" of the white militia, both of which he calls into question in correspondence to local planters and officials. Moreover, the reference to the free men of color in New Orleans is vague. Unlike almost every other reference to the free colored forces, he mentions no person of color by name, nor does he identify the company name that was allegedly organized. Finally, the governor neglects to describe what, exactly, these men did with "great exactitude and propriety." Likely, these men of color never left New Orleans, and their "Tour of duty" involved simply standing on guard and being prepared to defend the city. In the end, the German Coast rebellion appears to have been a conflict between white sugar planters and their slaves. The role of the free colored militia was minimal at best.

The second event to test the loyalty of free colored immigrants and militiamen was the Battle of New Orleans, for which there is a great deal more evidence—if not a greater variety of sources. Two companies of free colored militiamen fought in Andrew Jackson's most famous victory: one company of 250 natives of Louisiana and one company of 350 refugees. In the final battle on January 8, 1815, Jackson's forces defeated the British in the swampy regions east of the city in what has come to be known as the Chalmette battlefield. In the campaign leading up to the final battle, Jackson praised the courage and dedication of Louisiana's free colored soldiers: "I expected much from you, for I was not uninformed of those qualities that must render you so formidable to an invading foe—I knew that you could endure hunger and thirst, and all the hardships of war—I knew that you loved the land of your nativity and that, like ourselves you had to defend all that is most dear to man—but you surpassed my hopes."[65] After the victory, Jackson again commended the colored soldiers. He told the corps that they had "not

disappointed the hopes that were formed of their courage and persever-
ance in the performance of their duty."[66] In his praise, Jackson singled
out St. Domingue–born Joseph Savary, who had raised the company of
colored refugees. In the last significant skirmish of the battle, Savary
and a detachment of his men volunteered to clear the field of a detail of
British sharpshooters. Though Savary's force suffered heavy casualties,
the mission was carried out successfully. Jackson recognized Savary's
considerable influence and knew of his reputation as "a man of great
courage." On Jackson's orders, Savary became the first soldier of African
descent in the United States to achieve the rank of second major.[67]

While free men of color no doubt fought bravely in the Battle of New
Orleans, their eagerness to serve in the battle was more tempered than
Jackson's praise for them suggests, as evidenced by the correspondence
between Claiborne and Jackson in the months leading up to the battle. On August 12, 1814, soon after it became apparent that the British
would invade the Gulf Coast, Claiborne enthusiastically recommended
that Jackson make use of the corps, claiming that "under the Spanish
Government, the men of colour of New Orleans, were always relied on
in times of difficulties, and on several occasions, evinced [sic] in the
field the greatest firmness & courage."[68] Jackson eagerly accepted this
recommendation in a return letter to the governor. "The free men of
colour in your city are inured to the Southern climate and would make
excellent Soldiers. They will not remain quiet spec[ta]tors of the interesting contest. They must be for, or against us—distrust them, and you
make them your enemies."[69] Jackson enclosed with this letter an address
"To the Free Colored Inhabitants of Louisiana," soliciting the services
of the militia in the anticipated battle. In the address, Jackson promised
to pay to every colored volunteer "the same bounty" that white volunteer soldiers got paid, assured them that they would not "be exposed to
improper comparisons or unjust sarcasm," and claimed that they would
"undivided receive the applause, reward, and gratitude, of [their] Coun-
trymen."[70] The promises of Jackson's address suggest that free men of
color needed to be recruited to fight the English invaders.

Claiborne delayed presenting this address because, he claimed, he
had been having problems with certain colored officers. He wrote to
Jackson that "an unfortunate misunderstanding between the officers of
the Battalion of Colour, which excites much Interest, is the subject of

investigation before a Court of Enquiry now sitting; the difficulties will I hope be soon arranged, and in the mean time I have deemed it best to postpone giving the publicity to your address."[71] While Claiborne did not elaborate on the nature of this "misunderstanding," he informed Jackson that while he agreed with the general's plans to treat the free men of color on equal footing with white volunteers, "this mode of reasoning makes no impression upon some respectable citizens here."[72] Moreover, while in early September Claiborne had assured the legislature that the free men of color had "expressed their devotion to their country and their readiness to defend it," by the time of his October letter to Jackson, the governor had changed his views. "My impression is, that several companies composed of men of Colour may be raised upon the plan you suggest. But I cannot say to what number; such as are natives of Louisiana, are much attached to their families and Homes, and I am inclined to think would not inlist [sic] during the War; but such as have emigrated from St. Domingo and Cuba, may most probably be desirous to Join the army." Indeed, several prominent free men of color, demanding formal recognition for their sacrifices, offered to raise troops only after receiving commissions.[73] It appears, therefore, that Claiborne's early confidence about their enthusiasm to fight in the impending battle had been misguided.

The tempered enthusiasm of Louisiana's free colored militia on the eve of the Battle of New Orleans is not difficult to understand. From the very beginning of American rule, the white planters and merchants who composed the territorial assembly had deprived free men of color of the rights associated with citizenship. The policies of the state of Louisiana toward the free colored militia were slightly different than those of the Territory of Orleans, but no less discriminatory. While the territorial assembly had refused to recognize a free colored corps, Louisiana's state constitution of 1812 (perhaps in response to the German Coast rebellion a year before) allowed for the formation of the free black militia commanded by a white officer. Yet the same constitution limited suffrage to white males. Moreover, on September 6, 1812, the first state legislature authorized the organization of a militia corps of "a certain portion of chosen men from among the freemen of colour." These colored militiamen were "to be chosen from among the Creoles, and from among such as shall have paid a State tax," and they were to be commanded by a white man. The corps was not to exceed four companies of sixty-four men each, all of whom "must have been for two years previous thereto, owners, or sons of owners, of a landed property of at least the value of 300 dollars."[74] Thus, while the territorial government had denied free men of color rights while relieving them of martial duties, the state government denied them rights but still expected service. Perhaps Claiborne did not read Jackson's address to the free men of color, with all its promises of equal treatment, because he knew that the free men of color were not so gullible as to believe them. Nothing about their experience in the first ten years of American rule would have suggested that they would be placed on equal footing with whites.

Their treatment after the Battle of New Orleans confirmed the skepticism of free militiamen of color. Within weeks of the victory, Jackson removed the men from New Orleans to a remote site in the marshland east of the city. He assigned Colonel Fortier, "a respectable and rich merchant of New Orleans," and Major Lacoste, "a rich and respectable planter," both white men, to command these two companies as well as the battalion's free colored officers. He then ordered the battalions to do fatigue work repairing fortifications, work that white militia members refused to do.[75] Savary relayed a message to the general that his men "would always be willing to sacrifice their lives in defense of their country as had been demonstrated but preferred death to the performance of the work of laborers." Jackson was not pleased with the comments but refrained from taking any action against the troops.[76] After all, the general must have been thinking, he might need their services again.

*   *   *

Militia service had been the path to elevated status for free men of African descent in the Spanish period. This path was blocked by the Americans, despite the appeals of the free colored militiamen, beginning almost immediately after the Louisiana Purchase. Yet, while white Louisianans had denied free black militiamen many rights associated with citizenship during the territorial period and early statehood, they still asked them to serve their "country." Louisiana state officials had tried to appeal to the classical republican notion of civic virtue when recruiting free men of color in the Crescent City to fight in the war in anticipation that New Orleans could become a target of the British forces. But the appeal of civic virtue through militia service had diminished considerably because it was not accompanied by rights. As a result, the free colored militia disappeared after the War of 1812. This pattern was similar, in many respects, to the shifting treatment and attitudes of men of color in St. Domingue. People of color had to turn to other ways of gaining and protecting status, most notably, the accumulation of property. While this chapter has shown the ways in which men of color were denied the same political rights as white men on the basis of their race, the following two chapters demonstrate the circumstances that gave women of color much more economic and legal autonomy than white women. After chapter 4 examines the attempts and limitations of the law in regulating intimate relationships in New Orleans, chapter 5 focuses on the accumulation of property by free people of color and their use of the courts to protect this property and other rights. The final chapter then focuses on the use of the courts by free people of color to protect freedom itself.

4

Outside the Bonds of Matrimony

The New Orleans City Court's ruling on July 12, 1811, that ordered a white man named August Tessier to return a young slave to Fausette Bechillon, a free women of color, exposed flaws within the legal system that was structured around the twin pillars of patriarchy and racism. Tessier and Bechillon, both refugees of the Haitian Revolution, were former lovers who had two children together. Because Tessier was white and Bechillon was a "quadroon libre," they could not legally marry, and their children were "illegitimate." On June 21, 1808, Tessier made a gift to his six-month-old daughter, Eleanor Rosa, of a "black slave named Sophie," who was then seventeen years old. Bechillon formally accepted possession of the gift as the child's legal guardian and "tutress." For unknown reasons the couple's relationship deteriorated, and on January 8, 1811, Tessier retook possession of Sophie, prompting Bechillon to file suit in the City Court for breach of contract. The court entered judgment in favor of Bechillon, ordering Tessier to return the slave and pay Bechillon damages for the loss of Sophie's services at seven dollars a month.[1]

This chapter examines the impact and limitations of law in preventing interracial relationships and regulating the behavior of unmarried free women of color in early New Orleans. The domestic law of territorial New Orleans was made by slaveholders and supported the same premise that underscored their power—white men would rule over both their wives and their black slaves.[2] But the interplay of racism and patriarchy in the law combined with the peculiar demographics of the city to create openings for individuals to resist and, at times, contradict the intent of the law. While the law prohibited interracial marriages, it could not prevent many white men and women of color from forming unions together and struggling to live like husband and wife. Ironically, because interracial intimate partnerships were not recognized in the law, women of color were not legally subordinated to their white male lovers under the marriage laws, so white men did not have the same legal power over their colored mistresses that married men had over their wives. While white men in positions of power attempted to subordinate women of color outside of marriage, both through the law and outside of it, they were only partially successful. Most free women of color in the period, deprived of the benefits of marriage, struggled to maintain their dignity, autonomy, and property.

The Rights and Obligations of Husband and Wife

Marriage was both a religious and a legal institution in colonial New Orleans. As one of its seven sacraments, the Catholic Church defined marriage as "the conjugal union of man and woman, contracted between two qualified persons, which obliges them to live together throughout life." By the time of the Louisiana Purchase, however, marriage had come within the domain of the state. Marriages continued to be performed in churches, but not exclusively and only by the authority of the law. The *Civil Digest of 1808* stipulated that either a licensed "magistrate" or a "minister of the gospel" could conduct a marriage and defined marriage "in no other view than as a civil contract." Yet even though two people entered into this contract on their own accord, the state set the terms of the contract.[3] The governments of Orleans and Louisiana could and did regulate marriage in such a way as to promote white male superiority.[4]

First of all, the laws of the Orleans Territory assumed and reinforced white supremacy by prohibiting interracial marriages.[5] This prohibition was, of course, not unique to the region or to the civil law. Indeed, the first laws criminalizing marriage and sex between whites and blacks were enacted during the colonial era in the English colonies of Virginia and Maryland. First, in the 1660s, both colonies passed laws prohibiting marriages between whites and black (or mulatto) slaves and indentured servants. Then, in 1691, Virginia was the first English colony in North America to pass a law forbidding free blacks and whites to intermarry, followed by Maryland in 1692. Later these laws spread to others of the thirteen colonies, including those with far fewer slaves and free blacks, such as Pennsylvania and Massachusetts. At the time of American independence, seven out of the thirteen British colonies that declared their independence enforced laws against interracial marriage. And as the United States expanded, all the new slave states as well as many new free states, such as Illinois and California, enacted such laws.[6] Thus, the law of the Orleans Territory prohibiting interracial marriages was not exceptional in the United States at the time.[7]

Second, the marriage laws governing early New Orleans supported patriarchy. To be sure, the legal duties and obligations of husband and wife were different in early Louisiana than in the rest of the United States because the coverture laws of Anglo-America were never fully adopted in Louisiana. Under the English common law known as coverture, a married woman did not have legal rights or obligations distinct from those of her husband. She could not own property, sign legal documents, enter into contracts, or keep an income for herself.[8] In civil law jurisdictions, generally speaking, married women retained greater control of their property and the ability to sign legal documents and to appear independently in legal proceedings.[9]

Neither the Orleans Territory nor the state of Louisiana ever adopted coverture in its entirety, and the marriage and inheritance laws remained primarily civilian in nature. The marriage provisions did not completely subsume the legal identity of a married woman into that of her husband, allowing her to appear in court and to purchase, sell, or mortgage property with "the authority of her husband." Furthermore, if the husband refused to so empower his wife, she could appeal to the court for such permission. Moreover, a married woman who was deemed to be a "public merchant" had the power to "obligate herself for what relates to her trade."[10] Thus, the laws of early New Orleans granted wives at least minimal property and legal rights.

Nevertheless, under the laws of the *Civil Digest* the wife remained a dependent of her husband. She was bound to live with her husband and "follow him wherever he ch[ose] to reside," while he was obliged to "furnish his wife with the conveniences of life in proportion to his means and condition." The husband retained a right to deny his wife this independence, and it was no doubt risky for a wife to appeal to the courts against her husband's wishes. In fact, very few married women in New Orleans at this time availed themselves of these rights. Therefore, the differences between coverture and the marriage laws of the *Civil Digest* were overshadowed by their similarities. Both placed wives under the control of their husbands.

The laws of early New Orleans made it very difficult for either party to end a marriage. The "bond of matrimony" was legally dissolved only when either the husband or the wife died or the marriage was declared null and void because one or both of the parties had not legally consented to the marriage.[11] A party could sue for "separation from bed and board," which did not dissolve the marriage but did "put an end to their conjugal combination and to the common concerns which may subsist between them." But even this was difficult to do. The only legally sufficient causes for separation were attempted murder, abandonment, public defamation, excesses, cruel treatment, and adultery. The husband could claim separation if his wife committed adultery, but the wife had grounds for separation only if the husband kept a concubine in the common dwelling. Thus, the law allowed for the husband to carry on extramarital affairs outside the home. Furthermore, "cruel treatment" was grounds for separation only if "such ill treatment is of such nature as to render their living together insupportable."[12] Such vague language opened the door for "acceptable" physical abuse by husbands of their wives.

For the most part, the New Orleans courts were not sympathetic to wives suing for separation from bed and board. The City Court heard a total of seventeen legal separation cases in its eight years of existence, all of them initiated by the wife. Together, the various petitions claimed all of the legally sufficient grounds for separation, but most of them cited "cruel treatment" as the main reason. Fifteen of the legal separation cases involved white couples, while only two involved couples of color. The wife won in only three of the seventeen suits; all of the victorious wives were white, and all won by default judgment because their husbands did not answer the lawsuit. If the husband contested a suit against him in the City Court for legal separation, therefore, he was almost certain to win.[13]

The New Orleans courts' interpretations of the law regarding legal separation tended to favor husbands by making "cruel treatment" a difficult standard of proof for the wife to meet, as illustrated by several cases brought by white women against their husbands.[14] For example, in 1816, Lucie Bardon filed suit in the district court seeking a separation from bed and board from her husband, Louis Durand, on the grounds that Louis physically abused her on a regular basis. The trial court was not sympathetic and denied Bardon's petition. It found evidence that Durand had "ill treated" Bardon but agreed with Durand that his wife had behaved in an "outrageous" manner to him. In affirming the trial court's decision, the court of appeals stated, "The law on separation is made for the relief of an oppressed party not for interfering in quarrels where both parties commit reciprocal excesses and outrages." Rosalie Crousot had a similar experience in her legal separation lawsuit. She claimed that her husband, Joseph Brainpain, "treated her cruelly [and] occasionally kicked her out of the house." Brainpain answered that Crousot lived a "libertine lifestyle" and "left the house on her own free will." The court found that Brainpain was justified in his actions and denied Crousot's petition. Thus, the courts implicitly recognized the right of a husband to "correct" his wife for inappropriate behavior, even if such correction became abusive.[15]

The court's reluctance (or, perhaps, unwillingness) to grant a wife's petition for legal separation likely discouraged many women from filing suit in the first place or encouraged others, like Hannah Smith, to prematurely dismiss it. Smith sought a separation from bed and board on the grounds that her husband mistreated and beat her; he also had been charged with the attempted rape of Smith's granddaughter by another marriage who was only twelve years old at the time. Shortly thereafter, Hannah filed an affidavit with the court stating that the couple had reconciled their differences, and the case was subsequently dismissed. The record does not indicate what led to this reconciliation, but, given the heinous nature of the behavior of which John Smith was accused, one can imagine that Hannah Smith feared what her husband might do to her is she followed through on her lawsuit.[16]

In addition to their allegations of physical abuse, both Crousot and Smith claimed that their husbands had engaged in sexual indiscretions with women of African descent. Crousot alleged that Brainpain had "on separate occasions, lived with two mulatresses" while Smith alleged that her husband had sexual relations with several female slaves. Yet courts did not see white husbands' interracial affairs as worthy of punishment. As Bertram Wyatt-Brown explains, enslaved and free women of African descent "performed a useful service: their availability made possible the sexual license of men without jeopardizing the purity of white women. Prostitutes performed that convenient service in free societies; fallen women, it was thought, kept the rest of the world in good moral order. Slave companions did the same in the Old South."[17] Therefore, the City Court interpreted the marriage laws so as to allow white men great latitude to both "discipline" their wives and engage in extramarital affairs.

Women of color were involved in far fewer legal separation cases in the City Court, but they faced similar results. On April 12, 1810, Françoise Bacchus, a *negresse libre*, sought a legal separation from her free colored husband, Pierre Cassepare, on the grounds of both abuse and abandonment. Bacchus alleged in her petition that about three months after they were married, Cassepare "without any reason or just motive beat, mistreated and nearly killed" her, after which he left the house and abandoned her. A third-party witness testified that Cassepare refused to provide for Bacchus in proportion to his means, that he neglected the advice of his father and reverend to return home and provide for his wife, and that he offered his wife to another man in an attempt to avoid his responsibilities. Nevertheless, the City Court denied Bacchus her claim for separation from bed and board. A "quadroon libre" named Euphrosine Wiltz also had a troubled and violent relationship with her husband, a self-identified "homme de couleur libre" and prominent member of New Orleans's free black militia named Valfroy Trudeau. On May 21, 1807, Wiltz filed a separation suit alleging that her husband had brutally beaten her from the time they were first married to the point that she had to leave the house in fear for her life. Moreover, he had not only failed to provide for her in the manner to which she had become accustomed, but he had also left the house with a Negro slave named Marianne, who was Euphrosine's property as a part of her dowry, and made the slave his concubine. Wiltz asked the court to order a legal separation and the return of Marianne to her. While the court entered a temporary order that the sheriff seize Marianne and return her to Wiltz, it did not grant Wiltz her claim for separation.[18] Clearly, the New Orleans courts tended to interpret legal separation laws in favor of husbands regardless of the race of the parties.

Spouses could also ask the court to divide the community property, without ordering a separation "from bed and board," pursuant to book 3, title 5, chapter 3 of the *Civil Digest*. For example, Marie Agnes Mathieu, a *negresse libre*, and her husband, Joseph Mathieu, a free black man, both residents of the Faubourg Marigny, were married on July 2, 1806. In June 1809, Marie Agnes sued for separation of property, claiming that she brought to the marriage more than $8,000 "in the hopes that tradition states that her husband should have increased her fortune and those of her children that she had had before her marriage by the purchase of other estates." She claimed that she was deceived in that her husband was greatly in debt, her estate has been subjected to a list of creditors, and her dowry had already been consumed. She asked the court to order that her estate be separated from that of her husband. Joseph Mathieu did not answer the petition, and the court subsequently entered a default judgment in favor of Marie Agnes Mathieu, ordering a separation of their property and assigning the costs of the lawsuit to Joseph Mathieu.[19] The City Court heard five property division cases in total, all of them brought by the wife, and ordered a division of assets in four of these cases. The City Court, it appears, was more willing to divide the assets of a husband and wife than to order a separation from bed and board.

The laws of early New Orleans provided numerous incentives for intraracial marriages. Community property laws allowed husband and wife to pool their resources, while inheritance laws privileged the "legitimate" children of legally married couples and obligated these same children to provide for their parents in old age.[20] Moreover, while a husband may have had a lot of leeway to "correct" his wife with physical force, he was also charged with providing for and protecting her. Marriage was supposed to offer financial security and physical protection for women, who were deemed to be less capable than men of taking care of themselves. Because the husband was obligated to provide his wife with the conveniences of life, married women, in theory, did not need to support themselves by working outside the home. Thus, marriage offered a measure of protection for women even as it subordinated them to their husbands and potentially subjected them to abuse in their own homes.

Despite the law's incentivization of marriage, the majority of women of color in early American New Orleans were single, due to a combination of legal and demographic factors. In 1805, free women of African descent outnumbered free men of African descent by almost three to one. The 1809–10 immigration substantially increased the proportion of free blacks in the total population and slightly increased the proportion of women to men in the free population of color (see chapter 1 and table 1.1). When Fausette Bechillon filed her lawsuit in 1811, there were around 3,000 adult women of color living in New Orleans compared with only around 1,000 adult men of color. Because one could marry only within one's race and status, at least two-thirds of the city's women of African descent were single. Just because they were legally single, however, did not mean they were alone, as many women of color formed long-lasting—if not legally recognized—relationships with white men.

Intimate Relations across the Color Line

When stripped of the lore that envelops them, white male–colored female relationships in pre–Civil War New Orleans appear as understandable responses to the demographic and legal conditions of the time. If women greatly outnumbered men among the city's free people of color in the era of the Louisiana Purchase, the opposite was true in the white community. Augmented by the male-dominated white refugee population, men made up more than 60 percent of adult whites during the territorial period, ensuring a substantial number of single white men.[21] Given this complementary imbalance in the sex demographics of the free colored and white populations, therefore, it is not surprising that the early nineteenth century saw the greatest number of interracial relationships in pre–Civil War New Orleans. As figure 4.1 illustrates, the number of newly formed white male–colored female relationships rose steadily from the 1780s to the 1810s, at which point the numbers began to decline until reaching a low point for pre–Civil War Louisiana in the 1850s.[22] While its laws forbade interracial marriages, therefore, New Orleans's demographics in the era of the Louisiana Purchase all but ensured the development of intimate relationships across the color line.[23]

Figure 4.1. Number of Newly Formed Couples

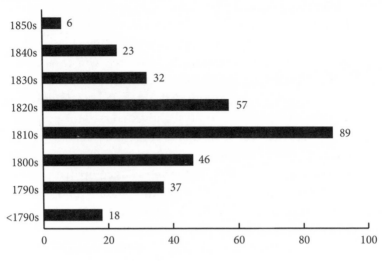

Number of Couples (per decade)

The majority of the women and men in these interracial relationships were francophone, and a significant number came from St. Domingue. Throughout the pre–Civil War era, 35 percent of colored women in inter-racial relationships were from St. Domingue, second only to Louisiana at 47 percent. The percentage of men from St. Domingue was significantly lower, but still noteworthy, at 8 percent, which was fourth behind France, Louisiana, and Spain. However, many of the men born in France may have been living in St. Domingue at the time of the Haitian Revolution. In the first two decades of the nineteenth century, when newly formed interracial relationships were at their peak, the percentage of women and men from St. Domingue was much higher. In the relationships formed during this twenty-year period, almost 50 percent of the women and 15 percent of the men were from St. Domingue. Some St. Domingan couples, like Tessier and Bechillon, met in Louisiana, but others met on the French island colony and fled together to the new American terri-tory. At least two of the couples had children together in St. Iago, Cuba, after they had fled Haiti but before coming to New Orleans.[24] Thus, the influence of the colony of St. Domingue and the Haitian Revolution on these intimate relationships across the color line is evident.

The number, openness, and "Frenchness" of interracial relationships in early New Orleans captured the attention of many Anglo-American travelers in the early nineteenth century who wrote accounts of their visits to the city. According to these traveler-authors, many of the city's most beautiful, elegant, and exotic women of mixed ancestry (often called "quadroons" whatever their degree of African ancestry) were the concubines of young white gentlemen of means who provided for the women, sometimes even buying them property, in exchange for their company and intimacy. This general depiction of white male–colored female relationships in early New Orleans, which has come to be called *plaçage*, originated with the travelers' accounts but has survived, and even thrived, to this day with the help of tourism-driven popular historians and novelists writing about exotic New Orleans.[25] The depiction is generally inaccurate but was accepted as truth because it only minimally challenged the patriarchal and racial ideologies of the society.

In these travelers' accounts and the subsequent literature, *plaçage* is often linked to another piece of New Orleans lore, the "quadroon balls"—dances in which only white men and women of color were permitted to attend. The general consensus in the literature is that quadroon balls were exceptionally refined affairs. Travelers compared the quadroon balls favorably with the other public balls in New Orleans, including the whites-only balls. Many of them commented on the exceptional beauty of the "quadroon" women, while others discussed their charm, refinement, and social graces that won the favor of white gentlemen.[26] In later and more detailed versions of the story, the quadroon balls were sites where *plaçage* relationships originated. A quadroon's mother took her daughter to the quadroon ball "as soon as [she] reached womanhood" and there displayed her "accomplishments in dancing and conversing with white men in attendance." If one of these men "fancied one of the girls he made the preliminary arrangements with her mother and was then permitted to pay court to the damsel of his choice."[27] Thus, as they are presented in the lore of the city, quadroon balls and *plaçage* are part of the same story.

This conflation of white male–colored female relationships with dances in which only white men and women of color were allowed to attend is understandable, especially considering the originator of New Orleans's quadroon balls was August Tessier, the man being sued by his former "quadroon" lover in the case that opens this chapter. Tessier was born in Paris in 1762 and immigrated to St. Domingue when he was in his early twenties. He left the island sometime around the 1791 slave uprising and went to New York City with his (white) wife, Eleanor Lapage, who died there around 1798 while the couple was still childless. Tessier arrived in New Orleans in 1804 soon after the Louisiana Purchase and worked there briefly as an actor and a dancer in the local opera company. Fausette Bechillon, the mother of Tessier's two mixed-race children, came to New Orleans from St. Domingue sometime after the Louisiana Purchase. The two likely met for the first time in New Orleans.[28] Maybe Tessier met Bechillon at one of the dances he hosted "pour les femmes de couleur libre." Or perhaps he got the idea for these dances after meeting her. In any event, Tessier hosted the city's first-ever quadroon ball on November 23, 1805. By the end of the year he was hosting quadroon balls twice a week.[29]

Nevertheless, the depiction of quadroon balls as sites where *plaçage* agreements were consummated is misleading. No evidence exists that the quadroon balls functioned as a form of debutante ball for young women of color to be introduced to wealthy white men. To be sure, society balls had become popular in New Orleans at the turn of the century, and ballroom operators tried to get "families of distinction" to hold their debutante balls in their ballrooms rather than private homes.[30] Yet all these announcements referred to the respectable and eligible young white women of New Orleans, and no similar announcements proposing to introduce young women of color into society appear regarding the quadroon balls.

Indeed, the quadroon balls developed out of the segregated public balls of the late Spanish period rather than the private society balls hosted by "families of distinction." From 1792 to 1800, a man named Filberto Farge had an exclusive license from the Cabildo to host pay-to-enter public balls for the city's white population. Farge held his dances in a crudely constructed barracks-like building that he called La Salle de Conde after the street on which it was located. As the city's population grew throughout the decade, so did the popularity, and profitability, of Farge's dances. Then, in 1799, a white man named Bernard Coquet petitioned the Cabildo for an exclusive license to operate public balls for free people of color. The Cabildo granted his petition, but with conditions and restrictions. First of all, Coquet was required to use some of his proceeds to subsidize the city's only theater, called the Coliseo. Next, whereas Farge had operated under two consecutive four-year licenses, Coquet received only a one-year license. Finally, the free colored dances were to be held on Sunday nights so as not to conflict with Farge's Saturday dances, they were to be held at Coquet's home at 27 Rue St. Phillip so as to keep the white and free colored spaces physically segregated, and no slaves were to be admitted without the written permission of their masters.[31] Despite the Cabildo's efforts to regulate and segregate the dances, however, "la Maison Coquet" quickly gained the reputation as a "den of vice," replete with gambling, drunkenness, lewd behavior, and racial intermixing. St. Domingue refugee Pierre-Louis Berquin-Duvallon referred to Coquet's dances as "tri-color" affairs attended by slaves, free people of color, and whites of the "low orders." Finally, on November 1, 1805, Coquet rented his house to August Tessier, who, later that month, hosted the first quadroon ball there.[32] It is unclear how Tessier met Coquet, but he was undoubtedly inspired by the "tri-color" dances at "la Maison Coquet." The first quadroon ball in New Orleans, therefore, was hosted by a St. Domingan refugee in the early American period, but was born from a public ball tradition with origins in the late Spanish colonial period.

In short, the story of young, beautiful, and "copper colored" concubines to wealthy white gentlemen in sexually charged relationships that began at quadroon balls romanticizes and distorts the reality of intimate relations across the color line in early New Orleans. Archival sources (as opposed to travelers' accounts) reveal details about hundreds of white male–colored female relationships in pre–Civil War New Orleans. The majority of the men in these relationships were of the middle ranks of society, not the elite wealthy gentlemen of the myth. The women were not necessarily young, beautiful, elegant, or well educated, nor were they necessarily "quadroon" or even of mixed ancestry. There is no evidence that any couple met at a quadroon ball or that white men negotiated with the quadroons' mothers for the right to "court" their daughters. Moreover, the relationships were, for the most part, neither transitory nor casual. Rather, most of them lasted many years and produced several children. Like most marriages, these intimate relationships across the color line often had an economic element to them, with women of color bringing financial resources to the partnership. These couples overcame tremendous obstacles to maintain long-term intimate and productive relationships.[33]

The laws created several deterrents to interracial coupling by placing unmarried couples at a distinct disadvantage vis-à-vis legally married couples. For example, the law prohibited those who "lived in open concubinage" from making gifts or bequests to each other. "Open concubinage" is not defined in the Civil Digest, but presumably the term applied to all couples who lived together without the formality of marriage. The term certainly applied to all interracial couples openly living together.

Yet many interracial couples found ways around this law. When his relationship with Fausette Bechillon was on good terms, for example, Tessier gifted the slave Sophie to his six-month-old daughter, Rosa Eleanor. He was almost certainly aware that Bechillon, as Rosa Eleanor's guardian until she reached majority, would be the main beneficiary of Sophie's labor for the next twelve years.[34] Whether Tessier knew it or not, Bechillon would not have had a cause of action against him had the gift been given to her instead of their daughter. Perhaps Bechillon, being knowledgeable of the law, caused Tessier to make the gift to their daughter.

Dozens of white men left property in their wills to women of color, claiming that it was compensation for services rendered as a "personal manager."[35] A white man named Nicholas Duquery gave a slave to a woman of African descent named Marie Louise Dupre as payment for the services she provided to his blacksmith business. Using a variety of legal devices, interracial couples succeeded in circumventing the "open concubinage" law.[36]

The laws dealing with inheritance also sought to discourage extramarital relationships, including all intimate relations across the color line, by establishing a hierarchy among heirs that subordinated children born outside of marriage. The law distinguished between "legitimate" children, born to a married couple, and children born out of wedlock. It also distinguished between "natural children," those simply born out of wedlock, and "bastards," those children born of adulterous or incestuous sexual encounters. Under the law of the Civil Digest, legitimate children, under all circumstances, stood to inherit their parents' estates to the exclusion of illegitimate children. Moreover, bastards were excluded

from inheritance altogether, even if their parents had no legitimate children from another relationship. For example, François Bernoudy was
married to a white woman but had no children with her. In his will,
Bernoudy left all his property to his free colored mistress, Rosette Jung,
and the children he had with her, only to have the court nullify the
legacies. First of all, Bernoudy had never formally acknowledged Jung's
children as his own. Louisiana law held that "illegitimate children,
who have not been duly acknowledged, may be allowed to prove their
paternal descent, provided they be free and white." More important,
however, the children were a product of an adulterous relationship. In
denying the claims to inheritance of Jung and Bernoudy's illegitimate
children, the court stated that the children were "under a double inca-
pacity, as illegitimate child[ren] of colour. [They could] not successfully
claim any thing from [their] natural father or his heirs, if [their] descent
be denied, because the law said [they] cannot prove it: as . . . adulterous
child[ren, they] cannot inherit."[37] Married white men, therefore, could
never leave property in their wills to children of color even if they had
no legitimate children.

   "Natural children" who were not born of adulterous or incestuous
relationships could inherit property from their parents under limited
circumstances. They stood to inherit from their mother or father only
when they had been "duly acknowledged" by one or both of them. Such
acknowledgment was "made by a declaration executed by a notary public in the presence of two witnesses." This could be any one of several
sacraments, a gift, or the will itself, as long as the document clearly
stated the maternity and/or paternity of the child.[38] Tessier did not
acknowledge his paternity of Rosa Eleanor in his gift to her of the slave
Sophie, and in his will he claimed to have no children, legitimate or natural. Bechillon, on the other hand, had her two daughters, Rosa Eleanor
and Maria Delores, baptized in the St. Louis Cathedral, naming Tessier
as their father. But, for legal purposes, these baptisms only served to
officially acknowledge her maternity, not his paternity.

   Even when "natural children" had been duly acknowledged, their
rights of inheritance under the intestate laws (which determine how the
estate is distributed in the event the deceased leaves no will) were very
limited. They had no right to the estate of the "lawful" relatives of their
parents (who could include their "natural" grandparents, cousins, aunts

and uncles, or their half brothers and half sisters). They had *no* intestate rights if the deceased left legitimate children. "Natural children" were "called to the legal succession" of their mother if she left no lawful children or grandchildren, "to the exclusion of her father and mother and other ascendants or collaterals of lawful kindred." They only inherited from their father, however, if he had "left no descendants, nor ascendants, nor collateral relations, nor surviving wife, and to the exclusion only of the territory." This distinction in the order of preference, which made it much more likely that a natural child would inherit from his or her mother than his or her father, likely presumes that most "natural children" in early New Orleans were born of white fathers and colored mothers. In such a case, the relatives of the mother are likely to be of African descent, while the relatives of the father are likely to be white. Thus, the distinctions in the intestate laws allowed for some minimal provision for "natural children" of color without (likely) preferring them to white heirs.[39]

The inheritance laws of the Orleans Territory even limited the ability of parents to give property to their natural children through a will. In the common law of successions, which prevailed in most of the United States at the time, a person had almost complete control over the distribution of his or her property and could disinherit his or her children if desired with a properly executed will. Under the principle of "forced heirship," however, a feature of the civil law tradition that survived the Louisiana Purchase, a person was required to leave a certain percentage of his or her property to living "legitimate" descendants or ascendants.[40] In the Orleans Territory, these rules applied to gifts during the lifetime as well as property bequeathed through a will. If a natural father or mother left legitimate children, he or she could not leave anything for his or her natural children "beyond what is strictly necessary to procure them sustenance." As was the case with intestate laws, the "forced heirship" laws also distinguished between mothers and fathers in the event that they left no legitimate children. In such cases the mother could leave all her property by will or gift to her natural children while a father could leave them only one-third of his property if he left legitimate ascendants, one-half if he left legitimate brothers or sisters, and three-fourths if he left collaterals below brothers and sisters. Another law allowed a parent leaving one or more legitimate children to leave as much as, but no more than, one-fifth of his or her property to someone other than these children. Yet this one-fifth portion could not be left to a "natural child."[41] Again, these laws, understood in the context of the racism and patriarchy that undergirded society, appear designed to ensure that white relatives (or even close acquaintances) would not be disinherited in favor of colored "natural children."

The several courts of early American New Orleans heard a number of cases interpreting the various "forced heirship" provisions of the *Civil Digest* in which white relatives of the deceased, or others on their behalf, challenged bequests to natural children of color. In the 1814 case of *Sennet v. Sennet's Legatees,* the petitioner, the brother of the deceased, brought suit challenging Sennet's disposition of his entire estate to his natural children of color. Sennet was a white man and had no legitimate children. The district court entered a judgment upholding the testamentary disposition, but the Supreme Court of Louisiana reversed the judgment. The high court noted that under the laws of the *Civil Digest,* when a father left legitimate brothers and sisters, his natural children could receive no more than one-half of his estate. After Monseiur Lardy, a white Frenchman, left all his belongings to the children he had with a woman of color named Geneviève Meteyer, the court, upon the request of the executor of Lardy's estate, ordered Meteyer to post a bond of $1,000 to secure the estate property while the executor determined whether or not Lardy had living heirs in France who had a legal claim to a portion of the estate. Almost twelve years later, the executor finally agreed that there were no absent heirs in France and the bequest by Lardy could be given to Geneviève and her children. In still another case, the mother of the deceased François Darby challenged his bequest of property to his natural children. While Darby only left one-third of his property to these children, as was allowed by law, his mother sued, unsuccessfully, to get the whole estate, claiming that her son had never acknowledged the heirs as his children or, alternatively, that they were still enslaved and had no rights of inheritance.[42] Many white relatives of deceased men who had been in intimate relationships with women of color knew their rights as forced heirs and sought to exclude mix-raced natural children from sharing in their fathers' estate.

Nevertheless, the majority of bequests from white men to their natural children of color went uncontested. These men either knew the law when drafting their wills or had lawyers to do the work. Dozens of men left the maximum amount they could to their natural children, and at times, this was their entire estate. The demographics were such that many white men in early New Orleans never married and thus had no legitimate children. And because many of these same men were immigrants from France or refugees of the Haitian Revolution, their direct ascendants and collateral kin were more likely to be estranged or dead.

Many women of African descent found creative (yet legal) ways around the laws of succession that discriminated against interracial relationships and prevented them from sharing in their partners' estates. A former slave named Marie Louis Dupre, mentioned in chapter 1, serves as an example. On March 14, 1810, Dupre sued the estate of Nicholas Duquery, a white man and longtime blacksmith in the Crescent City, claiming a partnership interest in Duquery's blacksmith business.[43] In her petition, Dupre alleged that through "great industry and economy" she had amassed the sum of $500, which she invested with Duquery in 1798 so that he could acquire a shop and the tools of his trade. Afterward, the petition continues, Dupre "faithfully labored" in the blacksmith shop for twelve years under the agreement that she was an equal partner in the firm. Dupre asked the court to order the defendants and coexecutors of the estate, Simon Saignal and Honoré Delinau, to liquidate Duquery's estate and to pay her the value of 50 percent of the blacksmith business.

In their answer to the petition, the defendants Saignal and Delinau invoked Dupre's race, sex, and previous status to justify their refusal to include her as a creditor of Duquery's estate. First, they challenged Dupre's right to bring the lawsuit, arguing that the rules of civil procedure required the Negress to prove her freedom before the court could consider the merits of her claims against the estate. Then, the defendants denied Dupre's allegations that she was a partner in Duquery's blacksmith firm, asserting that prior to filing the lawsuit she never made a claim to any portion of the decedent's estate and proclaiming it "difficult to believe that an intelligent businessman like Duquery would find himself so destitute as to solicit the measly sum of five hundred dollars possessed by an African wench."[44] Finally, the executors expressed surprise and disgust that a black woman who "owed her liberty" to

Duquery (if, indeed, she were free) had the audacity to seek monetary compensation from his estate.

The evidence supporting Dupre's free status and her contributions to Duquery's business was convincing to Judge Moreau-Lislet, who, on June 18, 1810, ordered the defendants to make an accounting of the estate and pay Dupre one-half of its value. Although the alleged partnership agreement had never been reduced to writing, Dupre attached to her petition a document purporting to be a "donation" to her from Duquery of a seventeen-year-old slave named Victoire. This document identified Marie Louise Dupre as a "free negresse" and stated that the gift was to compensate her for the years of excellent service she had provided Duquery. Three white men served as witnesses to the notarized "donation," adding further credibility to Dupre's claims.[45]

Despite the court's ruling, at least one white relative of Duquery was not convinced that her cousin and Dupre were business partners. More than a year after Moreau-Lislet's decision, a white couple from France appealed it. Marie Françoise Fiset claimed that she was "the first cousin and sole heir of the estate of Nicholas Duquery" and that Moreau-Lislet's "judgment was entered in favor of Marie Louise, aka Quinones, to the great prejudice" to herself and her husband, François Morin, who was also a party to the suit. The appellants argued that Dupre was the former slave and former lover of Nicholas Duquery, and that Dupre's lawsuit was an attempt to circumvent the territory's inheritance laws. The court was not convinced, however, and denied Fiset and Morin's appeal.[46]

The claims of the parties, the testimony of the witnesses, and the decisions of the courts suggest that Marie Louise Dupre and Nicholas Duquery were *both* business *and* intimate partners. Duquery never had any legal incentive to acknowledge an intimate relationship with Dupre because the two never had any children together. But other evidence certainly supports this possibility. Neither of them was ever legally married to anyone else, and they had lived together at the same residence for more than eleven years. Still, Dupre convinced the court that she had invested money and labor in Duquery's blacksmith business and that she was his business partner. Was Duquery's conveyance of a slave to Dupre a gift to a lover or compensation to a partner? It was likely both.

If Dupre and Duquery were lovers, they would not have been the only interracial couple to combine business and intimacy. For example, Angele Jacob, a *negresse libre* and native of New Orleans, contributed thirty-seven gowns and several expensive scarves to help stock the inventory of the father of her children, François Boutin, a Frenchman who came to New Orleans to become a merchant. Other women contributed their labor to their intimate partners' businesses, such as Dupre and Anne Charlotte Buteau, who worked in Jean Louis Laprune's general store that she helped him build.[47] Still other women of color brought land and/or cash to their relationships. Indeed, like most legal marriages in early nineteenth-century America, most of New Orleans's intimate relations across the color line were economic as well as intimate partnerships.

Thus, the white male–colored female relationships of early New Orleans resembled, in many ways, the complex and multifaceted partnerships shared by husbands and wives.[48] Some interracial couples sought a formal ceremony of some kind, even if it was not recognized by law, in what Diana Williams has called a "marriage of conscience."[49] For example, Jean Alujas, "un espagnol," and Adéle Rosalie Deslandes, "la negresse," were married on November 28, 1838, at the Ursuline Convent (downriver from New Orleans), even though the marriage was not legally valid. Others left the United States so that they could become legally married, such as Honoré Fortier and Arthemise Brulé, who moved to Puerto Rico, and Maurice Abat and Agathe Gireaudeau, who immigrated to France.[50] Most couples, however, did not bother with such formalities and simply lived together, informally, as intimate partners.

Still, the economic implications of these partnerships—the rights and duties of the men and women in them—differed depending on whether or not the couple was legally married. And because the law prohibited whites and free people of color from marrying, these implications were also racial. When a woman of color made a contribution to her white partner's business, it sometimes became a claim to equity in the business under the laws governing business partnerships, as was the case with Dupre. If a wife made the same contribution to her husband's business, however, it became part of the community property and was subject to the laws governing marriages. For example, through "hard work and industry," Hannah Smith contributed thousands of dollars to her marriage to the "lowly sailor" John Smith. This money helped the couple stock and operate a store in Faubourg St. Marie. When Hannah Smith wanted an accounting and division of these assets, however, she sued under the legal separation laws.[51]

In the end, therefore, intimate relationships across the color line were subject to a different set of laws than marriages, so women of color were not subject to the same restrictions vis-à-vis their male partners as were married women, white or colored. The two lawsuits of Euphrosine Wiltz and Fausette Bechillon, discussed earlier in this chapter, illustrate this difference. The cases are similar in that both petitioners sought the return of slave property from their intimate partners. Because she was not legally married to Tessier, however, Bechillon's claim was one in contract law. Wiltz, on the other hand, had to sue under the laws governing separation from bed and board. Bechillon won her lawsuit, but Wiltz did not win hers. One of the unintended consequences of the law preventing interracial marriages, therefore, was to create an increased independence for women of color in interracial relationships. And because the demographics of the time dictated that most free women of color would be single, most of them enjoyed this heightened autonomy.

Complications of Racism and Patriarchy

This community of independent free women of African descent was potentially subversive to the ideology of racism and patriarchy that governed society and served as the premise to its laws. As a result, the elite white men who sat at the top of the social hierarchy attempted to reassert their authority in at least three additional and interrelated ways. First, they passed laws seeking to subordinate unmarried free women of color (who were living outside the bonds of matrimony and of slavery). Second, after failing to prevent or minimize illicit interracial relationships, they sought to institutionalize them in a way that did not subvert the social order. Third, as we have already seen in chapter 3, white men took steps to emasculate men of color. As the rest of this chapter will show, these efforts met with resistance from different quarters, were difficult to enforce, and at times contradicted each other.

The Orleans territorial government passed laws that subordinated all people of color to whites but seemed particularly targeted to women of color. One of the most obvious examples of legal attempts to sexually subordinate women of color was the law regarding rape. In 1805, the territorial legislature passed a law that stated that only white women could be victims of rape and provided that the punishment for rape was to be imprisonment at hard labor for life. Yet a little more than a decade later, in an effort to "clarify any doubts or confusion" arising from incongruity of texts, the legislature stated that if any free or enslaved person of African descent committed "rape on the body of any white woman or girl," he would, "on conviction thereof, suffer death."[52] The letter of the law itself, therefore, created separate penalties for white and black perpetrators of sexual violence on women and stipulated that only white women could be victims. In this way, the laws tacitly permitted white men to use sexual violence as a way of subordinating women of color.

The laws also supported racial and gender hierarchies by requiring that free people of color defer to whites. Section 40 of the 1806 Black Code admonished free people of color "never to insult or strike white people, nor presume to conceive themselves equal to whites: but on the contrary that they ought to yield to them in every occasion." While the language of this provision applied to the behavior of all free blacks, it seems to have been intended especially for free women of African descent. Several cases in the City Court stemmed from the perceived impertinence of free women of color who refused to defer.

The 1807 case of *Raby v. Forstall* illustrates the potential connection between the legislature's omitting free women of color from rape law and requiring free people of color to defer to whites. In August of that year, Clarice Raby, a free woman of color, filed suit for battery against Edmund Forstall, a white man. Raby's petition claims that Forstall inflicted "injuries to her arms, torso, and head" and asked for compensation in the amount of $2,000. While Raby did not claim that she was sexually assaulted, the racialized language of the laws likely would have deterred her from such a claim and caused her to frame her lawsuit as one of battery. In his answer to the petition, Forstall did not deny inflicting the injuries but claimed that he acted in self-defense after Raby leveled a series of insulting words and gestures. Forstall further claimed that Raby had assaulted him and that he hurt her in the act of defending himself. Finally, Forstall implicitly invoked section 40 of the Black Code by pointing out in his pleadings that Raby was a woman of color and he was a white man, though neither the petition nor the citation identified Raby's race. The jury returned a verdict in favor of Forstall, implicitly acknowledging the right of white men to "discipline" women of color under certain circumstances.[53]

In subsequent cases, however, the court placed limitations on the ability of white men to extralegally enforce section 40 of the Black Code. For example, the unfavorable verdict for Raby did not prevent Henriette Massant, another free woman of color, from obtaining a favorable judgment in her civil assault and battery suit against a white man named François Veda. As mentioned in the introduction, in August 1812 Massant verbally reprimanded Veda's daughter after Massant was soiled with the contents of a chamber pot while passing by Veda's house. A few hours later, Veda physically abused Massant in her own home. Massant then sued Veda for assault and was awarded a $500 judgment.[54]

While the different outcomes in the *Raby* and *Massant* cases appear to be contradictory, they can be explained on several possible grounds. One possible explanation is that Massant won her case because the factual disputes were resolved by a judge, whose main concern was with upholding the law, whereas Raby lost hers because the factual disputes were resolved by a jury of white men, who may have been concerned with upholding social hierarchies.[55] Or perhaps the different outcomes are tied to a respect (in the law itself) for the sanctity of the home. Under this explanation, had Forstall beaten Raby on Raby's own property, he would likely have been found liable. Most likely, however, the two cases demonstrate that while the law upheld and even promoted racial subordination, the court placed limits on its extralegal enforcement. Forstall claimed to be acting in self-defense, which, if believed, is a legitimate exonerating factor. Veda, on the other hand, could not have asserted this defense due to the lapse of time between the two altercations. Rather, he appeared to be taking the law into his own hands. Several decades later the Supreme Court of Louisiana made it clear that it would not tolerate vigilante enforcement of the Black Code. In upholding the conviction of a white man found guilty of killing a free man of color, the court, referring to section 40 of the code, opined that while whites did not have to suffer insults or abuse from blacks (slave or free), they had adequate recourse in the courts.[56] Therefore, the courts demanded respect for the law even when its proper application disrupted the race- and sex-based social hierarchies.

Unlike the other two white men who felt disrespected by women of color, Louis Durand did not take matters into his own hands but sought recourse in the courts, where he invoked section 40 of the Black Code. Before he was the defendant in the legal separation lawsuit brought by his wife (described earlier in this chapter), Durand was the petitioner in a lawsuit against his neighbor, a free colored woman who shared his last name. On or around May 15, 1812, Lucie Bardon, Louis Durand's wife, sent her "domestic" to wash the sidewalk in front of their house. In order to clear space, the slave moved rubbish to the front of the house of the next-door neighbor, a free woman of color named Félicité Durand. Watching from a window with her two daughters, Mrs. Durand told her own domestic slave to push the trash back to the front of Louis Durand's house, which led the two slaves to quarrel. Bardon, having heard the commotion, went outside to investigate, and when she learned what was happening, she summoned her husband. These are the stipulated facts of the case.

What happened after Louis went outside is disputed. Louis told the court in his petition that Félicité Durand and one of her two daughters, Félicité Foucher, began insulting him and his family. According to Louis, after his daughter, Demoiselle Aspasie, warned the women of color that they would be put in jail if they did not get away from her father, Foucher responded, "You little hussy, only an old sow like your mother would have us put in jail. Do what you will!" Louis then took his family inside his house so that they would no longer be exposed to these insults, determined to teach these women of color a lesson. Louis Durand also told the court that this was not the first incident involving Félicité Durand and her daughter. In fact, he claimed, his family had been daily exposed to disparaging insults from these two women of color. Just three months earlier, Louis had lodged a complaint with Mr. Decourneau, a justice of the peace, who reprimanded the women of color and ordered them to apologize to Louis and his family. He had hoped that this reprimand would change things (that these woman of color would learn their place in society and give him the respect owed to whites), but his hopes were in vain. Louis annexed to his petition a copy of section 40 of the Black Code, admonishing people of color to submit to whites and speak to them with respect. In his lawsuit, he sought reparations and punishment in the amount and severity that the court deemed fit. Defendants Félicité Durand and Félicité Foucher filed an answer on June 27, 1812, in which they admitted that the elder Félicité had ordered her slave to push the rubbish back in front of Louis's house but denied insulting him or anyone in his family. The women of color further alleged that Louis Durand had a reputation for snobbery and defensiveness. Finally, the defendants demanded that a jury decide their case. There is no judgment in the court records, and it appears that the case never went to trial.[57]

Although it is not clear why the case was never tried, Louis Durand may have dropped the lawsuit out of fear that his reputation in the community would be damaged by a drawn-out jury trial, a fear that could have stemmed from the parties' common last name. The caption on the pleadings reads *Louis Durand v. Felicité Durand and Felicité Foucher,* but Louis never acknowledged that the elder Félicité shared his last name. In affidavit testimony in support of the petition, moreover, Louis's (and Félicité's) neighbors, Jean Baptiste Giquel and Sieur Berquier both made it a point to say that they did not know the names of the defendants. Giquel "confess[ed]" that he "never knew the name of this girl of color," while Berquier referred to the "women of color whose names [he] did not know but who live next door to Madame Durand." It seems more likely that Louis was intending to dispel any suggestion of a connection between himself and Félicité Durand than that neither Giquel nor Berquier knew her name. While it is difficult to know for sure what else, if anything, Louis and Félicité shared besides a last name, the claims of the parties leave a lot of room for speculation. Even if one believes Louis Durand's version of the facts, why did he react so strongly to a few insulting words from his next-door neighbor? Was he really concerned with maintaining proper social etiquette, or was he, as Félicité suggests, merely being defensive? In either case, the antagonism between the parties gleaned from Louis's narrative of events suggests a keen familiarity between the two Durands. Maybe this is why Félicité was so bold around Louis and why he was so defensive. Indeed, could Louis have dropped the lawsuit fearing what Félicité might reveal (to a jury, not only a judge) during the course of the trial? Although all of this is speculation, it seems clear that Félicité Durand did not think of Louis Durand, her next-door neighbor, as her social superior.

Raby, Massant, and *Durand,* the only three cases heard by the City Court involving section 40 of the 1806 Black Code, all involved white men seeking to put unmarried women of African descent in their place. Yet, as the cases show, the law was an imperfect tool for this purpose. The legal separation cases discussed earlier, on the other hand, demonstrate that husbands (white and colored) had a much easier time "correcting" their wives in the home than white men did in subordinating free women of color. While Clarice Raby, Henriette Massant, and Félicité Durand faced the threat of punishment from their white male "social superiors," they were no more exposed to physical abuse than were married women, colored or white.[58]

White men in power sought not only to subordinate potentially subversive free women of African descent but also to dictate the terms of socialization and intimacy between the races and to emasculate men of color. One area of concern for the governments of both Spanish colonial Louisiana and American territorial Orleans was interracial dancing in New Orleans. On February 7, 1800, less than a year after Spanish governor Lemos had granted Bernard Coquet his exclusive license to offer public balls for free people of color, Attorney General Don Pedro Dulcido Barran filed a petition seeking its immediate termination or, alternatively, a method to ensure that only free people of color (no whites or slaves) attended the dances. Barran cited the "impropriety" of whites and coloreds mixing in the ballroom setting. According to the attorney general, white men dancing and flirting with women of color showed a weakness of character similar to those who gambled and drank too much. More important, the open and unapologetic "mingling" of the races blurred the racial distinctions justifying the racially based social hierarchy. Barran also decried the inappropriate behavior of the free people of color at these dances. He claimed that Coquet's dance had become "a ridiculous imitation of Farge's dance," where free people of African descent openly "imitate[d] the luxury of the whites."[59] By dressing in their finest formal wear and dancing to cotillions and waltzes, the community of free people of color was appropriating a culture that was, in Barran's view, not theirs. Although many members of the Cabildo supported Barran's petition, the majority of the governing body decided to permit the dances to continue for the short time remaining in the license agreement but reject the petition of Coquet and his partner Antonio Boniquet for its renewal in April 1800.[60] Perhaps Cabildo officials were reluctant to immediately shut down the dances due to the revenue produced by the license fee. Or, perhaps, some of the Cabildo officials attended the dances themselves.

Some members of the free colored militia were equally concerned with the interracial mixing at Coquet's house, if for different reasons, but adamant about retaining the free colored dances. The October 24, 1800, petition of four militia members, discussed at length in the previous chapter, specifically asked the Cabildo to renew the dances but to provide guards at them in order to prevent the "disturbances" caused by white men. Notably, the petitioners did not ask to be permitted into white dances. Indeed, they noted that their proposed dances, to be held on Sundays, would not interfere with the white people's Saturday dances. This was possibly an implicit (and reluctant) acceptance that whites had been attending and would continue to attend free black dances. Still, the militiamen asked the Cabildo to police the dances to prevent white men from disrespecting and abusing women of color at them. Underpinning their petition to retain the dances, therefore, was a power struggle for sexual control. Shortly after receiving the October petition of the four militiamen, Governor Nicholas Maria Vidal and the Cabildo reinstated Coquet's license on the condition that slaves no longer be admitted, with or without their masters' permission. Yet they denied the request to post guards at the dances to prevent disturbances. The free colored militiamen were able to retain the free colored dances, but they could not prevent whites from coming.[61]

Indeed, many white men in New Orleans must have wanted the free colored dances to continue because many of them, including, possibly, members of the Cabildo, attended these dances. Even if they did not attend, Cabildo members may have preferred that white men continue to attend the dances at "la Maison Coquet," as long as the events continued, because it allowed them to monitor the dances and assert white male superiority. Thus, while the petition of the free colored militiamen was an expression of masculine civic virtue, the Cabildo's refusal to prevent the attendance of white men at Coquet's dances or to monitor their behavior can be seen as an attempt to emasculate these same free men of color.

Because white men in power could not prevent extramarital inter-racial mixing, they turned, instead, to institutionalizing it in a way that would promote white male superiority. Lawmakers in charge after the Louisiana Purchase, unlike the Spanish colonial government, did not grant exclusive licenses to ballroom proprietors. Thus, August Tessier did not need permission from the government to hold quadroon balls, but he did not have protection from it either. Operating in a free market, Tessier took a variety of steps to attract patrons. He played upon (and contributed to) the exoticized image of quadroon beauty by renaming the ballroom La Salle de Chinoise. He provided accoutrements that had been theretofore unavailable at other public balls, black or white, such as consommés, wines, soups, the finest chocolate, and a carriage ser-vice.[62] If the numerous advertisements Tessier placed in the newspapers are any indication of popularity, La Salle de Chinoise was a hot spot for the 1805–6 carnival season. Yet the free market ultimately undermined Tessier, as the success of his dances spurred others to imitate them. Within a few years, other entrepreneurs directly competed with Tes-sier by opening new venues that hosted quadroon balls. By April 1806, Bernard Coquet was holding quadroon balls at his Tivoli Ballroom on Bayou St. Jean. In 1810, he opened a much larger and more convenient venue, the St. Phillip Street Theatre, which eventually drove La Salle de Chinoise out of business. By the 1830s, there were half a dozen ball-rooms hosting quadroon balls.[63]

While the American government after the Louisiana Purchase did not grant exclusive licenses to dance hall proprietors for segregated dances, as the Spanish government had done, it did, on occasion, attempt to regulate interracial dancing. On several occasions, the city government prohibited masked balls so that attendees could not hide their racial identity. Masks not only made it more difficult for propri-etors to police the racially exclusive dances but also provided a con-venient excuse for their failure to do so. Thus, in February 1806, the city council passed an ordinance imposing a twenty-dollar fine on anyone who advertised for a masked ball, permitted masked partici-pants at his dances, or wore a mask to a ball. The ordinance expired on its own terms and was not immediately renewed, but the concern did not subside. Three decades later the city council, worried about the "unrestrained freedom at masked balls for colored people two or three times a week," asked the acting mayor of New Orleans, John Culbertson, to use his police powers to monitor these balls. Culbertson also had concerns about "the composition of the masquerade balls." According to the mayor, too many white women were attending masked balls intended for colored women and were bringing "with them unprincipled men who have been expelled from other states, and who find here, in consequence of the disguise they are allowed to assume, and the protection of those females, every opportunity of following their swindling career." Preventing the entrance of white women, Culbertson claimed, would "place the masked balls of the colored women on a more eligible basis."[64] The *bals de masques* had been a long-standing part of New Orleans's dancing tradition, but in a time of heightened concern about the inappropriate mixing of the races, the opportunity to conceal one's racial identity in the ballroom setting caused concern among the white men in power.[65]

Yet neither the government nor the private sector could prevent the "indiscriminate" mixing of the races at public dances. Berquin-Duvallon's criticism in 1802 of the "tri-color balls" of "la Maison Coquet" was echoed decades later in references to the quadroon balls. When members of the city council paid a visit to a quadroon ball at the Washington Ballroom in November 1835, they were "surprised to find that two-thirds at least of the females present were white women." And Belgian traveler Isidore Lowenstern claimed to have seen "privileged men of color" at a quadroon ball he attended in 1837. The hosts of quadroon balls either had difficulty keeping out uninvited guests or did not care to do so.[66] Judging from comments of government officials and travelers to the city, however, these attempts had only limited success.

*   *   *

The laws of early New Orleans regulating marriage and inheritance were designed, in part, to support the racial and gender hierarchies on top of which sat white men. Yet these laws were an imperfect tool for doing so, in large part because the city's demographics combined with its laws to create a large, semiautonomous community of free women of color. Lawmakers passed additional legislation, outside of domestic law, to try to subordinate this community, but even these laws met with limited success. By prohibiting interracial marriages, the lawmakers forced the majority of free women of color to accumulate property and provide for themselves rather than rely on support from a husband. The next chapter focuses on another contradiction in the legal system that could not be fully reconciled: the need to neutrally apply property laws in a racially based slave society with a large community of property-holding free people of color.

5

Owning So as Not to Be Owned

In October 1812, a jury in the New Orleans City Court returned a verdict favorable to the defendant Sannite Hazaca against the petition of Louis Mallet, which alleged that Hazaca had misappropriated slave property rightfully belonging to Mallet and his sisters as an inheritance from his deceased brother Nicholas Mallet. This ruling was the culmination of two decades of legal battles between these two parties concerning the distribution of Nicholas Mallet's estate. It played out in three separate courts in three different legal systems.

The dispute originated in the southern province of St. Domingue prior to the outbreak of the Haitian Revolution. Hazaca, a free woman of color, lived with Nicholas Mallet, a white man, from 1784 until Mallet died in 1800 on a coffee plantation near Cap Dame Marie. The Mallet siblings, Louis, Marie Magdelaine, and Marie Louise, also lived in the southern province, near Anse à Veau, west of Cap Dame Marie. Although Hazaca claimed that she lived with Mallet "in the capacity of housekeeper or manager," she also testified that she had children with him. In his last will and testament Nicholas Mallet named these children as heirs to part of his estate. Although Louis Mallet challenged this bequest in a Les Cayes court, a Judge Berly validated the will sometime in 1801. The same court in Les Cayes, again against the protests of Louis Mallet, named Hazaca as the manager of Nicholas Mallet's estate on behalf of her children. Only one of these children, a young man who called himself Rousseau, survived the Haitian Revolution.[1]

While Nicholas Mallet had been a successful planter in the 1780s and early 1790s, the Haitian Revolution reversed his fortunes. He had owned two plantations near the western tip of the southern province. Both had been profitable and likely worked by dozens if not hundreds of slaves. But these slaves were freed by the French National Convention in 1794, and the violence of the Haitian Revolution, especially the War of the South from 1799 to 1800, made Mallet's hold on his real estate tenuous at best. After Nicholas's death, Hazaca began to manage the plantations with the help of a merchant in Anse d'Hanault named Mssr. Latasie. The plantations continued to be productive—as late as October 24, 1802, Hazaca sold 1,000 pounds of coffee on credit to Louis Mallet. Hazaca, Rousseau, and the Mallet siblings held out for as long as they could, but in December 1803, on the eve of Haitian independence, all of the parties "evacuated the island for St. Iago de Cuba." Hazaca managed to bring with her "two negro boys aged between eight and nine years old, and an old "domestique" around sixty years having a child around twelve years old," all of whom she claimed as her slaves.

Once settled in Cuba, the parties reignited their dispute. Hazaca demanded payment for the coffee, and in response, Louis Mallet sued for possession of the four Negroes held by Hazaca, claiming that he had inherited them from his deceased brother. In effect, Mallet asked the Cuban court to ignore not only the ruling of Judge Berly in Les Cayes but also the legitimate claims that the blacks had to their freedom.[2] According to Mallet's petition in the New Orleans City Court, on March 7, 1805, Judge Pedro Herresuelo ordered Hazaca to deliver the four Negroes to Mallet, but she "defied the decree and refused to deliver the slaves." There is no documentary record of this case, however, and it is unclear if, when, and how the Cuban court ruled on the matter.

Hazaca, Rousseau, and the living Mallet siblings all left St. Iago for New Orleans as part of the massive 1809–10 immigration. Two years later, the adversaries found themselves back in court. First, Hazaca sued Mallet in the New Orleans City Court for $300, representing the price of 1,000 pounds of coffee at thirty cents a pound. Then, Mallet filed a separate lawsuit against Hazaca in the same court, alleging that he and his two sisters were the only lawful heirs to the Nicholas Mallet estate, that they were unable to claim their inheritance in St. Domingue due to the extraordinary conditions of the revolution, and that Hazaca had evaded him and defied her obligations under the law. The petition also claimed that Hazaca had fraudulently sold one of the four "slaves," an elderly woman named Angelique, to a "planter named Rousseau." Mallet asked for a judgment in the amount of $6,640 and an order that Angelique be returned to him.[3] Hazaca and Rousseau filed a joint answer to Mallet's petition. Hazaca claimed that she was entitled to the slaves as a creditor of the estate of Nicholas Mallet for the services she had performed in managing the plantation over the course of sixteen years, and Rousseau claimed that he had legally purchased Angelique from Hazaca. The first lawsuit was decided by Judge Moreau-Lislet, without the aid of a jury. He awarded Hazaca the requested amount of $300. The other lawsuit, the one filed by Mallet, was decided by a jury, which returned "a verdict in favor of Sannite Hazaca, allowing for one hundred percent of all claims against the estate." It also found that Rousseau was a legal heir to his father as determined by the "judgment of the tribunal at Les Cayes." Finally, the jury reprimanded Louis Mallet for his attempts to "distress the defendant who is now sixty years old and imprisoned at the insistence of the petitioner." Hazaca and Rousseau, therefore, had achieved complete legal victories in the New Orleans City Court.[4]

The City Court lawsuits involving Sannite Hazaca and Louis Mallet, like dozens of others in the same court, illustrate the interconnections of property ownership, freedom, and racial slavery in New Orleans in the context of the Haitian Revolution. The court's highest priority was to enforce the property rights upon which any slave society rested. This gave free people of color a tool that they could use to defend themselves—both to defend their rightful property and to establish a clear legal record showing that they had a rightful claim to themselves as property—so long as they were willing to abide by the rules of the slave society. This chapter argues that for free people of color, especially displaced refugees whose freedom was precarious, property ownership was one of the most important ways of securing liberty. This chapter begins by examining the relationship of property to freedom in the discursive traditions informing the Age of Revolution and ways that racial slavery and the Haitian Revolution intersected with this discourse. Then it addresses the impact of the revolution and subsequent refugee flight on the economies of both St. Domingue and New Orleans, specifically with regard to free people of color. Next it provides an overview of the approximately 200 New Orleans City Court property disputes in which free people of color were involved, showing that the court exhibited little racial or gender bias in its decisions. The chapter concludes by focusing on a particular type of property dispute in which free people of color were parties, that involving slave property. Together, these cases show that as free people of color sought to protect their rights as property holders in the courts, they did so in a way that both supported slavery and fed the notion of a racial distinction between "people of color" and "Negroes."

The "Inviolable" Right to Property

In the ideologies that informed the Age of Revolution, property and liberty were inextricably intertwined. The republicanism espoused by James Harrington and the Baron de Montesquieu associated freedom with independence, which they believed could only be achieved through landownership. Furthermore, John Locke argued in *Two Treatises of Government* that political society existed for the sake of protecting property, which he identified as a person's life, liberty, and estate. The sanctification of property in revolutionary ideology is encoded in two iconic documents of the age, the American Declaration of Independence and the French Declaration of the Rights of Man. The last clause of the Rights of Man insisted that "the right to property [was] inviolable."[5] In essence, liberty in Enlightenment ideology was defined by property holders who desired to keep and protect their propertied interests.

By naturalizing the right to property and placing it on the same level of importance as the rights to life and liberty, Enlightenment ideology recognized different levels of freedom, all tied to property ownership. The freest of all were the independent landowners, large merchants, and bourgeoning capitalists. Less free were artisans and the petit bourgeois, whose survival was dependent on the whims of the market. Finally, indentured servants, temporarily, and slaves, permanently, were, as forms of property themselves, excluded from the political community altogether. The political goal of the American and early French

Revolutions was to establish equality not among all people but among all property holders. In other words, it was to make the political power of propertied men of nonnoble origin commensurate with their economic power.

The exclusion of some from the political community and the different levels of freedom within this community were expressed in the language of citizenship, which helped to reconcile liberty and equality with social hierarchies and subordination. Only people with a stake in society (namely, those who owned land) could be truly independent citizens. Edmund Morgan writes that "John Locke, the classic explicator of the right of revolution for the protection of liberty, did not think about extending the right to the landless poor."[6] Moreover, revolutionary ideology distinguished between "active" and "passive" citizens. In the discourse of the early French Revolution, as Robin Blackburn explains, "only propertied French men could be 'active' citizens (with a vote and right to stand as a candidate); French women and children were 'passive' citizens (with no vote or right to represent others)."[7] Some citizens, therefore, were more independent than others.

Given the important relationship of property to liberty, the reconciliation of Enlightenment ideology with New World racial slavery was not difficult. First of all, while the right to "liberty" was considered a "natural right," only members of the political community (most important, property holders) were entitled to the realization of this right. The language of race also fostered this reconciliation, as members of a different (and inferior) race were easily excluded from the political community. Indeed, as Robin Blackburn puts it, "Since slaves were indubitably a sort of property as well as arguably a prop of public utility, the qualification of natural liberty seemed robust enough to reassure the many colonial proprietors in the French Assembly."[8] Not coincidentally, slaveholders were some of the biggest advocates of "inviolable" property rights.

The intertwined relationship of liberty and property in the context of racial slavery took on added significance for free people of African descent in the New World. Throughout most of the slave societies of the New World, slaves were prohibited by law from owning property. New Orleans was no exception in this regard, with section 15 of the 1806 Louisiana Black Code stating, "As the person of a slave belongs to his master, no slave can possess anything in his own right or dispose, in any way, of the produce of his industry, without the consent of his master." The logic of the Black Code, therefore, was that *as* property, slaves could not *own* property. To be sure, customary rights to property in both Louisiana and Anglo-America were well established. But for purposes of determining the status of a person of African descent, the difference between legal and customary rights to property was enormous. If the law prohibited slaves from owning property, then establishing one's legal rights to certain property was the equivalent of establishing one's status as free. Thus, in the absence of documentation or social networks of people who could acknowledge their liberty, legal ownership of property, especially in land or slaves, was the most important means by which free people of color could protect their freedom.

The Haitian Revolution significantly modified Enlightenment ideology by privileging liberty above all other rights and denying that people could be property. The reaction to the Haitian Revolution in England, France, and the United States diverged in two different directions. One was to retreat from revolutionary ideals, and the other was to push them further. In Great Britain the one gave way to the other. As Blackburn tells his readers, "Widespread slave revolt and revolutionary turmoil provoked such a panic after 1792 that it undercut British abolitionism. But eventually the consolidation of Toussaint Louverture's regime and the emergence of a black state filled the gaps that yawned in the discourse of liberty and set the scene for a rebirth of abolitionist practices."[9] The reaction in France followed a different trajectory. After tens of thousands of slaves in St. Domingue had effectively won freedom for themselves, Léger Félicité Sonthonax took the radical step in 1793 of formally freeing the slaves in St. Domingue, followed by the National Convention's Act of 1794 that abolished slavery in all of France's colonial possessions. By 1800, however, France had reversed course as Napoleon tried to reinstitute plantation slavery in the Caribbean, with limited success. In the United States, the sentiments diverged geographically. Elites in both the North and the South abhorred the atrocities of the Haitian Revolution but placed the blame on different sources. Those in the slave states blamed abolitionism, while those in the free states blamed the cruelty of slavery itself.

Prosperity Disrupted

While the plantation system in St. Domingue was exceedingly oppressive for the slaves, it had proved to be extremely profitable for a privileged few. Before the Haitian Revolution, St. Domingue had been the richest colony in the New World, creating great wealth for planters and merchants, many of whom were important players in the bourgeois revolution in France. The wealth of the colony came in three main forms: staple crops (primarily sugar, coffee, indigo, and cotton), land, and, of course, slaves. On the eve of the French Revolution, St. Domingue produced 40 percent of the world's sugar and more than half of the world's coffee. More than 450,000 slaves worked 2.5 million acres of land. There were more than 7,800 plantations raising and processing agricultural commodities, including 793 sugar, 3,117 coffee, 3,150 indigo, and 789 cotton plantations.[10] For good reason, late colonial St. Domingue was known as "the Jewel of the Antilles."

By the late eighteenth century, free people of African descent in St. Domingue shared in the colony's wealth to a greater degree than free people of color of any other New World slave society. After the Seven Years' War, the *gens de couleur libre* greatly benefited from the coffee boom in St. Domingue, which was concentrated in the southern province where many free people of color had lived for a couple of generations. Established sugar planters, for the most part, did not move into the coffee-growing regions, and free people of color were more accustomed to the climate and more prudent investors in the plantation system than newly arriving whites. By 1789, many wealthy free people of African descent in St. Domingue were poised to participate in and share the benefits of the bourgeois revolution.[11]

The Haitian Revolution, the greatest freedom struggle of the modern world, was devastating for the propertied interests of St. Domingue. Plantation owners saw their crops destroyed and their slaves freed. Those who abandoned their land had it confiscated by the government and distributed "among the good and loyal Republicans."[12] Salvaging as much property as they could, thousands of refugee planters and merchants hastily fled the island with sugar, coffee, indigo, cotton, and people of African descent whom they claimed as their slaves. Whether or not certain blacks were treated as slaves in their new homes depended on the local laws and

courts, not what Louverture, Sonthonax, or the French National Convention had to say on the matter.[13] In Philadelphia, Boston, and New York,
three popular destinations for the refugees, slavery had been outlawed,
while it was legal in St. Iago, Baracoa, Norfolk, Charleston, and New
Orleans. While Congress had banned the importation of slaves from outside of the United States on January 1, 1809, it made a special exception to
this law in order to facilitate the 1809–10 immigration into New Orleans.
For the *gens de couleur* refugees in Louisiana, the exception was a double-
edged sword. It provided them the opportunity to import slaves from St.
Domingue and Cuba, but it also created the danger that they, themselves,
could be enslaved. This danger will be discussed in chapter 6.

Many refugees in New Orleans used salvaged commodities and
reenslaved human property to help them reestablish themselves in
Louisiana. While most white refugees moved to rural Louisiana hop-
ing to become planters, free colored refugees tended to abandon plantation life for other opportunities in New Orleans. Some leased or
mortgaged their "slaves" to get ready cash but maintain legal rights to
the slave; others sold their "slaves," often at discounted prices.[14] Some
seemed concerned about how the laws of their new destination would
treat their human property. Just prior to leaving St. Iago, Cuba, for New
Orleans, the executor of the estate of Joseph Rey sold a "negress named
Sophy and her child" to Fanny Lugois, a free mulattress, for the paltry
sum of $200. Perhaps the executor of the Rey estate was simply trying
to settle affairs quickly, but perhaps he was unsure of the estate's legal
rights to Sophy, or even of her status as a slave.[15]

The influx of thousands of immigrants into the city in a matter of
months presented logistical problems but also created economic opportunities for both New Orleans's existing free colored population and
refugees of color. Free colored artisans helped construct hundreds of
houses in the Vieux Carré and the faubourgs and built improvements
on sugar plantations in the region. Other free people of color opened or
expanded inns and boardinghouses to provide temporary accommoda-
tions for new arrivals to the city and opened and expanded small businesses to meet their everyday needs. Several free colored refugee *arma-
teurs* (ship owners) transported refugees from Cuba to New Orleans for
a fee. Some free people of color purchased promissory notes for a fraction of their value, risking that they would not be able to collect.

Of course, the very nature of refugee flight implies crisis, and few refugees had the time or the means to settle all their accounts before leaving. Those who left St. Domingue or Cuba with unpaid debts might have thought that they had at least escaped their obligations. They would be mistaken. The confusion created by the clash of legal cultures and refugee immigration was partially resolved in the New Orleans court system. Because the city's rapidly expanding commercial economy required legal certainty and consistency, part of the process of restoring order involved the City Court's adjudicating disputes regarding obligations incurred in St. Domingue and Cuba.

Property Disputes in the New Orleans City Court: An Overview

One of the most important functions of bourgeois law in the revolutionary era was to enumerate and protect private property rights. Two of the three books of the *Civil Digest of 1808* were dedicated to identifying the "different modifications of property" (property law) and "the different manners of acquiring property and things" (contract law).[16] While the legal structure in early Louisiana supported patriarchy and racism, more than anything else it protected private property rights. Nothing in the *Civil Digest* prevented free people of color from owning property, and the City Court exhibited little gender or racial bias in its application and interpretation of property and contract law. Neither judges nor juries in the New Orleans City Court appear to have discriminated against men or women of color when deciding cases. In territorial New Orleans, as in all liberal societies, the appearance of neutrality was important to establishing and maintaining the court's authority.

Free people of color were litigants in approximately 200 property disputes in the New Orleans City Court, nearly 60 percent of all the lawsuits in that court to which they were parties. These cases ranged from relatively commonplace lawsuits involving unpaid debts that arose from loans or credit purchases of real estate, goods, and/or services, to more extraordinary cases that arose from elaborate schemes to deprive someone of his or her property. While most petitioners sought monetary damages, others sought specific performance, or orders from the courts that particular pieces of property be delivered to them. Most specific performance cases involved either real estate or slave property, which took on special significance for free people of color because landownership and slave ownership were not only forms of wealth but also badges of freedom.

Most free colored litigants had lawyers representing them. Approximately sixty total lawyers appear representing parties in the City Court during its existence, with about a quarter of them representing free people of color at least once. Of course, this does not mean the other lawyers refused to represent people of color or that those who did had a heightened sense of egalitarianism. Rather, some lawyers had specialized clientele, while others represented whoever could pay them. A half dozen attorneys repeatedly represented free people of color, including Samuel Young, Jean Rodriquez, P. F. L. Godefroy, Alfred Hennen, A. R. Ellery, and Jacques Cesar Paillette. At least two of these lawyers, Jean Rodriquez and Samuel Young, had intimate relationships with women of African descent. Indeed, Rodriquez was sued for default after he failed to repay money he borrowed to purchase the freedom of a black female slave named Magnon whom he took as his lover.[17] Godefroy, on the other hand, used his position to take advantage of a free woman of color named Babet Lartigue. After recovering a judgment on Lartigue's behalf for the sum of $728, Godefroy negotiated with the defendant for a reduced payment and kept the proceeds for himself. Lartigue sued her former lawyer and recovered a default judgment, but Godefroy, who was in dire financial straits, was unable to pay it.[18] No other lawyer representing free people of color was as demonstrably unscrupulous as Godefroy, but all of them, it appears, expected to get paid.

Free people of color appeared as both petitioners and defendants in City Court property disputes. Table 5.1 provides a breakdown of the types of cases in which and the side of the docket on which free men and women of color appeared. The most common property disputes in the New Orleans City Court were cases seeking collection of debts, including promissory notes, accounts, general debt, services rendered, as well as some of the real estate and slave property cases. Men and women of color were petitioners in about the same number of property lawsuits overall, but men appeared as defendants more frequently, especially in debt collection cases. Perhaps not as many women of color borrowed

Table 5.1. *Property Disputes Involving Free People of Color
in the New Orleans City Court*

	Free Women of Color Petitioners	Free Women of Color Defendants	Free Men of Color Petitioners	Free Men of Color Defendants	Total
Real estate	8	11	8	22	49
Promissory note	7	7	8	14	36
Account	3	4	2	10	19
General debt	2	1	3	8	14
Services rendered	5	6	14	6	31
Slave property	8	17	2	5	32
Fraud	3	1	4	6	14
Estate litigation	4	3	1	1	9
Total	40	50	42	72	204

money or purchased goods on credit as did their male counterparts. Or maybe free women of color were able (or forced) to pay off their debts in ways that free men of color typically were not. In any event, men of color responded to lawsuits much more often than they initiated them, while women of color did both about equally.

The success of free colored litigants in the City Court property disputes was mixed. A precise determination of the percentage of free black litigants who won their cases is difficult for a couple of reasons. First, the court records of many cases contain no judgment, indicating that the case probably settled out of court. Second, the judgment was at times a "split decision" in which the plaintiff recovered partial relief but not everything he or she requested. As a general rule, however, for cases in which there is a recorded judgment, plaintiffs won more than two-thirds of them. Likely, potential petitioners and their lawyers knew what constituted a winning lawsuit. Free women of color won a higher percentage of their cases than free men of color, in large part because they were defendants far less often. The judgments and verdicts in the cases heard in the City Court suggest that judges and juries respected the property rights of free people of color and took their claims seriously. Free people of color played a crucial role in the New Orleans economy, and it was important for the court to validate obligations to them. While free people of African descent who recovered favorable judgments were not always able to collect on their judgments, all petitioners, including white men, faced this risk.

The most common form of debt collection lawsuit involving free people of color in the New Orleans City Court was the real estate default case. Free people of color were involved in twenty-nine such cases, four as petitioner, twenty-four as defendant, and two as both.[19] Typically, the petitioners in these cases sought a judgment for the amount of the debt plus interest, as well as an order of foreclosure on the property to satisfy the debt. More than a dozen free people of color lost their homes in foreclosure proceedings. Another free person of color also lost his home in Faubourg Marigny in two different foreclosure proceedings intended to satisfy debts incurred outside of the purchase of his home.[20]

Of the twenty-six real estate default cases filed against free people of color, Bernard Marigny, after whom Faubourg Marigny was named, was the petitioner in twenty of them, all filed between June 1809 and May 1812. But Marigny did not discriminate—he filed even more real estate default lawsuits against white defendants during the same period. Marigny sold hundreds of lots in the period in question, most of which were unimproved (vacant) but all of which were secured by a mortgage. The price of most unimproved lots in Faubourg Marigny was around $350 to be paid either in two to three installments or in a single payment at a future date with an interest rate of 8 percent. None of the free colored defendants to Marigny's real estate default lawsuits challenged the allegations of the petition, and Marigny recovered a default judgment in all but a couple of them. Likely, Marigny filed a lawsuit only after exhausting all efforts to negotiate a settlement with the defendant.

While the vast majority of free colored defendants in real estate default lawsuits did not dispute the claims of the petitioners, three people of color filed wrongful foreclosure lawsuits. A free Negro named Magloire Durand did not deny that he had owed money to Jean Dupuy, for example, but claimed that he had satisfied that debt by more than two years of service to Dupuy from 1805 to early 1808. Nevertheless, despite a court order stating that Durand had satisfied his debt, Dupuy obtained a new judgment against Durand in May 1808 from a justice of the peace named Rouzier. The justice of the peace commissioned a constable named Canmi to sell a house on Bienville Street that Durand had purchased for $500, as well as another piece of land near the same value that was owned by a ten-year-old "free mulatto" named Saneville. The constable sold both properties for a fraction of what they were worth without having obtained either an estimate of their value or the permission of either Durand or Saneville's guardian. Durand asked the court to order Dupuy to pay him $2,000 plus his expenses for bringing the lawsuit.[21] This case illustrates the potential pitfalls for those carrying real estate mortgages. Creditors had no problems finding purchasers of real property to satisfy debts, especially if it was sold at a discounted price. While the creditor was under a duty to get close to the fair market value of the property at the foreclosure sale and to refund any excess over the debt to the mortgager, it behooved the debtor to oversee this process because creditors were not above abusing it.

If people of color were overwhelmingly defendants in real estate default cases, they tended to be petitioners in lawsuits arising from nonpayment for services rendered. Many of New Orleans's free colored coopers, masons, and especially carpenters had to go to court to seek payment for their work. Many of the cases arose from nonpayment for construction of houses in Faubourg Marigny. Artisans of color also show up in cases involving work they performed on new plantations of white refugees, including that of a man named Anfoux. François Lalande was one of five free colored carpenters who built a sugar-manufacturing house on the plantation of Anfoux and never got paid for his work. In addition, Marcellin Gilleau and Bernard, both free men of color, did some masonry work on the same plantation and were not paid. Anfoux then sold the plantation to Bernard Marigny, who assumed the obligations of Anfoux. In separate lawsuits, the carpenters and masons won judgments against Marigny for a total of more than $500. While women were excluded from the skilled trades, several women of color were petitioners in lawsuits to recover for nursing services or child care. These women were not concubines providing "services," but caregivers who assisted the needy with the expectation that they would eventually be paid.[22] These skilled laborers won twelve of the thirteen cases for which there is a recorded judgment.

New Orleans's commercial economy ran on credit transactions, with small-business owners, including those operated by free people of color, often exchanging goods and/or services as payment. But sometimes this credit system led to a domino effect of defaults and lawsuits. For example, a white general store operator named Francis Wells had similar credit arrangements with two different free colored business owners. First, from September 2, 1808, until March 2, 1809, Wells leased a house on Conty Street from a free woman of color named Rosette Jung, who owned several lots of real estate in the city and its faubourgs. Then, Wells left the Conty Street house to rent a room in an inn owned and operated by a free man of color named James Ash. In neither case did Wells pay cash for his lodging, but instead credited what he owed for room and board against items he supplied from his general store. Yet Wells died before he settled his accounts, and shortly thereafter his estate was embroiled in litigation. The curator of Wells's estate, Thaddeus Mayhew, obtained a judgment against Ash on March 19, 1810, but a month later Ash filed his own lawsuit against Mayhew. According to Ash, Mayhew had inflated Ash's account to make it appear that the balance favored the estate of Wells. Mayhew denied Ash's allegations and won the case; Ash was ordered to pay the costs of the lawsuit.[23] Rosette Jung fared better against the Wells estate. She demanded payment from Mayhew for the sum of $184, which represented the balance on the account for back rent less the credit for goods she acquired from his store. Mayhew responded by filing an action with the justice of the peace for fifty six dollars representing the value of the goods that Jung received from his store. Jung then filed her own lawsuit in the City Court, which Mayhew did not answer. Jung won a judgment in the amount she demanded.

In another example of the domino effect of credit system defaults, Bernard Marigny's increasing unpaid receivables led to unpaid debts and lawsuits. Several free colored artisans sued Marigny in the New Orleans City Court. As he foreclosed on dozens of lots, Marigny sometimes assumed the debt incurred for improvements made to the property. For example, a free man of color named Jean Blanchard did some carpentry work in 1811 valued at ninety dollars on a house in the Faubourg Marigny being purchased by another free man of color named Jean Bouquet. But when Bouquet failed to make one of the installment payments, Bernard Marigny foreclosed on the house in early 1812. Blanchard then demanded payment from Marigny and, when Marigny refused, filed a lawsuit against him. Bouquet was himself a carpenter who was the petitioner in another lawsuit to recover payment for his part in constructing a house for a "mullatre libre" named Martin Narcisse. The agreed-upon price was $800 to be made in four installments of $200, the first to be paid prior to the beginning of construction, the last to be paid after completion, and the middle two payments to be made at various stages of progress during construction. Bouquet alleged that Narcisse refused to make the third payment on the contract. Narcisse answered that he stood ready to fulfill his part of the bargain, but that the work remained incomplete. The case was decided by a jury, which awarded Bouquet $324.[24]

Very few debt collection cases in the New Orleans City Court involved refugees of color, but those that did reveal a lot about the way the court dealt with debts incurred outside of its jurisdiction. Three women of color successfully sued on promissory notes signed in St. Domingue. Two other women of color, including Hazaca, won judgments for the value of staple crops sold in St. Domingue. Finally, the City Court awarded $138 to two free men of color for the balance due on an account for labor and materials provided on a job done on a plantation in Cuba. The City Court was not constitutionally obligated to enforce these contracts, but the court needed to create legal certainty in order to promote the commercial economy. This involved adjudicating disputes arising from obligations incurred in St. Domingue and Cuba.[25]

Fraud lawsuits were far less common in the New Orleans City Court than debt collection lawsuits, but they were at least as revealing of the social position of free people of color in New Orleans and the influence of the refugee immigration. The City Court heard nine fraud lawsuits involving free people of color—three as petitioners (or alleged victims), three as defendants (or alleged perpetrators), and three as both. Women of color were petitioners in three cases and defendants in one; men of color were petitioners in three cases and defendants in five; and white men were petitioners in three cases and defendants in three. Essentially, the petitioners in fraud cases alleged that the defendants had induced a contract under false pretenses.[26] Most fraud cases involved real estate or slaves, probably the two most important types of property a person of color could own because such ownership helped to verify his or her freedom.[27]

One of the fraud cases arose because a white man looked to exploit the fears and take advantage of the weaknesses of a free woman of color. Babet Bienvenu was an attractive target for unscrupulous con artists because she was illiterate, elderly, devoutly religious, and deeply concerned about her spiritual fate after death. Alexis André played on all these factors when he defrauded Bienvenu out of her house and lot on St. Anne's Street. Calling himself the "King of the Hiboos," André persuaded Bienvenu that he had special priestly powers to save her soul. He convinced his victim to transfer the St. Anne's property to him on the promise that after her death he would sell the property, use the proceeds to give her a proper burial, and give any money left over after the funeral to the woman's son, Batiste Bienvenu. After Babet Bienvenu learned that Alexis André was a fraud in April 1809, she sued him and won. The court's judgment rescinded the deed to him of her land.[28]

In two cases, free men of color gained the confidence of free women of color in order to defraud them out of their property. A free black woman named Marie Lalande turned to François Durand, a free man of color, to borrow $100 after several white potential lenders had refused her the loan. Lalande agreed to secure repayment of the loan with a mortgage on a house and half lot she owned on Hospital Street (present-day Governor Nichols Street in the French Quarter) and trusted Durand to draft and file the mortgage agreement. However, Durand, taking advantage of the woman's trust, drafted a deed of sale rather than a mortgage of the property, obtained Lalande's signature, and then filed the documents with a notary public. In another case, a former slave named Jeannette Moraud had unsuccessfully tried to purchase the freedom of her enslaved daughter Annette from the girl's white owner, when a free man of color named Terance Voisin convinced Moraud that he could succeed where she had failed. Claiming that Annette's owner owed him a favor, Voisin offered to act as a broker in the purchase of the young girl's freedom. A trusting Jeannette Moraud gave Voisin $300 for this purpose, but Voisin kept the money and left the city. Both Lalande and Moraud successfully sued their perpetrators.[29] Lalande, Moraud, and Bienvenu exposed themselves to fraud not only because they were women of African descent and otherwise perceived to be vulnerable but, most important, because they owned property.

At times, free black women may have used their perceived vulnerability to their advantage in the courtroom, and judges seemed receptive of appeals to their assigned role as protectors of the weak. Jeanette Moraud, for example, alleged that "by hard work and economy" she had amassed the sum of $300, the "only fruit of ten years of labor," in order to purchase the freedom of her daughter Annette, "the most important person in [her] life." After years of frustrated attempts, she was "easily manipulated" by Voisin's offers to intervene. Some courts were willing to take extreme measures to protect the property rights of black women, as illustrated by the case of *Masson v. Dobbs*. In August 1812, Marie Monier, a free woman of color, sued a Mr. Masson for breach of contract in the court of a justice of the peace named H. M. Dobbs. Apparently, Masson did not respect Monier's legal rights because he began to insult Dobbs for even considering the allegations and testimony of Monier. Dobbs promptly entered judgment in favor of Monier and found Masson in contempt of court, ordering that he be confined in the public jail for twelve hours or until he paid the judgment, whichever came last.[30] Judges demanded respect for themselves and the law and would punish white men who acted as if racial or gender bias trumped this respect.

The refugee presence was much greater in fraud cases than in debt collection cases. Three of the nine fraud cases involved refugees of the Haitian Revolution. One of them was the only fraud case in which a free woman of color was the defendant. In his March 1810 petition, a white refugee named Nicholas Jean Pierre alleged that he purchased a Congolese slave named Azor, around thirty-five years old, from Marie Noel, a "femme de couleur libre," for the price of $350. Noel, a recent arrival from Cuba, claimed to be representing Sieur Audee David but never had any legal rights to sell Azor. Jean Pierre sued for a refund of the purchase price plus additional expenses he incurred in filing the lawsuit. He won the case, but it is unclear whether he was able to collect the money from Marie Noel.[31]

A free colored refugee named Pirron was the petitioner in another fraud case that involved a complicated confidence scheme. Pirron purchased the schooner *Brisbane* in St. Iago, Cuba, on May 12, 1809, from a Mr. Dalillet for the sum of $1,500. Dalillet had purchased the ship in April of the same year from a Mr. Robinson. According to Pirron, Robinson then "fraudulently tried to sell the same schooner, again, to a Mr. Rooke, the defendant in this case." Upon learning of the second sale, Pirron then entered into an agreement with Rooke that until the title to the schooner could be cleared up, Rooke would act as master of the schooner and be paid an appropriate salary. Instead of holding the ship in trust, however, Rooke stripped it of its sails and tackle. Pirron then sued Rooke, asking for an order that gave him title to the schooner and required Rooke to return the appropriated tackle and sails. Pirron won the case—the court determined that Pirron was the rightful owner of the ship and ordered Rooke to deliver it to him. Robinson and Rooke appear to have conspired to defraud Pirron, and Mr. Dalillet may have also been involved in the conspiracy.

Slave Property Disputes

Perhaps the most significant type of property dispute involving free colored litigants was that regarding the ownership of slave property (the slave property dispute).[32] The City Court heard a total of nineteen slave property disputes involving free people of color. They were petitioners in four cases (with a white defendant), defendants in ten cases (with a white petitioner), and both in five cases. The slave property disputes carried heightened significance because with all the claims of people of color to slave ownership came the necessary implication that they were not slaves themselves. While the slave property disputes were decidedly not freedom suits, the subject of the next chapter, they did share one thing in common: in both types of cases the defendants were defending against challenges to their slave ownership. And as the analysis here and in the following chapter reveals, both types of cases played an important role in judicial race making.

Slave property disputes had the greatest number of refugees of color of all property lawsuits in the City Court. In twelve of them at least one of the parties was a refugee, and in eleven cases both were. Most of the City Court disputes regarding the legal rights to slave property sprang from the chaos created by the Haitian Revolution and subsequent

refugee immigration. The uprooting of thousands of former slave owners and slaves, twice within a decade for many, separated immigrants
from their possessions, and the conflicting slave laws of different jurisdictions created confusion with regard to their legal rights to their
"slaves." Several of the petitioners explicitly blamed the turmoil of the
revolution for their inability to secure their human property.[33]

In most of the slave property lawsuits, as in the case of *Mallet v.
Hazaca* that opened this chapter, both parties had a relationship with
the previous owner by which relationship they claimed slave ownership rights. Typically, one or both of the parties claimed the right to the
slave(s) as either an heir or a creditor of the slaves' former master. Fourteen of the parties claimed to have inherited the slaves, one claimed the
slaves as a creditor, and two, including Hazaca, alleged both. If the former master died insolvent, then a trustee could initiate proceedings on
behalf of the creditors to collect as many assets as possible to satisfy
them, including any human property. For example, a white Louisiana
planter named Joseph Yellies owned several slaves but was deeply in
debt at the time of his death. A free woman of color named Catherine
Clerge (aka Pouponne), who had lived with Yellies for many years, left
the plantation with eight of his slaves, including a mother with her
three children and four other adults. The executor of the estate, Paul
Lanusse, called a meeting of the creditors and appointed a merchant
named Phelippon as trustee. Phelippon then filed suit asking the court
to order Pouponne to return the eight slaves to the estate and to pay
damages for the lost labor of the slaves. Pouponne had no claim to the
slaves as an heir, but she may have had a claim as a creditor of the estate.
There is no final judgment in the documents, so the outcome of the case
is unclear.[34]

Free women of color were prominent in slave property disputes in
the New Orleans City Court. They were at least one of the parties in all
but two of the nineteen lawsuits. They were defendants twice as many
times as they were petitioners (fourteen vs. seven), meaning that they
were most often the person in possession of the slave(s) at the time
the lawsuit was filed. Free men of color were parties to only two slave
property disputes.[35] Most often the opponents of free women of color
in slave property disputes were white men. In the most common sce-
nario, the woman of color had been living with the decedent prior to

his death and thus had access to and a relationship with the alleged slave. The petitioner, on the other hand, was typically a white relative of the decedent or creditor of the estate and lived away from the slave(s) in question. Nine of the nineteen lawsuits fit this profile. The outcomes of the cases indicate that the court did not discriminate against women of color in these lawsuits. The petitioner won six of the lawsuits, the defendant won five, and there is no recorded judgment in eight. Women of color were defendants and white men were petitioners in all five defendant victories. Furthermore, colored female petitioners defeated white male defendants in two cases. A white male petitioner defeated a colored female defendant only once.

Indeed, the City Court slave property disputes reveal a lot about the social position of free women of color in prerevolutionary St. Domingue, where they "were a major economic, social, and cultural force." Many of the women of color involved in City Court slave property disputes would have taken the title in St. Domingue of *ménagère,* a position that combined the roles of "professional manager and personal companion."[36] Sannite Hazaca, for example, was a *ménagère* on Nicholas Mallet's coffee plantation. Sometimes these arrangements were formalized in contracts so that the *ménagère's* services to the estate were documented and could be claimed as a credit against the estate.

This type of arrangement, without the formal title, also existed among some *ancienne habitants* of Louisiana. For example, a free woman of color named E. A. Burel lived for many years on the Louisiana plantation of Sieur Mieullan as both his personal companion and the manager of his estate. After Mieullan died in early 1811, Burel left the plantation with a young adult Negress named Marianne. Pierre St. Amant, an heir of the estate of Sieur Mieullan, then sued Burel, claiming that Marianne belonged to Mieullan's estate. St. Amant asked the court to order Burel to return Marianne, pay money for her lost services, and pay the expenses of the lawsuit. In her answer to the lawsuit, Burel argued that Marianne belonged to her as partial payment from Sieur Mieullan for managing his affairs. She also claimed that because Marianne had been with her for more than five years, it was too late for Mieullan's heirs to claim her. Burel won the lawsuit. She was allowed to keep Marianne, and St. Amant was ordered to pay her legal expenses.[37] In *St. Amant v. Burel* and several other cases like it, the City Court held that services provided by women of color on the plantations of deceased white men could be claimed as credit against the estate.

Yet not all slave property disputes between white men and women of color turned on the question of whether a woman of color had legal rights to her deceased lover's former slaves. In a couple of cases women of color illegally absconded with "slaves" in the midst of the confusion of refugee flight. For example, a free woman of color who called herself Lise Gautier left Cuba with a ten-year-old black child named Beljance. Gautier, who later admitted that she did not have any legal rights to Beljance, paid for the child's fare from St. Iago to New Orleans because Beljance's former master had died and left her without a home. Once Gautier was in New Orleans, two different relatives of Beljance's former master, Damonette and Charles St. Martin, claimed inheritance rights to the young girl. After Gautier delivered Beljance to Damonette, Charles St. Martin filed a lawsuit. Gautier answered that she was willing to abide by the court's decision as to who was the proper owner of Beljance. The court ordered Gautier to return the "young negress" to Charles St. Martin but ordered St. Martin to reimburse Gautier for passage fare and to pay for her legal expenses. The case of *St. Martin v. Gautier* illustrates that even when the court sided with a white male petitioner, it scrupulously sought to respect the property rights of the free woman of color who was being sued.[38]

If white men thought that they could use their status to take advantage of women of color in the courtroom, they were mistaken. In December 1810, a white St. Domingue refugee named Jean Joseph Convignes filed suit in the New Orleans City Court on behalf of himself and his sister, Emilie Convignes, against a free woman of color named Marie Joseph Foure. Convignes alleged that Foure held "a slave named Anne and her three children," who rightfully belonged to him and his sister as heirs of the estate of their parents, who had owned land and slaves in Jean Rabel Parish, St. Domingue. The petition claimed that Foure "unjustly appropriated" Anne and her children because the Convignes siblings "were not able to claim the property that is rightfully theirs through inheritance by reason of the circumstances and the environment of the revolution in St. Domingue." Foure responded that "she purchased [Anne and her children] from Convignes in 1799 in front of witnesses." Apparently, Foure produced evidence of this purchase because she won the case and was allowed to keep Anne and her children.[39] Again, the court took seriously its role of objectively evaluating the evidence in property disputes without racial or gender bias.

The 1811 case of *Vincent v. Laroche*, in particular, illustrates both the vulnerability of free women of color refugees and their potential influence and status. The petitioner, a "femme de couleur libre" named Victoire Vincent, came to New Orleans from Cuba in August 1809 with seventeen individuals she claimed as her slaves. Once she arrived at the port of New Orleans, she registered all of these "slaves" with New Orleans mayor James Mather, who provided her with a certificate of ownership.[40] The city had passed an ordinance requiring all immigrants to register their slave property, but the law was honored in the breach— Vincent was one of the few who obeyed it. A little more than two years after Vincent's arrival, for reasons that are unclear, a constable named Laroche came to Vincent's home and took from it "a negress named Helene and her two children." Vincent then filed her lawsuit, complaining of the "illegal and unjust act committed by Sieur Laroche to whom your petitioner owes nothing and with whom she has never had any dealings or agreements." She attached to her petition the mayor's certificate indicating ownership of Helene and the children. With this conclusive evidence the City Court ordered that "the negro woman named Helene and the two children in the petition mentioned be delivered over to the Plaintiff." Moreover, although Laroche denied that he did anything wrong, the court reprimanded him for his "illegal and unjust" actions.[41] According to the court, therefore, Victoire Vincent's right to her slave property could not be infringed even, perhaps especially, by a government official.

As the cases discussed so far illustrate, the New Orleans City Court did not hesitate to enforce contractual obligations formed outside of the United States. The court allowed evidence of wills, deeds of sale, and service contracts drafted and executed in both St. Domingue and Cuba. Again, the court was under no obligation to do so and could have declared that it had no jurisdiction to hear these cases. But to refuse to hear the cases would have only added to legal and commercial uncertainty, rather than alleviate it.

Nevertheless, Moreau-Lislet's court selectively enforced the rulings of outside courts. At times, it had to decide between conflicting rulings. For example, while the jury in *Hazaca* found that Rousseau was a legal heir to his father as determined by the "judgment of the tribunal at Les Cayes," the same jury ignored the decision of a Cuban court that granted possession of the slaves in question to Louis Mallet, Hazaca's opponent.[42] Other times the court had to decide whether or not it would defer making a decision pending the decision of a court in another jurisdiction. After Elizabeth Daquin, a widow named Poiney, "formerly an inhabitant of the District of Arbonite in the island of Santo Domingo," sued Leonard Durand in the City Court for the value of "a negro woman named Dorothea now aged about twenty five years," Durand answered that Poiney could not maintain her action because a similar case was pending before "a Spanish tribunal in St. Iago de Cuba." The court rejected this defense, however, and awarded Poiney the sum of $500.[43] In two other cases, one of the parties asked the court to recognize the judgment of a court in Cuba regarding the ownership of slave property; each time the court refused.

Most significantly, the City Court refused to recognize the legal claims to freedom of the objects of slave property lawsuits. In the lawsuits involving refugees of the Haitian Revolution, the court was not only adjudicating property disputes but also judicially validating the reenslavement of thousands of men and women of African descent who had gained their freedom during the course of the Haitian Revolution. The City Court could have explicitly declared the objects of those lawsuits to be free or implicitly acknowledged their right to freedom by refusing to hear the cases—but it did neither. Instead, by adjudicating the disputes, the City Court implicitly rejected the revolutionary laws freeing the slaves. This is not surprising considering Haiti had been ostracized and isolated by the European imperial powers. Indeed, by the time of the slave property lawsuits in the New Orleans City Court, even France had repealed its own laws with regard to slavery in its colonies. For the court to acknowledge the legitimacy of these laws would have threatened to undermine plantation slavery in the lower Mississippi valley by validating abolitionism.

Given that no European or American power recognized the laws that freed the slaves during the Haitian Revolution, why did the objects of the lawsuits, those claimed as slaves, leave the one place where their freedom was secure? Maybe they believed that their freedom would be respected in their new home or that emancipation would not last on the island they left behind. After all, never before had slaves successfully overthrown slavery. Perhaps they preferred being the slaves of people familiar to them to freedom on the war-ravaged island from whence they came. Most likely, however, they did not have a choice. Almost half of the objects of these lawsuits were children under sixteen, and nine of the nineteen cases involved mothers and their children. Such people were less likely to take up arms in the revolution and were more vulnerable to force and manipulation by would-be slaveholders.

There were limits, however, to the extent to which courts would tolerate reenslavement, as illustrated by the companion cases of *Floté v. Aubert* and *Aubert v. Martineau*. A young Negress named Anne had been one of the slaves of Sieur Floté in St. Domingue. After Floté and his wife, Dauphine, died during the revolution, Anne remained on the island living as a free person until well after Haitian independence. In 1807, however, a man named Dominique Soux took Anne on board a ship off the coast of St. Domingue and "enslaved [her] by force." Soux then sold Anne in Baracoa, Cuba, to one Eugene Martineau, who, in turn, sold the young girl to a free woman of color named Marie Magdelaine Aubert in St. Iago for 350 pesos. In 1809, Aubert and Martineau fled Cuba for New Orleans, where they encountered Honoré Floté, the only legitimate child of the deceased Sieur Floté. In March 1810, Honoré Floté sued Aubert for possession of Anne. During the course of the trial, the circumstances under which Anne was enslaved were revealed, and the court declared her to be free. Aubert then sued Martineau to recover the money she paid for Anne, and won. The court distinguished between those "slaves" who left St. Domingue "on their own volition" during the course of the revolution and those who were taken from the island by force.[44] Thus, while the court refused to enforce the laws of revolutionary France and St. Domingue in New Orleans, it did recognize as free those former slaves who had remained in postindependence Haiti.

As the story of young Anne indicates, the objects of slave property disputes could sometimes influence the outcome of a case. It is doubtful that Martineau would have sabotaged his own case by testifying as to the circumstances of Anne's enslavement—he might not have even known them. Rather, it is more likely that Anne herself conveyed this information to Aubert, who then notified the court. Moreover, slaves could create procedural hurdles for certain people by choosing to leave St. Domingue or Cuba with others. Those who claimed legal rights but did not have possession were forced to bring the lawsuit and, as petitioners, carried the burden of proof. In such cases, unless the petitioner had evidence of ownership other than the testimony of interested persons, they were not likely to win the case. Finally, in one case the court, invoking the principle of prescription, granted ownership of a slave to the defendant based on the defendant's open and uninterrupted possession of the slave for more than five years. The slaves in these slave property disputes may have actually been trying to choose one master over another.[45]

The relationship between a person's perceived complexion and his or her position within the New Orleans City Court slave property disputes is striking. Twenty-two of the twenty-three people of African descent who were parties to slave property disputes were of mixed ancestry, with only one "free negress" defendant. The objects of the slave property disputes, on the other hand, were almost exclusively "Negroes."[46] Thus, even if the decisions in the slave property disputes did not hinge on presumptions of freedom for people of color and of slavery for Negroes, they certainly helped to create these presumptions. The implicit legal categorizations of race in slave property lawsuits became explicit in freedom suits, as discussed in chapter 6.

* * *

It is too much to say that the decisions in these slave property cases represent the court's intentions to reestablish the social hierarchies of prerevolutionary St. Domingue. Indeed, recent work on colonial St. Domingue has shown that the community of free people of African descent was incredibly diverse economically, socially, politically, and even racially. Many of them were of mixed African and European ancestry, but many were not.[47] Nevertheless, the influence of the refugees of the Haitian Revolution in these early slave property disputes is undeniable. In attempting to protect the property rights of the refugees, the City Court normalized slave ownership for *gens de couleur* and slave status for *noirs*.[48]

The specific purpose of the court in these property lawsuits, however, was not to create a racial order but to adjudicate property disputes. Its larger purpose was to legitimize a socioeconomic system in which property rights, including property in human beings, were considered "inviolable." For free people of color, who were vulnerable to being enslaved, property rights took on added significance because property ownership helped them get a firmer grasp on their own freedom. The irony is that people of color needed to own property in order to minimize the chances of becoming property themselves, a very real threat that is the subject of the next chapter.

6

"When the Question Is Slavery or Freedom"

In September 1809, Adèle Auger discovered that her uncle was making arrangements to sell her in the New Orleans slave market. Auger
had been born in the mid-1790s to a free family of color on the French
West Indian island of Guadeloupe. After the death of her mother, Auger
was entrusted to the care of her maternal uncle, a recent Guadeloupean
immigrant to New Orleans named Frederick Beaurocher. Auger spent
several years in a boarding school in New York City before Beaurocher
sent for her to come to New Orleans in the spring of 1809, when she was
probably in her early to middle teens. After living with him for almost
four months, under unusually close supervision, Auger became aware
that her uncle had taken her freedom papers and was claiming that she
was his slave.[1]

Within days of this discovery, Adèle Auger filed a lawsuit in the
New Orleans City Court seeking a declaration that she was free. She
presented no evidence of her freedom other than her own testimony,
which was countered by the testimony of Beaurocher. Nevertheless, the
City Court's presiding judge, Louis Moreau-Lislet, entered judgment
that the teenager be "returned to her former state of freedom to which
she appears justly entitled." On appeal to the Superior Court of Orleans,
Beaurocher's lawyer argued that the trial court erred because Auger did
not meet her burden of proof. As the person bringing the lawsuit, Auger

was required to establish the facts at issue in the case by a preponderance of the evidence.[2] Despite the lack of evidence corroborating her own testimony, however, the Superior Court affirmed the lower court's decision, stating, "Although it is in general correct, to require the plaintiff to produce his proof before the defendant can be called upon for his, it is otherwise, when the question is slavery or freedom." Taking note of Auger's "yellow" complexion and perceived mixed European and African ancestry, the court proclaimed, in a landmark decision, that "persons of color may have descended from Indians on both sides, from a white parent, or mulatto parents in possession of their freedom. Considering how much probability there is in favor of the liberty of those persons, they ought not to be deprived of it upon a mere presumption." If the plaintiff were a Negro, the court explained, she "perhaps would be required to establish [her] right by such evidence as would destroy the force of presumption arising from color; Negroes brought to this country being generally slaves, their descendants may perhaps fairly be presumed to have continued so, till they show the contrary."[3] Thus, the Superior Court decision in *Adele v. Beauregard* created a dual standard for burden of proof in suits of this type based upon the race of the petitioner. "Negroes" or "Africans" were presumed to be slaves, while "mulattoes" or "persons of color" were presumed to be free.[4]

This chapter examines the ways in which the relationship of race and status was contested, compromised, and defined in freedom suits in the New Orleans courts. First, it identifies the precariousness of freedom for free blacks in the young United States, especially in the states that recognized slavery and those states that bordered them. The illegal enslavement of free blacks in the antebellum United States, while driven by market forces, was facilitated by legal systems that equated people of African descent with slavery. The chapter then broadly examines lawsuits for freedom brought by people of African descent in the slave states. Next, it narrows the focus to freedom suits in the New Orleans City Court, showing the ways in which they were similar to and different from freedom suits generally. Finally, it shows how the precedent created in these cases, especially the case of Adèle Auger, led to the legal construction of three races in Louisiana. The freedom suits in the New Orleans City Court and the three-tiered legio-racial regime expressed in *Adele v. Beauregard* reveal the important impact of the Haitian Revolution on ideas of race and status in antebellum New Orleans. As the courts tried to restore order out of the confusion created by the revolution and consequent refugee immigration, they crafted a set of rules that would help them determine who was to be enslaved and who was entitled to freedom. In the process, they were making race.

The Precariousness of Freedom

Freedom for free people of African descent throughout the United States in the pre–Civil War era was precarious because members of the "black" race were under constant threat of illegal enslavement. It is impossible to know just how many free blacks were illegally enslaved in the United States prior to the Civil War, but the numbers were likely in the thousands at least. One should be skeptical of abolitionists who may have exaggerated the numbers in order to highlight the problem, such as John Parrish, who claimed that "in six months alone" during 1806, "six hundred persons" were kidnapped.[5] But more than a thousand free people of color claimed to have been kidnapped in lawsuits filed during the years 1792 to 1860, and if abolitionist literature may have overcounted the number of illegally enslaved blacks, then court records certainly undercounted it. In the words of Ulrich Bonn Phillips, "Kidnappings without pretense of legal claim were done so furtively that they seldom attracted record unless the victims had recourse to the courts."[6] One would think, therefore, that for every illegally enslaved black person who sued to gain his or her freedom, many more did not, due to lack of knowledge, insufficient resources, or fear of retaliation. If ten free blacks were kidnapped into slavery for every one of them that sued for his or her freedom, then perhaps 10,000 or more people were illegally enslaved in the United States during the antebellum period.[7]

Illegal enslavement occurred in every state and territory of the United States between the American Revolution and the Civil War. According to Carol Wilson in her book *Freedom at Risk*, "The vast majority of kidnappings took place . . . in the border states of Pennsylvania, Delaware, and Maryland."[8] Her evidence for this assertion comes from the statements and writings of abolitionists, specifically the Underground Railroad conductor Levi Coffin and the antislavery pamphleteer Jesse

Torey. To be sure, the people of these three states (along with Massachusetts) made kidnapping a political concern by petitioning their respective state legislatures for harsher penalties and greater enforcement of kidnapping laws. But evidence from court records suggests that Missouri, Kentucky, and Louisiana should also be added to this list. Regardless of where the free person of color was abducted, he or she was almost always moved—at least to another county and more often to another state. Free blacks abducted in free states had to be removed from the state if they were to be claimed as slaves, but free blacks in slave states also needed to be moved in order to minimize the likelihood that friends, neighbors, and/or acquaintances could identify them as free.

Once abducted, the person of African descent faced two likely fates. Some perpetrators sought to make use of his or her labor. For example, Claire Drouin kidnapped Melanie Chalon when the latter was a young teenager and used her as a sex slave in both Charleston, South Carolina, and New Orleans, Louisiana. More often, however, perpetrators looked to quickly sell their victims in the slave market in order to both profit and rid themselves of the living evidence of their crimes. George Lewis of Jamaica was sold five times in four different cities in a matter of months. Presumably each sale garnered a profit—but, just as important, each sale further disguised the original illegal act.[9]

Louisiana was unique among the states with high numbers of kidnapped free blacks in that it was part of the Deep South where slavery was more firmly entrenched than in the border states. Indeed, Louisiana was the ultimate destination of many free blacks who were kidnapped in other states, as represented in the story of Solomon Northup.[10] Nothing contributed to and symbolized the precarious freedom of free blacks more than the slave market, and in the nineteenth century, New Orleans was the hub of North America's slave trade.[11] The Crescent City invited slaveholders and slave traders from all over the South; some of them carried "stolen" human property they hoped to sell, while others sought a good labor source at a good price, paying little heed to the legality of the transaction. Slaves varied in price, but even a young female slave could garner several hundred dollars in the slave market. Kidnappers who lived in New Orleans, like Frederick Beaurocher, had quick and easy access to hundreds of potential purchasers of slaves each day. Kidnappers from other parts of the United States commonly sold their victims to professional slave traders, who then trekked to the nation's largest slave market to dispose of their property. Perhaps the slave traders were aware of the original illegal act and purchased their victims at discounted prices.

Throughout the country, as in New Orleans, free blacks were illegally enslaved in a variety of ways, but almost all of them involved forceful abduction, deceit, or both.[12] Some people of color unwittingly set themselves up for illegal enslavement by entering into employment relationships that were, on their surface, indistinguishable from the master-slave relationship. Amand Langlois, for example, was a carpenter's apprentice when his *master* carpenter, Roland Gallier, sold him to a slave trader named Rose in 1809. Similarly, Hervey des Romain was induced by a certain Albers to come to Charleston, South Carolina, on the promise that Albers would procure him a trade. Once in Charleston, however, Albers sold des Romain to a slave trader named Gilbert.[13] In each case the victim of illegal enslavement remained unwitting of his fate until his seemingly legitimate employer chose to sell him. If a free black employee had no readily available proof of freedom, the owner of his or her labor could easily claim to be the owner of his or her person.

Other free people of African descent were simply hauled into slavery through violence or the threat of violence. Some were severely beaten, others deprived of food and water, and still others imprisoned or confined. Women were sometimes threatened with sexual abuse. George Lewis was locked in a sugar house for several days, and Thereze and *la fille* Bouvais were both confined in jail pending their trials. One slave trader named Kohn threatened that if his victim, William Jones, told anyone that he was free, the trader would "blow his brains out" or "run him through with his sword."[14]

While nearly every free person of African descent faced the threat of being kidnapped and sold into slavery, certain segments of the population were more susceptible than others. Both nationally and in New Orleans, kidnappers targeted children, women, and, among adult men, sailors.[15] The disproportionate victimization of women and children can presumably be attributed to their perceived or actual physical weakness. Sailors, on the other hand, lacked community ties, not physical strength. Adèle Auger, being a young female who had been uprooted from her social networks of people who could verify her freedom, was especially vulnerable. Indeed, in early nineteenth-century New Orleans, when the *Adele* case was heard, the chaos of war, revolution, and refugee flight created conditions especially ripe for illegal enslavement.

Many laws, both federal and state, facilitated the efforts of kidnappers of free blacks. First and foremost were the Fugitive Slave Laws of 1793 and 1850. Backed by a clause in the Constitution, these acts of Congress gave slaveholders the right to retrieve their runaway slave property that had escaped into a state or territory where slavery was illegal. The question remained, however, whether or not the person in question was really who the slaveholder said he or she was. The 1793 law left the determination of this issue to the legal system of each individual state. In 1842, however, the Supreme Court decision in *Prigg v. Pennsylvania* gave slaveholders a right to "self-help," meaning that the slaveholder did not need to use any state's legal system. The *Prigg* decision left both sides dissatisfied. Northerners claimed that it provided carte blanche for kidnappers of free blacks in northern states, while southerners claimed that it deprived them of needed assistance from northern state officials. In 1850, southerners procured a more slaveholder-friendly federal Fugitive Slave Law that nationalized the process by which persons of color were returned (or in some cases, no doubt, sent for the first time) to slavery. The struggle over the procedural method for determining who was and was not a fugitive slave became one of the major political and constitutional controversies over slavery leading to secession and, ultimately, the Civil War.[16]

The laws of many southern states also facilitated illegal enslavement. In some states freed slaves could be legally reenslaved if they fell into debt. A North Carolina law called for enslaving free blacks who failed to pay their taxes. Other state laws simply created conditions ripe for illegal enslavement. For example, when Charity Oxendine could not pay a fine levied on her for having a child out of wedlock, she was sold as an indentured servant to someone who could, a man named Thomas White. White then sold Oxendine's labor to Thomas Ingles, who left the state with Oxendine and her two children, claiming that all three of them were his slaves. Perhaps the most publicized and controversial state laws that facilitated illegal enslavement were the infamous Seamen Acts that required free black sailors to be confined in jail during their stay in southern port cities. In 1822, after the Denmark Vesey conspiracy, South Carolina enacted the first Negro Seamen Act. While the U.S. Circuit Court in Charleston declared the act unconstitutional in 1823, South Carolina officials ignored the decision and continued to confine free black sailors.[17] Louisiana enacted similar legislation in 1841 that, according to some, had nefarious consequences. John Pearson, a ship owner out of Boston, claimed to have "certificates" proving "more than one thousand imprisonments, within three years, at the port of New Orleans alone."[18] Once confined in jail, free black sailors were vulnerable to claims that they were actually slaves.

Some of the biggest legal obstacles to freedom for free blacks were not substantive but procedural, especially with regard to admissibility of evidence. Most southern (and some northern) states had laws that prohibited blacks, enslaved or free, from testifying against whites. Thus, sometimes even when there were witnesses to a kidnapping, if the witness was black, a white perpetrator could not be convicted.[19] Louisiana did not have such a law, however, as free people of African descent were allowed to testify against whites. This was not an issue in the *Adele* case, since her uncle and enslaver was also a person of color, but in most cases in Louisiana and elsewhere the kidnapper was white.

Freedom Suits in Southern Courts

While the laws and legal systems of the United States and southern states, in some respects, facilitated illegal enslavement, they also provided the mechanisms by which victims of the crime could win back their freedom. Kidnapping was illegal in almost every state and territory of the United States, and courts would, upon sufficient proof, grant freedom to an illegally enslaved person. Vermont led the way with a law in 1787 that punished the kidnapping of free blacks that was mimicked by every northern state except Rhode Island. Pennsylvania's law of 1826 was one of the harshest. It punished offenders with a fine of as much as $2,000 and a maximum prison sentence of twenty-one years. Several slave states, including Delaware, Virginia, Tennessee, Georgia, and Mississippi, as well as the District of Columbia, passed anti-kidnapping laws in the late eighteenth and early nineteenth centuries. Louisiana passed an anti-kidnapping law in 1819 that carried a maximum penalty of fourteen years in jail and a fine of $1,000 dollars.[20]

The eastern border states of Maryland, Delaware, and Pennsylvania, home to many free blacks and many antislavery Quakers, were particularly concerned with curtailing the crime. The abolition societies of Delaware and Pennsylvania led the way in the anti-kidnapping campaign. From 1816 to 1818, the Delaware legislature received twenty-six different petitions signed by almost 900 citizens of the state who were alarmed by the rising number of free black kidnappings. These petitioners asked the legislature to pass laws with a severe enough penalty to discourage those who would seek to profit from the unscrupulous activity. In 1817–18, legislators from Delaware unsuccessfully pushed Congress for a national anti-kidnapping law. Quakers from all the Mid-Atlantic states continued to lobby Congress throughout the antebellum period.[21]

Even in the Deep South, while there were no mass petition campaigns, some individuals were enthusiastic about curtailing the kidnapping of free blacks. According to Mississippi attorney general Richard Stockton in 1826, outside of his state "there is no community that holds in greater abhorrence, that infamous traffic carried on by negro stealers."[22] Joshua Boucher of Tuscaloosa, Alabama, labored to secure the release of Cornelius Sinclair, a freedom suit petitioner who had been sold by his kidnapper to an Alabama planter. Duncan Walker was a Mississippi lawyer working to prosecute kidnappers and secure freedom for the kidnapped.[23] Many different lawyers in New Orleans offered their services to freedom suit petitioners. Most of these men were themselves, at one time, slaveholders.

Why would southern slaveholders who undoubtedly believed in the inferiority of "Negroes" champion the cause of illegally enslaved free blacks? One obvious explanation, in the case of lawyers for freedom suit petitioners, is that they were getting paid. While few illegally enslaved blacks had the resources to hire lawyers, many benefited from antislavery organizations that paid their expenses. Yet many white southerners were, undoubtedly, driven to restore freedom by compassion. Moreover, the desire for certainty in the law and the need to legally legitimize slavery also factored in. For much of the antebellum period, the conflicting laws of free and slave states were resolved by the principle of comity: "the courtesy among political entities (as nations, states, or courts of different jurisdictions) involving especially mutual recognition of legislative, executive, and judicial acts."[24] In short, slaveholders in the South agreed to respect the right of northern states to prohibit slavery so that the governments of the North would respect southern laws permitting and enforcing it.

The freedom suit was the main avenue by which a slave (or person being treated as a slave) could legally arrive at his or her freedom. With rare exceptions, Dred Scott's second trial being one of them, almost all of these cases were tried in state (as opposed to federal) courts. Collectively, the courts of the various slave states heard thousands of cases litigating the status of a person of color. The bulk of these were in five states: Missouri, Delaware, Louisiana, Maryland, and Kentucky.[25] All but Louisiana were border states; indeed, Louisiana was the only one of these states that joined the Confederate States of America in 1861. Because, as a general rule, slaves could not sue, legislatures and courts carved out exceptions to allow alleged slaves to bring suits for freedom. As David Konig has pointed out, freedom suits "had their origins in actions brought *in forma pauperis* under statutes made in Tudor times, which, a Virginia lawyer commented in the nineteenth century, had by that time 'in practical operation been confined to suits brought by persons of colour to recover their freedom.'"[26] With regard to the Territory of Orleans, the *Civil Digest of 1808* stated that the slave cannot be a party in any civil action either as plaintiff or defendant, "except when he has to claim or prove his freedom."[27]

Freedom suits in the United States were different in several respects from *coartacion* proceedings in Spanish Cuba and Louisiana. The latter were not trials per se but hearings in which colonial administrators were charged with determining the price of a slave's freedom. With very few exceptions, the issue in *coartacion* cases concerned not whether a slave was entitled to freedom but how much that freedom would cost. Freedom suits, on the other hand, were adversarial proceedings in which plaintiffs claimed the right to freedom and defendants claimed the right to ownership of the plaintiff. Most important, for purposes of the argument presented here, freedom suits, like all adversarial proceedings, involved issues of burden of proof whereas *coartacion* proceedings did not.

Freedom suits in the slave states can be divided into four main categories.[28] One type was found almost exclusively in Delaware and Maryland. Delaware, by its constitution, prohibited the importation of any new slaves into the state, and a 1793 act provided the penalty of such slave gaining his or her freedom. Maryland passed similar legislation in 1796.[29] The vast majority of the freedom suits in the Delaware and Maryland courts involved masters ignorant of these laws and former slaves who were the beneficiaries of such ignorance. In a second type of freedom suit, framed in contract law, the petitioner alleged that her master had promised to free her, but that he (or his heirs) had failed to fulfill this promise. A Negress named Marie, for example, claimed that her former master, Françoise Algue, had granted Marie her liberty just prior to Algue's death. Marie later learned, "at the time of the announcement of the inventory of the estate of Françoise Algue," that she "was listed as part of that inventory."[30]

A third type of freedom suit involved issues of conflict of laws and the use of comity (defined earlier in this chapter). In this type of suit, the petitioner invoked the "freedom principle," claiming that she had gained her freedom by virtue of living in a jurisdiction that did not recognize slavery.[31] In the United States, the existence of both free and slave jurisdictions raised important questions regarding conflict of laws. If the slave entered free territory, did he or she gain freedom? The Fugitive Slave Clause and Fugitive Slave Act answered this question in the negative with regard to runaway slaves but did not answer it with regard to slaves who were taken into free territory voluntarily by their masters. The latter question was answered "in comity" by the domicile/sojourn distinction. Judges and juries were called upon to decide whether the master had been *living* in the free jurisdiction, in which case the petitioner was judged free, or simply *visiting* it, in which case the petitioner remained a slave. This was a "question of fact" but really involved interpretation of facts.[32]

In theory, the same principle applied if the petitioner had spent time in a jurisdiction outside of the United States that did not recognize slavery. Indeed, several petitioners won their freedom by virtue of having lived in England or France. Yet, while St. Domingue's commissioners abolished slavery in the colony in 1793, and the French National Convention abolished slavery in all French colonial possessions in 1794, courts in the United States were reluctant to recognize the freedom of a person on the basis of these laws. Sue Peabody analyzed thirty-one cases in four different states involving the claims to freedom of refugees of the Haitian Revolution. She found that very few petitioners, none before 1809, claimed freedom on the basis of St. Domingue's or France's general emancipation laws. Furthermore, only one petitioner, a refugee woman of African descent living in Tennessee, *won* her freedom on this basis.[33] Thus, while southern courts regularly acknowledged the freedom principle of the northern United States and Western European countries, they generally refused to recognize the abolition of slavery in the French West Indies.

Finally, the fourth type of freedom suit alleged that the petitioner had been legally free when he or she was kidnapped and taken or sold into slavery. These cases were usually framed as criminal complaints for kidnapping or private lawsuits for false imprisonment or for assault and battery. In these cases the finder of fact was asked to determine who was lying and who was telling the truth. In the case that opens this chapter, for example, Beaurocher claimed that he had owned Auger since she was a newborn, but Auger claimed that she had been born free and had lived that way all her life. Both could not have been telling the truth.

In the false imprisonment–based freedom suit, the petitioner faced the sometimes daunting task of providing sufficient evidence, documentary or testimonial, that he or she had been legally free prior to being kidnapped. The best possible evidence was a certified and notarized fiat proclaiming the person's freedom, commonly known as "freedom papers." If a free person of African descent possessed freedom papers, however, he or she probably would not have been in court. Many petitioners, including Adèle Auger, alleged that one of the first things their kidnappers did was confiscate or destroy their freedom papers.[34] Barring documentary evidence, the next best evidence came from third-party witnesses who could testify to the freedom of the petitioner. White witnesses were preferable, and sometimes necessary, because most states prohibited free blacks from testifying against whites. Without documentary evidence or third-party witnesses, a freedom suit simply came down to the petitioner's word against the defendant's. In these cases, in every southern state but Louisiana, the petitioner was at a disadvantage because he or she carried the burden of proof. Thus, the ruling in *Adele,* which placed the burden of proof on the defendant in cases in which the petitioner was a "person of color," was exceptional in many respects.

The legislation and court cases dealing with illegal enslavement produced mixed results. On the one hand, kidnappers were rarely punished. Many of them never even saw the courtroom. Some law enforcement officers could not enforce the anti-kidnapping laws even when they wanted to, as the plight of Sarah Hagerman illustrates. Hagerman, a free black girl, had been abducted and sold as a slave to Jesse Cannon of Norway's Fork Bridge, Maryland. When a concerned John H. Willits traveled there to rescue her, a Maryland sheriff named John Brown explained that he could not help Willits because Cannon lived in Delaware, outside of his jurisdiction.[35] Those kidnappers who were brought into court were likely to escape penalty, even when a court found that a person of color deserved freedom. In Louisiana, as Judith Schafer has shown, from the date the anti-kidnapping law was passed in 1819 until the outbreak of the Civil War, there was not a single criminal prosecution for kidnapping.[36]

The legal systems were more effective at freeing the kidnapped than they were at punishing the kidnappers. The majority of petitioners in freedom suits nationwide gained their freedom. Most likely, only those petitioners with the best cases had the courage and resources to sue in the first place. The success rate in Louisiana was 60 percent. Of the five states with the most freedom suits, Delaware had the highest success rate at 90 percent, and Missouri petitioners had the lowest success rate at 42 percent. The percentage in Delaware can be explained, in large part, by its unique laws. In addition to the constitutional provision and supporting law referenced earlier, a 1787 Delaware law banned the sale of Delaware slaves to the Carolinas, Georgia, and the West Indies and was expanded in 1789 to include Maryland and Virginia. These laws helped make slave owning in the state increasingly unprofitable. Finally, in 1797, all Delaware slaves sold out of the state were declared automatically free.[37] Delaware makes for an interesting comparison with Louisiana. While the laws of Delaware, a nominal slave state, preferred freedom for all, the laws of Louisiana, a state where slavery was firmly entrenched, preferred enslavement for "Negroes" but, after *Adele*, freedom for "people of color." How this came to be is the subject of the rest of this chapter.

Freedom Suits in the New Orleans City Court

New Orleans–based courts heard an unusually high number of freedom suits by U.S. standards. Only St. Louis, Missouri, and Dover, Delaware, were home to more such lawsuits than the Crescent City. For its part, the New Orleans City Court, in its eight years of existence, adjudicated sixteen freedom suits—for an average of two per year. Eight different slave states adjudicated fewer than sixteen total. Indeed, during the entire pre–Civil War era, Alabama (6), Arkansas (2), Florida (4), Georgia (5), Mississippi (3), South Carolina (1), and Texas (1) heard a total of twenty-two freedom suits combined, just six more than the New Orleans City Court heard in an eight-year period. Thus, the frequency with which the City Court determined the status of people of African descent was not typical.[38]

A breakdown of the numbers of New Orleans City Court freedom suits reflects both the vulnerability of women and children to illegal enslavement and the influence of the Haitian refugee immigration in early New Orleans. Five of the sixteen freedom suit petitioners were adult women, and six were children under the age of sixteen. Furthermore, the petitioners in ten of the sixteen City Court freedom suits were from the French West Indies, as were both of the judges of the City Court, Louis Moreau-Lislet and James Pitot.

The majority of the freedom suits adjudicated by the City Court were of the kidnapping variety. The petitioner in eleven of the sixteen freedom suits claimed to have been illegally enslaved. Eight of these claimed to have been born free, while three claimed to have been former slaves who had legally acquired their freedom. Significantly, seven of these eleven petitioners were from St. Domingue, another (Adèle Auger) was from Guadeloupe, and still another was from Jamaica. Eight of the nine West Indian (and seven of the eight French West Indian) petitioners in the kidnapping suits were people of perceived mixed ancestry. The only Negress lost her case. Thus, the typical freedom suit heard in the New Orleans City Court involved a petitioner of mixed ancestry, either a woman or a child, who had been born free in the French West Indies and then illegally enslaved in the chaos created by revolution and refugee flight.

The City Court also heard several freedom suits framed as breach of contract claims. One of them, the 1812 case of *Lafite v. Dufour*, shows some problems inherent in contract claims brought by people held as slaves. In this case, Jeannette, born a slave in St. Domingue, claimed that in 1797 her master, the late Louis Victor Dufour, freed her "as gratitude for her service and her fidelity." Dufour confirmed this grant of freedom in his will executed on February 18, 1803. Jeannette had been "living without problem as a free person since 1797 in St. Domingue, in Cuba and in New Orleans," during which time she had three children, Marie, Jean Jacques, and Norbert. Theodore Lafite claimed that at the time of making his will, Louis Dufour was not solvent and was indebted to Lafite in the sum of $22,000. Thus, according to Lafite, the will was made "in fraud of the decedent's creditors." On March 9, 1812, Lafite had the sheriff seize Jeannette and her three children as his property—giving rise to the lawsuit. The question for the court was whether Jeannette was legally freed by the 1797 promise, in which case the contract was valid, or by the 1803 will, in which case the freeing of Jeannette was void as a fraudulent transfer.[39]

The case of *Metayer v. Noret* further illustrates the problems associated with suing for one's freedom under contract law. In this, the first of many cases adjudicating her status, Adelaide Durand (aka Adelaide Metayer), a "mulatresse libre" and native of St. Domingue, alleged that in Cap Français sometime in 1801 she paid her former master, the tailor Charles Metayer, the sum of 350 piastres in order to be released from service to him.[40] At the time, according to the petition, Durand had a child who was not included in the transaction, her master having said that "he loved the child" and did not want to part with him until he was older. She had two more children after gaining her liberty who were, presumably, born free. Charles Metayer later died, after which the defendant, Louis Noret, who was the creditor of Charles Metayer's brother, Louis, seized Durand and all three of her children to satisfy his claim. Blaise Cenas, the sheriff of New Orleans, enforced the seizure of the three children and was planning to sell them at auction on May 28, 1810, when Adelaide Durand filed a suit to suspend the sale. In a separate lawsuit, Durand sought a judgment declaring herself and all three of her children to be free.

In making his ruling, Judge Moreau-Lislet seems to have misunderstood the nature of the contract in question, and he balked at admitting evidence of the 1801 transaction because it had not been notarized. Yet the laws of St. Domingue did not require notarization of the transaction in question.[41] In the end, the City Court took the easy way out. It allowed the seizure of Durand's oldest child, who had not been included in the transaction, but declined to rule on the status of Durand herself.[42]

Tellingly, the New Orleans courts did not extend comity to the abolition laws of revolutionary St. Domingue and France. Indeed, not one of the French West Indian freedom suit petitioners in the City Court claimed to be entitled to freedom by virtue of the general emancipation laws of 1793–94. Jeannette and Adelaide Durand, who both lived in St. Domingue at the time of the general emancipation, framed their freedom suits in the New Orleans City Court in contract law rather than on the basis of the freedom principle and comity. Cases in other New Orleans courts after the City Court had been discontinued illustrate the ineffectiveness of appealing to French revolutionary law. In a second freedom suit, this time in the Parish Court, Adelaide Durand's lawyer invoked the emancipation laws of the French West Indian colonies. The jury agreed that she should be freed, but the Louisiana Supreme Court reversed the jury's verdict, implicitly refusing to acknowledge the abolitionist laws of France and St. Domingue. More than twenty years later, in June 1845, Marie Françoise, a free woman of color also known as Dauphine, argued to the New Orleans District Court that her sons, whom she claimed were born free, were being held as slaves by the administrators of the estate and tutors to the heirs of Augustin Borie. Marie Françoise contended that she was the daughter of a free woman of color named Isabelle, who was born in St. Domingue, where she had been legally freed under the French colonial government of the island led by Sonthonax. Isabelle and Marie Françoise came to Louisiana, via Cuba, in 1809 with Augustin Borie and his wife, Valérie Samanos. She served the couple and their family for many years in Iberville Parish, during which time she gave birth to four sons. After Valérie Samanos's death, however, Augustin Borie "retained" ownership of her four sons, "maltreating" one of them. When Borie died, the administrators of his estate retained "possession" of Marie Françoise and her children and collected income by hiring them out to the municipality. Marie Françoise asked the court to free her sons and give her $15,000 in damages from the administrators, George Deslonde and Cyprien Ricard, and from the adult heir named Paulin Ricard. The district court dismissed her lawsuit, however, holding that the Louisiana law did not recognize the freedom granted by the French revolutionary government in St. Domingue.[43] Thus, as Sue Peabody has shown in her broad study, lawyers did start basing claims on the freedom principle as the country moved deeper into the antebellum period. In New Orleans, however, these claims fell on deaf ears.

Nor did the Louisiana courts respect British policy emanating from the Haitian Revolution, as evidenced by another case decided in the district court on April 15, 1819. In this case, Zephir, a free man of color, alleged that he was "being illegally held in slavery by Simon Gallien Preval." Zephir claimed that he was Preval's slave in St. Domingue when, in 1794, the British invaded the island, offering planters 400 pounds for each slave enrolled into a newly organized "regiment of Blacks." Availing himself of the offer, Preval received the money for Zephir, and Zephir became a grenadier in the new regiment. In 1798, after the "capitulation" of the British to Toussaint Louverture, the regiment was disbanded and its members declared free by the authority of the British government. However, Zephir was "induced by various pretences" to remain with Preval, and the latter continued to exercise "every right of ownership" over him. The court denied Zephir his claim and, presumably, he continued to live as a slave.[44] Apparently, the courts in New Orleans were not inclined to honor any law coming out of the French or Haitian Revolutions that was hostile to slavery.

Other freedom suit petitioners sought freedom in the New Orleans City Court on the basis of the laws of Spanish colonial Louisiana. Jean Baptiste, the petitioner in the case that begins chapter 2, could not convince the court of his claim to freedom under *coartacion*. But a woman named Geneviève had more success. In the 1790s, John Arnould sold Geneviève and her child, as slaves, to Francis Bouligny for the sum of $1,160. The documents never identify Geneviève as a Negress, mulattress, or woman of color, just as a slave. After Geneviève had stayed in the possession of Bouligny for some time, a Spanish court ruled that she and her child were to be freed, declaring them to be Indians. Still, they continued to live with Bouligny. After both Bouligny and Arnould died, Bouligny's widow, Maria Louisa Dauberville, Geneviève, and her child all brought suit before a Spanish tribunal to take notice of the previous court ruling and recover $1,160 from the widow Arnould. The suit was undecided at time of the Louisiana Purchase. In 1807, Dauberville and Geneviève brought yet another lawsuit in the City Court seeking declaration of freedom. Recognizing the laws of Spain and the decisions of Spanish tribunals in colonial New Orleans, the City Court held that Geneviève and her child were free.[45]

On the whole, the freedom suit petitioners in the New Orleans City Court were more successful than the national average, the Louisiana average, or even the Delaware average. Out of the fourteen cases for which the judgment is known, twelve petitioners won their freedom. The only two people to lose were the "Negress" Caroline and the "Negro" Jean François, both of whom had been born slaves.[46] Adelaide Durand, another former slave and a woman of color, saw her son seized and ordered into slavery. But her status remained undetermined by the City Court, and she eventually won her freedom in another court. Therefore, the New Orleans City Court not only adjudicated an unusually high number of freedom suits but also ruled in favor of freedom in an unusually high number of them.

The petitioners in the New Orleans City Court freedom suits received assistance from a variety of sources in their efforts to protect their freedom. First of all, many of these petitioners were minors and required court-appointed or court-approved representatives to act on their behalf. In the absence of a relative, the court appointed a "next friend" to represent a minor party's legal interests.[47] Adèle Auger's next friend was a merchant in the city named William Lester, while Caroline's was a free colored artisan named Pierre Adrian Jesse. Caroline was one of the few petitioners to lose, but there is no indication that Jesse breached any of his duties that cost Caroline her case.[48] Without the use of court-appointed next friends, the City Court would not have adjudicated so many freedom suits.

Moreover, all sixteen of the freedom suit petitioners in the City Court had lawyers. These lawyers were apparently diligent in collecting evidence and occasionally clever in formulating and presenting arguments. One petitioner's lawyer succeeded in freeing his client by getting the ruling of a justice of the peace overturned on a procedural error.[49] It is difficult to know with certainty what motivated lawyers to represent petitioners in freedom suits, but there is no evidence that they took the cases pro bono.[50] The court records suggest that lawyers in New Orleans may have been more willing to take on a freedom case than lawyers elsewhere in the Deep South and perhaps more competent. George Lewis tried to hire a lawyer to sue for his freedom in Charleston, but no one would take the case. Eventually, he was taken to New Orleans. Harry Oxendine had a lawyer in Claiborne County, Mississippi, named Peter Vandorn, who was charged with procuring Oxendine's freedom. Vandorn dragged his feet for almost two years, however, until Oxendine's enslaver finally took Oxendine by force to New Orleans in the winter of 1811. William Jones procured the services of a lawyer in Natchez named Shields to bring suit for his freedom, but Shields took his time in filing suit and failed to secure Jones's protection in the interim. Eventually, Jones's enslaver learned of the black man's plans to sue for his freedom in Natchez and took him to New Orleans and there sold him to the slave trader Kohn. All three men found lawyers in New Orleans who helped them win their freedom in the City Court.[51]

Five of the sixteen petitioners received help from third-party witnesses who testified on their behalf. William Jones submitted the affidavit testimony of three white men who had known him in his native Pennsylvania. Robert Randolph, William Moore, and Abraham Seldis all verified that Jones was a free man in Orange County (formerly Crawford County), Pennsylvania, who "was hiring himself out and receiving his own wages."[52] Randolph did much more than just testify; he helped Jones escape from his enslaver's custody and hired a lawyer named Mr. Earle to file suit for his freedom.[53] Three of the nine West Indian petitioners had witnesses testify on their behalf. Amand Langlois's claim to freedom was supported by "a number of credible witnesses" who knew "both the father and the mother of the plaintiff to be free." Although the witnesses had last seen Langlois "in his infancy," they were able to identify him by "a scar on the right side of his forehead in consequence of a blow caused by a pistol with which he wounded himself in his infancy, which proved by inspection, to be the fact." In each of these cases, the witnesses provided valuable support for the petitioners' legal claims to freedom.[54]

The City Court freedom cases are noteworthy, however, for the lack of testimony offered by third-party witnesses. In two-thirds of the cases (11 out of 16 overall, and 6 out of the 9 cases involving West Indians), the only evidence supporting the petitioner's claim was his or her own testimony. These cases essentially became contests over whose testimony (the plaintiff's or the defendant's) was more believable. In *Chalon v. Drouin*, for example, the petitioner, Melanie Chalon, testified that she had been born free in St. Domingue, kidnapped in Charleston by Claire Drouin, and taken to New Orleans. The defendant, Drouin, testified to a jury that she had possessed Melanie Chalon as her slave since the latter was born in 1791. The jury believed Chalon's testimony, and in September the court entered judgment on the jury verdict, ordering that Chalon and her child be restored to freedom, "to which they appear justly entitled," and that Drouin pay the costs of the lawsuit.[55] It is not surprising that West Indian refugees of color, who had been uprooted from their social networks, had little evidentiary support from others. What is surprising, however, is that all but one of them won his or her case based only on his or her own testimony.

The only unsuccessful West Indian petitioner in the City Court illustrates the importance of both complexion and cultural capital to the success of a freedom suit petitioner. On December 1, 1812, a young Negress named Caroline filed a freedom suit through her next friend, Mr. Jesse. Caroline's petition alleged that she was born a slave in St. Domingue to a Mssr. Duval, but that Duval had freed Caroline and her mother by his will in April 1802. Caroline enjoyed her freedom, the petition continues, until the evacuation of St. Domingue in 1803, at which time Jean David, a free man of color, convinced Caroline's mother to let him take Caroline to Cuba on the promise that he would treat her as one of his own children. Caroline alleged that while in Cuba she was treated well by David but that after they arrived in the Crescent City in 1809, David began to pretend that he owned Caroline by virtue of being one of the heirs of Duval. She asked the court to issue an order declaring that she was free. Jean David's answer to the lawsuit was a boilerplate general denial.[56] He offered no evidence of his ownership of Caroline other than his own testimony. On April 5, 1813, the court entered a judgment declaring Caroline to be David's slave, stating that Caroline had "failed to produce sufficient proof to support her action."[57] Caroline's case may have been hurt by the fact that she admitted to have been a former slave. Ultimately, however, she failed to carry a burden of proof that was hers by virtue of the fact that she was a "Negress" rather than a "person of color."

Judges and juries may have also based their decisions, at least in part, on their perceptions of the defendants in freedom suits. The defendants in the *Auger* and *Chalon* cases, for example, were, respectively, a severely indebted man of color and an unmarried white woman of low repute. The defendant in Adelaide Durand's freedom suit, on the other hand, was a successful white merchant. Perhaps the former two were not believable as slaveholders whereas the last one very much was.

While some people used the courts to try to gain their freedom, others used the courts to deny it to others. The City Court heard eight enslavement suits in its short existence. An enslavement suit petitioner alleged that the defendant was pretending to be free but was legally the petitioner's property. French West Indian refugees dominated enslavement suit litigants in the City Court; they were petitioners in five cases, defendants in six cases, and both in four. Thus, the profile of defendants in enslavement suits very much resembled that of petitioners in freedom suits.

The stakes of both freedom suits and enslavement suits were, for all intents and purposes, the same: whether or not a person or persons of African descent would enjoy freedom or suffer slavery. Yet the process by which this was determined differed in small but important ways, as illustrated by the case of *Saloman v. Berton*. Suzanne Dubois Saloman was the executer of the estate of the late Jean Baptiste Barutteaut, a doctor in Cap Français. In a suit filed in the City Court on September 30, 1809, Saloman alleged that the doctor had purchased a slave named Pauline in 1792, but when he left to fight the slave insurgency, Pauline escaped amid the chaos. For the next sixteen years, Saloman claimed, Pauline pretended to be free in St. Domingue, Cuba, and New Orleans, successively, and when she arrived in New Orleans in 1809, she "fraudulently registered herself in the mayoralty records" as a free Negress named Pauline Berton. In her lawsuit, Saloman asked the court to declare that Pauline was a slave belonging to the Barutteaut estate.[58] Pauline Berton quickly hired a lawyer who filed an answer to Saloman's petition. The answer claimed, among other things, that the petitioner had failed to carry her burden of proof, having no evidence of the estate's ownership other than the executor's testimony. The court entered a judgment in favor of the defendant Pauline Berton, acknowledging her freedom.[59]

If Pauline Berton was a slave living as free—if the allegations in the petition were true—she was exceptional in many ways. First of all, she was demonstrably literate (she signed her own court papers) and possibly formally educated. Moreover, few of the enslaved refugees would have had the opportunity, much less the acute awareness, to register themselves as free before Mayor Mather. It is unclear with whom, if anyone, Berton fled Cuba for New Orleans, but apparently nobody claimed her as a slave when she first arrived in the Crescent City. Still, there must have been other former slaves who passed as free upon arriving in New Orleans. Just as there are likely many times more undocumented than documented cases of illegal enslavement of refugees of color, the same is probably true for formerly enslaved refugees who passed as free.

The *Berton* case illustrates that burden of proof could be a significant obstacle facing petitioners in enslavement suits, perhaps explaining why the City Court saw twice as many freedom suits in the territorial period as enslavement suits. By physically taking possession of a black person and forcing him or her to sue, as opposed to suing oneself, one could, in theory, shift the burden of proof onto the would-be slave. This burden could be hard to meet if the petitioner did not have documentary proof of freedom. Perhaps some enslavement suit petitioners resorted to the courts only after their self-help efforts had failed.

Nevertheless, despite the procedural hurdle for enslavement suit petitioners, the outcomes of enslavement suits proved to be a harsh counter to those of freedom suits for people of African descent. Four of the eight defendants in enslavement suits in the City Court lost their cases and were ordered into slavery. This was in contrast to only two of fourteen petitioners of African descent who lost their freedom suits.[60] Thus, more people of African descent were ordered into slavery after the enslavement suit than remained in slavery after the freedom suit. To some degree, this is likely because only petitioners who had strong cases sued in the first place. In other words, perhaps most petitioners, whether seeking freedom or seeking slave property, were telling the truth. But in questionable cases with little evidence, such as *Berton* or *Adele*, who had the burden of proof might have determined the outcome of the case. And the City Court seemed more comfortable with procedural hurdles for would-be slaveholders than for would-be slaves, regardless of which one was the petitioner and which one was the defendant. Thus, it created the presumption of freedom for people of color as expressed in *Adele*.

Just as most of the litigants in early post-Purchase New Orleans freedom and enslavement suits came from the French West Indies, so too did the judges who decided their fate. Pierre Derbigny, who heard several status suits on appeal as a justice on the Louisiana Supreme Court, and James Pitot, who replaced Moreau-Lislet on the City Court bench, both had lived in St. Domingue before coming to New Orleans. Judge Louis Moreau-Lislet held out on the island much longer than these men, leaving only on the eve of Haitian independence in late 1803. Yet Moreau-Lislet was not a radical. Although he had worked for Toussaint Louverture in 1800 and 1801, he was not a supporter of the Haitian Revolution's challenges to slavery and racial oppression. According to his biographer, Alain Levasseur, Moreau-Lislet "did not seem to be, actually far from it, a partisan for the liberation or equality of the black people." He was a slave owner in both St. Domingue and New Orleans, and as a member of the Louisiana Senate in 1828 he took a stand against a bill that was to allot certain slaves a required time for their emancipation. Whatever his connections to Toussaint Louverture, therefore, Moreau-Lislet did not identify with the most radical elements of the Haitian Revolution.[61]

Still, the jurist did not seem troubled by the prospect of a large community of free property-holding people of African descent. Elaborating on his order granting the petitioner his freedom in *Langlois v. Labatut*, Moreau-Lislet explained that the petitioner's mother, a mulatto, and his grandmother, a Negress, had "enjoyed the condition and prerogatives of free persons" long before the French Revolution. The distinction between enslaved blacks and free blacks "was vigorously enforced on that island," and Moreau-Lislet would see it enforced in his new home.[62] The judge's intent on making a firm distinction between free people of color and slaves in early Louisiana, therefore, was the product of his experience of social hierarchies in St. Domingue. While he was presiding judge, the City Court granted the petitioner his or her freedom in all but two freedom suits.[63] In every one of those cases, the petitioner either produced documentary or third-party testimonial evidence or the burden of proof had been shifted to the defendant because the petitioner was a person of mixed ancestry.[64]

In enslavement suits, Moreau-Lislet showed reluctance though not an unwillingness to judge a person of color living as free to be a slave. If the petitioner in an enslavement suit produced enough evidence of slave ownership, the judge would order someone into slavery. In November 1810, for example, he ordered the seizure and return to Theodoseus Fowler, a resident of New York, of "a young Negro named George," whom the judge deemed to be an escaped slave living as a free person in New Orleans since 1806.[65] On the other hand, Moreau-Lislet denied Suzanne Saloman's claim to ownership of Pauline Berton, entering a judgment that the defendant, Berton, was free. Unfortunately, Moreau-Lislet did not provide the rationale for his decision in the *Berton* case. He may have been convinced that Berton had never been a slave. This seems unlikely, however, because Berton's answer never specifically denied this allegation, and Berton never explained whether she had been born free or how she had obtained her freedom.[66] In the end, the judge may have felt that the plaintiff Saloman had simply failed to meet her burden of proof. If the petitioner did not show strong evidence that the defendant was his or her property, however, an enslavement lawsuit could backfire. For example, Moreau-Lislet ordered Bernard Bayle to pay costs of court after his unsuccessful bid to have a mulatto girl named Fanny seized as his slave. Bayle had failed to meet his burden of proof.[67] Nevertheless, this decision must not have served as much of a deterrent because the cost to Bayle was low compared with the hoped-for payoff. Thus, one's complexion and relation to the docket created presumptions that were not insurmountable but were difficult to overcome.

Judge Moreau-Lislet's impact on the cases, though important, was not all-encompassing. At least thirteen of the sixteen freedom suits were decided by juries. And while the judge offered instructions to the jury on how to read and weigh the evidence, most notably with regard to burden of proof, the ultimate determination of factual issues in jury trials rested with the members of the jury. There is no evidence of a significant difference in the outcome of a status suit based on whether or not a jury decided the factual issues. A jury of eleven white men found Adelaide Durand to be free in her parish court freedom suit. In the words of Rebecca Scott, "However committed these eleven residents of New Orleans may have been to the institution of slavery, they seem to have balked at the prospect of letting Louis Noret, armed with a power of attorney from a man in New York, barge into the house of a woman living as free and seize her children."⁶⁸ Both judges and juries in the New Orleans City Court understood and respected that there were clear distinctions between enslaved and free people of African descent. And while they may not have initially seen these distinctions in racialized terms, such was the collective impact of their decisions.

Although next friends, witnesses, lawyers, judges, and juries all played important roles in freedom and enslavement suits, the West Indian litigants themselves possessed a "cultural capital" that helped to create the presumption of freedom for "people of color." Many of the West Indian freedom suit petitioners came from families of significant wealth, and several of them, including Adèle Auger, had been formally educated. The socioeconomic and cultural background of the West Indian freedom suit petitioners is reflected, in part, in the way they presented their cases to the court. Many of them described their family history of freedom, and several highlighted their partial European ancestry. Amand Langlois's petition, for example, alleged that he was born free in Port-au-Prince, St. Domingue, that his father was white, and that both sets of his grandparents had been free and property holders in his native land. Finally, most of the petitioners asked the court not to declare them to be free but to "restore them to their former state of freedom."⁶⁹ Indeed, unlike freedom suits in much of the country, the freedom suits in the New Orleans City Court were not part of an antislavery campaign. These petitioners did not appeal to the lofty freedom principle but, instead, emphasized that which made them different from enslaved blacks.⁷⁰

The freedom suits in the New Orleans City Court were the product of the dynamic place and time that was New Orleans in the Age of Revolution. As free black litigants sought to distinguish themselves from slaves, the New Orleans courts, inspired by the revolutionary ideology of the day yet confined by the socioeconomic reality of the plantation system, read this distinction in racialized terms. Race justified the enslavement of human beings, but it also explained the existence of a large, educated, and relatively wealthy population of free people of African descent. Thus, the law presumed that one race, "Negroes" or "Africans," were slaves while another race, "mulattoes" or "persons of color," were free.

While the presumption of freedom or slavery expressed in *Adele* ostensibly rested on complexion or ancestry, skin color alone did not determine whether one was a "Negro" or a "person of color" in the eyes of the law. Other factors, such as dress, behavior, and education, could also shape racial identity. Although described as a "negress" in the court pleadings, for example, Pauline Berton had, in many ways, assumed an identity as a member of the *gens de couleur*. In her sixteen years of living as a free person, she had learned to read and write in three different languages. Upon her arrival in New Orleans, she took on a last name and had acquired real property in the city's French-speaking Marigny suburb. The Negress Caroline, on the other hand, had not distinguished herself from the African slaves. She did not have a last name, was illiterate, and had never lived independently. While the skin color of these two women may have been similar, therefore, their lifestyles set them apart from one another.[71]

Furthermore, the complexion of a person of African descent was, to a certain extent, subjective and the perception of it malleable. For example, Harry Oxendine is described as a "yellow man" in the court records by someone who knew him to be free but as having a "sun burned brown" complexion by a man who thought Harry was a slave. In addition, Marie Louise Dupre was identified as a "black" slave in New Orleans records until she acquired her freedom sometime around 1798. Several years later, her former master, a Mr. Quinoner, and then business partner, a white blacksmith named Nicholas Duquery, continued to refer to Marie Louise as a "negress." After Duquery's death in 1810, however, Dupre filed suit against the estate seeking one-half of the value of the business. In the caption of this case, as well as another case in which she was the plaintiff suing on an account, the court identifies Marie Louise as a "free woman of color."[72] Therefore, skin color itself was at times a matter of perception that could be shaped by context.

The City Court status suits produced peculiarities in Louisiana law, including several legal double standards. First of all, petitioners in enslavement suits had the burden of proof, but petitioners in freedom suits (as long as they were perceived to be "persons of color") did not. The Orleans Territory was the only jurisdiction in the U.S. South that carried such a presumption of freedom for certain freedom suit petitioners. The statute enacted by the legislature in the Territory of

Louisiana (in what was to become the state of Missouri), by contrast, expressly stated that petitioners in all freedom suits carried the burden of proof and made no exceptions for people of perceived mixed ancestry.[73]

Second, would-be slaves got the benefit of prescription—a legal principle akin to adverse possession—but would-be slaveholders did not. According to one of the laws of the Siete Partidas, which governed Louisiana during the Spanish colonial period, a slave living as free for ten years in the same country as the master or for twenty years in a different country gained his or her freedom through prescription. This particular law had not been officially incorporated into the *Civil Digest of 1808*. Still, nothing in the digest superseded it, and the courts later ruled that any laws of the Spanish colonial period that had not been superseded by statutes passed since, remained in effect. The issue of prescription came up in two of the cases involving Adelaide Durand, both of which were appealed to the Louisiana Supreme Court. In the first (1816), the court ruled that Durand had been living as free since 1801, the year she bought herself out of her service obligation to Charles Metayer. This was not long enough to meet the statutory requirement. In the later case, however, the court, based on new evidence, declared that she had been living as free since 1793 (until 1818), which exceeded the twenty-year requirement.[74] After eight years of legal battles in three different New Orleans courts, Durand finally acquired judicial recognition of her freedom on the basis of prescription. One of Pauline Berton's arguments in her successful defense to a lawsuit that would have enslaved her was that she had acquired her freedom through its continued and uninterrupted possession for a period of sixteen years. Given the twenty-year requirement when master and slave are in different countries, it is unlikely that the court's decision was based on prescription. But the fact that Berton had lived on her own for so long may, nevertheless, have contributed to her successful defense.

On the other hand, the City Court would not allow similar claims to the possession of slave property. In an unusually long judgment in the case of *Langlois v. Labatut*, for example, Moreau-Lislet felt compelled to justify his decision in light of "the silence which [Langlois] kept during six years, without claiming his freedom at Charleston where he was in the service of Gallier." The judge understood why a person in Langlois's position would not come forward given the uncertainty in his ability to prove his freedom in Charleston. Only when he came to New Orleans, according to Moreau-Lislet, was he able to procure witnesses to testify on his behalf. Moreau-Lislet applied the same reasoning in the freedom suit of Hervey des Romain, who had spent more than four years as a slave in Charleston before he sued for his freedom in the New Orleans City Court. A little more than a decade later, in the appeal of another freedom suit brought by a refugee of the Haitian Revolution, the Supreme Court of Louisiana confirmed that prescription was not "pleadable" to those seeking a ruling of enslavement. "If a man be free," Justice Porter opined, "no matter how long he may be held by another, as a slave; his state or condition cannot be thereby changed; nor can he be reduced to slavery, in any manner whatever, on account of the time he may have been held in servitude." Therefore, while a slave could, in some circumstances, acquire his or her freedom through its adverse possession, the would-be slaveholder could not by the same method acquire slave property.[75]

The shift in burden of proof to the defendant in freedom suits brought by "people of color" and double standard in the application of prescription were not due to the freedom-loving nature of New Orleans in comparison with the rest of the South. Rather, they were the product of the influence of West Indian immigrants on social hierarchies and of the evident cosmopolitanism of West Indian *gens de couleur*. The City Court judge as well as the free colored litigants from St. Domingue and Guadeloupe had developed attitudes about the important role of free people of African descent in slave societies and the clear distinction between free and enslaved people of African descent.

In addition to producing legal double standards, status suits, specifically *Adele*, helped to clarify the role of judicial precedent (of judge-made law) in a legal system engulfed in a battle between civil law and common law jurists. As discussed more fully in chapter 2, the main difference between civil law and common law lies in the methodological approach to codes and statutes. In civil law jurisdictions, legislation is seen as the primary source of law. Courts in the civil law tradition base their judgments on the provisions of codes and statutes, from which solutions in particular cases are to be derived. By contrast, in the common law system, cases are the primary source of law, while statutes are seen only as incursions into the common law and thus interpreted narrowly. Even though Moreau-Lislet and many of the lawyers and judges operating in the Louisiana courts were trained in civilian law, the three-tiered legio-racial system that developed in New Orleans was not derived from this legal tradition. The *Adele* decision was not an application of any existing legislation but, instead, was judge-made law.[76]

The Legal Construction of Race

Chronologically speaking, *Auger v. Beaurocher* was the third of fifteen freedom suits in the New Orleans City Court, but, without question, it was the most significant. It was the first freedom suit to be appealed to the Louisiana Supreme Court, whose opinion became precedent for subsequent cases. Yet the significance of *Adele v. Beauregard* as precedent had little to do with freedom suits. While defendants in freedom suits brought by "people of color" carried the burden of proof, they only needed to meet the minimal standard of "preponderance of the evidence," a much lower threshold than "beyond reasonable doubt," which is the standard of persuasion in criminal trials.[77] Indeed, Rebecca Scott concludes that in the case of Adelaide Durand's son, "the courts seem to have been willing to accept the most fragile oral evidence as sufficient to rebut the presumption of freedom."[78] With the possible exception of the *Adele* case itself, the shift in burden of proof may not have been the deciding factor in any City Court freedom suit.

Rather, the significance of the precedent set in *Adele* lies in the way it helped to create a particular racial identity. The three-tiered society that is reflected in the status suits of early American New Orleans is not simply a product of combined considerations of race and status, or what the Spanish called *calidad*.[79] To be sure, the influence of *calidad* can be seen in certain aspects of early New Orleans, such as Louisiana's marriage laws delineating three groups that were prohibited from intermarrying and the mayor's categorizations of the refugee immigration.[80] Yet, while these legislative and executive acts distinguished between free and enslaved people of African descent, the decision in *Adele* took it a step further by presuming enslaved status for Negroes and free status for people of color. To be sure, in all slave states people of perceived mixed ancestry had certain advantages over darker-skinned blacks, but Louisiana was the only state in the United States, North or South, to identify a *legally* distinct third race.[81] This distinct identity is what prompted Justice King, in the case that opens the introduction to this book, to claim that Louisiana's free people of color were "a different class of persons" from free blacks in "the slave states generally."

Adele v. Beauregard shaped perceptions of race in antebellum Louisiana because the decisions that cited it reflected evolving perceptions of race in that era. The Louisiana Supreme Court cited *Adele* as precedent six times before the Civil War, the earliest being in 1812 and the latest being in 1856. *State v. Cecil*, decided in 1812, expanded the *Adele* rule to hold that "persons of color are competent witnesses against whites in criminal cases." And the 1828 decision in *Hawkins v. Vanwickle* made precedent what had been dicta in *Adele*, that Negroes were presumed to be slaves.[82] These two decisions contributed to the understanding of a racial distinction between "Negroes" and "people of color."

Perhaps the most unusual case to cite *Adele* as precedent is the 1845 case of *Miller v. Belmonti*, a freedom suit brought by a white woman. In this case, the plaintiff, Sally Miller, claimed that she was born free of European parents and had emigrated from Germany in 1817 or 1818. Belmonti, the defendant, asserted that he had purchased the petitioner, whom he called Bridget, from John Fitz Miller. John Miller testified on Belmonti's behalf, swearing that when he purchased the petitioner in 1822, he was told that she was a twelve-year-old mulatto girl and that he still believed her to be of African descent, and a slave for life. The district court dismissed the plaintiff's petition, and she appealed. The court of appeals reversed the trial court's decision based, in part, on the Superior Court's decision in *Adele*. The *Miller* opinion stated:

> The first enquiry which engages our attention is, what is the color of the plaintiff? . . . Ever since *Adele v. Beauregard* . . . it has been the settled doctrine in the Supreme Court that persons of color are presumed free. Slavery itself is an exception to the condition of the great mass of mankind, and, except as to Africans in the slave-holding States, the presumption is in favor of freedom, and burden of proof is upon him who claims the colored person as a slave. . . . The proof in the record of the complexion of the plaintiff is very strong. Not only is there no evidence of her having descended from a slave mother, or even a mother of the African

race; but no witness has ventured a positive opinion, from inspection, that she is of that race. One of the most intelligent and candid witnesses on the part of the defense says she is as white as most persons: but that he has seen slaves as bright as the plaintiff. He added that he always thought that she had something resembling the colored race in her features, but this opinion may have been induced by the fact that he had always seen her associating with persons of color.[83]

This opinion illustrates both the use of race to justify slavery and the difficulties of racial classifications. After pronouncing that slavery was the "exception to the condition of the great mass of mankind," the court made clear that it was the rule for "Africans in the slaveholding states." Yet the dispute as to the "color of the plaintiff" is striking. One would think that the court could have answered its "first enquiry" merely by looking at the plaintiff, but it had to examine evidence of Sally Miller's ancestry to help answer this question. The court further acknowledged the unreliability of complexion as a racial indicator by admitting that the company one kept could influence one's racial identity.

By the eve of the Civil War, *Adele* had come to stand for not only the presumption of freedom for "people of color" but also the unique character of free people of African descent in Louisiana as compared with the rest of the U.S. South. The 1856 Louisiana Supreme Court case of *State v. Harrison* cited *Adele* for the proposition that "in the eye of Louisiana law, there is, (with the exception of political rights, of certain social privileges, and of the obligations of jury and militia service,) all the difference between a free man of color and a slave, that there is between a white man and a slave."[84] Of course the court's expressed defense of the legal equality of free blacks to whites may reflect the especially uncomfortable existence in the 1850s of free blacks in slave societies. In this period of intense sectionalization, pro-slavery forces in the slaveholding states, including Louisiana, united to limit the growth, wealth, and movement of free people of African descent. But in many ways the legal defense of a distinct free black identity was successful. Free people of color in Louisiana retained property rights and legal rights that every other slave state denied them.[85]

*   *   *

According to its language, the opinion in *Adele v. Beauregard* called for a modification of the burden of proof "when the question is slavery or freedom." But the case represented and came to stand for much more than a minor procedural shift; it stood for the principle that "people of color" were racially distinct from "Negroes." The *Adele* standard was born out of the incredibly dynamic era that was New Orleans in the Age of Revolution. In the early years of American rule in New Orleans, when the legal system was malleable and the specter of Haiti loomed large, these refugee litigants used the courts not only to protect their freedom but also to assert their identity. In the process, they brought a confused social hierarchy to order. At the same time that Louisiana's legal system and law of race and slavery were in flux, litigants and jurists from the French West Indies made their indelible mark on the laws. While the concept of race was not new to the lower Mississippi valley in the first decade of the nineteenth century, it did take on greater significance in explaining and justifying social hierarchies as New Orleans made the transition to a slave society. But just as race was deployed to justify the enslavement of human beings by claiming that Negroes were inferior to whites and thereby suited for slavery, it was also used to explain the existence of free people of African descent who were ill suited for slavery in a society so dependent on the labor of enslaved Africans.

Free people of color enjoyed more privileges and rights in Louisiana than anywhere else in the antebellum South (while slaves in the region certainly fared no better than slaves elsewhere in the U.S. South) based, in large part, on the perception that free blacks were racially distinct from enslaved blacks. The influx of more than 3,000 *gens de couleur* alongside the same approximate number of African-born slaves into a newly emerging slave society did much to create this perception. But the legal distinction between "Negroes" and "persons of color," as expressed in *Adele*, ensured that New Orleans's three-race system would remain intact until the Civil War. This book does not intend to pinpoint a precise date at which a three-race system was born in early New Orleans. Yet, while the origins of race may not have fixed dates, court cases and laws do, and *Adele v. Beauregard* indisputably changed in important ways how race was perceived in Louisiana law. Thus was the role of the courtroom in making race.

From *Adele* to *Plessy*

The 1811 case of *Adele v. Beauregard* judicially recognized a racial distinction between "Negroes" and "people of color." Another court case arising out of New Orleans at the other end of the nineteenth century, one much more well known, obliterated this legal distinction. *Plessy v. Ferguson* is best known, for good reason, as the case that constitutionalized Jim Crow laws. It also reshaped the racial identities of people of African descent in New Orleans. The U.S. Supreme Court not only upheld the Louisiana Separate Car Act, which required railway carriers to segregate on the basis of race, but also implicitly classified all people with any degree of African ancestry, from former "Negro" slaves to "octoroons" whose ancestors had been free for generations, as belonging to the same race.[1] In other words, while *Adele* helped to create a three-race social order in antebellum Louisiana, *Plessy* helped to establish a biracial system in postbellum Louisiana.

The *Plessy* case was initiated by a New Orleans–based civil rights organization called the Comité des Citoyens. Formed on September 1, 1891, at the instigation of a prominent "Creole of color," Aristide Mary, the committee set out to overturn Louisiana's Separate Car Act, claiming it violated the Fourteenth Amendment to the U.S. Constitution.[2] Yet the committee's legal strategy appealed to practical concerns as well as constitutional principles. Any legal system that classifies on the basis of race must also, of necessity, determine who belongs to what race. This may have seemed to be a simple task. Is not appearance, especially complexion, a marker of race? Yet the committee sought to illustrate the difficulties of enforcing the Separate Car Act in New Orleans, where a large number of people of African descent could, and did, pass as white.

The outcome of *Plessy v. Ferguson* is well known, and the opinion is today considered one of the most nefarious in the history of the U.S. Supreme Court. While Plessy's lawyers argued that the Separate Car Act violated the due process and equal protection clauses of the Fourteenth Amendment to the Constitution, the Supreme Court rejected this argument with what is now known as the infamous doctrine of "separate but equal." The opinion of Justice Brown was long on racist ideology and short on logic. He asserted, for example, that "legislation is powerless to eradicate racial instincts or to abolish distinctions based upon physical differences." Yet the Separate Car Act actually *created* distinctions based on perceived physical differences and prohibited people from acting upon their *instincts*. Brown also claimed that "the underlying fallacy" of Plessy's argument was the "assumption that the enforced separation of the two races stamps the colored race with a badge of inferiority." Clearly, however, that was precisely the intention of all Jim Crow laws. In his lone dissent, Justice Harlan correctly predicted that future generations would view the majority opinion as "pernicious."[3]

The named plaintiff in the now infamous case, Homer Plessy, was a self-identified "octoroon" with no discernible trace of African ancestry. The Comité des Citoyens assigned him the task of sitting in the whites-only car and allowing himself to be arrested precisely because his racial ambiguity exposed the practical difficulties of enforcing the Separate Car Act in New Orleans. Both of his parents and three of his four grandparents were "people of color," while his paternal grandfather was a white Frenchman. All had been born free. One of Homer Plessy's great-grandmothers on his father's side was a former slave named Agnes Mathieu, the petitioner in one of the legal separation cases discussed in chapter 4. Before she married her husband, Joseph, she had an intimate relationship with a white man from Marsailles named Mathieu Deveau. When Deveau met Agnes, she was the slave of Barbara Hertelin. Deveau hired Agnes as a domestic, and within a few months she had purchased her freedom under *coartacion*, against Hertelin's wishes. Deveau appears to have contributed a substantial portion of the purchase price. Perhaps Deveau helped Agnes gain her freedom because he loved her. Perhaps Agnes used her sexuality to gain her freedom. The records remain silent on this point. Whatever the nature of their relationship, however, Mathieu Deveau and Agnes Mathieu had several children together. One of these children, Catherine Mathieu (aka Cathiche), was involved in a long-term relationship with a Frenchman named Germain Plessy, Homer Plessy's white grandfather.[4]

The three generations of Plessys who lived in the nineteenth century represent three different and important formative moments in the history of race in Louisiana. François Germain Plessy was born in Bordeaux circa 1777 and immigrated to New Orleans sometime prior to the Louisiana Purchase. Germain's older brother, Dominique, left Bordeaux for St. Domingue sometime in the 1780s. He came to New Orleans later, perhaps after having spent some time in Cuba.[5] It is not clear how Germain Plessy, a bookkeeper by trade, met Cathiche Mathieu, but they had their first child together in April 1804, just a month after Orleans officially became a territory of the United States. There were ten more children to follow, including Joseph Adolphe Plessy, Homer's father, who was born in 1822.

Homer Plessy's grandparents on his mother's side, Josephine Blanco and Michel Deberque, were both quadroons; they were the children of two separate white male–colored female relationships of the late Spanish colonial period.[6] As shown in chapter 4, the period between the 1790s and the 1820s was when white male–colored female intimate relationships were at their peak, due, in part, to demographic factors. Thus, Homer's grandparents lived in New Orleans during the Age of Revolution, the period covered by the six chapters of this book, when intimate relationships across the color line were widespread and racial classifications were in flux.

While Homer Plessy's grandparents lived in an era when racial identity was fluid, Plessy's parents lived at a time when the three-tiered racial order had become more entrenched. Homer Plessy's father, Joseph Adolphe Plessy, and mother, Rosa Deberque, were both self-identified quadroons. Adolphe was born in New Orleans in 1822, one of the last children of Germain and Cathiche, and Rosa was born in 1835. The two were legally married in Enunciation Catholic Church in 1855.[7] During their childhoods, Louisiana's population of free people of color grew rapidly, from 10,000 in 1820 to almost 17,000 in 1830 and to 25,500 in 1840.[8] A concerned Louisiana legislature took steps to both limit this growth and ensure that social distinctions between people of color and whites were not breached. An 1830 law required that all free people of

African descent who had come to Louisiana after 1825 leave the state within sixty days or face a penalty of one year's hard labor. Moreover, slaves who were freed after the passage of the act were required to leave the state within one month of manumission. While this law was ignored or evaded more often than not, the legislature took further steps in the 1840s and 1850s to limit the growth and rights of Louisiana's free colored population. Finally, in 1857, it outlawed manumission altogether.[9]

The impact of these measures was twofold. First, while there was a lag time, the laws significantly decreased the size of the free population of color in both Louisiana, in general, and New Orleans, in particular: from 25,500 and 19,226 in 1840 to 17,500 and 9,905 in 1850. There are several reasons for this decline. Some free people of color moved north, others moved out of the country, to France and to Haiti, and still others likely passed as white. The second, related, impact of the draconian laws of the Louisiana legislature was to create clearer lines of distinction and less intermingling between slaves, free people of African descent, and whites. In the last three decades of the antebellum period, there were far fewer long-term intimate relationships across the color line than in earlier decades and many more endogamous marriages among free people of color. This trend is represented in the difference between Germain Plessy's extramarital relationship with Cathiche Mathieu and Adolphe Plessy's marriage to Rosa Deberque.

While the legislature was passing laws designed to curb the growth of Louisiana's free population of color, the Louisiana courts continued to recognize the special status of this group of people relative to free blacks in the other slave states as evidenced by two cases examined in this book. Both the 1847 case of *Levy v. Dreyfous,* which opens the introduction, and the 1856 case of *State v. Harrison,* discussed in chapter 6, exalted the "intelligence, industry and habits of good order" of Louisiana's free colored population. The concern among lawmakers, it seems, was over the newly freed slaves and free Negroes from other states, not the community of free people of color who were the product of the Age of Revolution or earlier.

Even before he joined the Comité des Citoyens, Homer Plessy lived through one of the most dynamic periods in U.S. history, encompassing the Civil War, Reconstruction, and Redemption. He was born in New Orleans on Saint Patrick's Day 1862, a little more than a month before

Union forces captured and occupied the city of his birth. Three and a half years later, the Thirteenth Amendment to the Constitution obliterated legal distinctions of status—all people became formally free. Of course, cultural distinctions between whites, Creoles of color, and former slaves could not be so quickly dissolved, and Creoles of color took what they saw as their natural positions of leadership in New Orleans's postbellum black community. They concentrated their efforts in part on improving the position of the freedmen by giving substance to the formal freedom granted to all black people by the Thirteenth Amendment. Yet they also sought to elevate their own social position by giving meaning to the formal U.S. citizenship and equal protection granted to them (and to former slaves) by the Fourteenth Amendment. The result of their efforts was the most progressive constitution of the Reconstruction era. The Louisiana Constitution of 1868 "went to unprecedented lengths to achieve complete equality for black Louisianans." It banned discrimination of the basis of race in places of public accommodation, required state officials to take an oath recognizing civic and political equality for all men, regardless of race or previous condition of servitude, and forbade segregation in public schools.[10]

The radical constitution of 1868 was short-lived, however, as ex-Confederates pushed back against the progressive forces behind the document. In 1868 alone, white supremacist groups such as the Knights of the White Camelia terrorized and murdered blacks and white Republicans in an effort to prevent them from exercising their right to vote. The violence reached its peak with the Colfax Massacre following the disputed gubernatorial election of 1872. Throughout the rest of the decade, white supremacists used terrorism and violence as a means of dismantling Reconstruction in Louisiana. By 1879, after Federal troops had been removed from the South, Louisiana had a new constitution and, like all states of the former Confederacy, had embarked on a path toward segregation and disenfranchisement of the former slaves. The Louisiana Separate Car Act of 1890 was part of this effort.

When Homer Plessy intentionally violated the Separate Car Act by sitting in a first-class car reserved for whites only, he, like the rest of the Comité des Citoyens, sought to make history. But the conditions under which he sought to make it were not of his choosing—they were transmitted to him from the past. Indeed, the actions of people of color within each of the three generations of Plessys helped to create the conditions under which succeeding generations acted. This book has been a close examination of one of these generations, represented by Germain Plessy and Cathiche Mathieu. It makes no attempt to argue that all legal and cultural constructions of race ended in the Age of Revolution. Indeed, as the title of this book suggests, race is less a category than it is a process, continuously being made and remade.

NOTES

NOTES TO THE INTRODUCTION

1. Justice King referred to "certain districts" in Louisiana that had a history of privileged people of color. He was likely referring to Orleans Parish, where New Orleans is, and the Cane River area of northwest Louisiana, where Natchitoches is located.

2. *State v. Levy*, 5 La. Ann. 64, Louisiana Supreme Court (1850).

3. *Adele v. Beauregard*, 1 Mart. (o.s.) 183 (La. 1811).

4. For an enlightening analysis of the role of courts in New World slave societies during the Age of Revolution, see Sue Peabody and Keila Grinberg, *Slavery, Freedom, and the Law in the Atlantic World: A Brief History with Documents* (Boston and New York: Bedford/St. Martin's Press, 2007). According to Peabody and Grinberg, "One of the most important sites where people thrashed out the meanings of slavery and freedom was in the judicial courts. Court cases created a rhetoric to describe slavery and freedom and had specific, physical consequences. Kings and politicians might pronounce laws, but when disputes arose, it was the judges and juries who ruled on them, creating immediate, tangible results in people's lives. Slaves and free people of color could in certain circumstances claim rights in court, framing their interests in a new, emerging language of citizenship, natural law, and humanity" (2).

5. Some of these books and articles include Daniel Usner, *Indians, Settlers, and Slaves in a Frontier Exchange Economy* (Chapel Hill: University of North Carolina Press, 1992); Gwendolyn Midlo Hall, *Africans in Colonial Louisiana: The Development of Afro-Creole Culture in the Eighteenth Century* (Baton Rouge: Louisiana State University Press, 1992); Carl A. Brasseaux and Glenn R. Conrad, *The Road to Louisiana: The Saint-domingue Refugees, 1792–1809* (Lafayette: Center for Louisiana Studies, University of Southwestern Louisiana, 1992); Kimberly Hanger, *Bounded Lives, Bounded Places: Free Black Society in Colonial New Orleans, 1769–1803* (Durham, NC: Duke University Press, 1997); Thomas Dargo, *Jefferson's Louisiana: Politics and the Clash of Legal Traditions* (Cambridge, MA: Harvard University Press, 1997); Caryn Cosse Bell, *Revolution, Romanticism, and the Afro-Creole Protest Tradition in Louisiana, 1718–1868* (Baton Rouge: Louisiana State University Press, 1997); Paul F. Lachance, "The

1809 Immigration of Saint-Domingue Refugees to New Orleans: Reception, Integration, and Impact," *Louisiana History* 29 (1998): 109; Thomas Ingersoll, *Mammon and Manon in Early New Orleans: The First Slave Society in the Deep South, 1718–1819* (Knoxville: University of Tennessee Press, 1999); Alecia Long, *The Great Southern Babylon: Sex, Race, and Respectability in New Orleans, 1865–1920* (Baton Rouge: Louisiana State University Press, 2004); Rebecca Scott, *Degrees of Freedom: Louisiana and Cuba after Slavery* (Cambridge, MA: Harvard University Press, 2005); Nathalie Dessens, *From Saint-Domingue to New Orleans: Migration and Influences* (Gainesville: University of Florida Press, 2007); Jennifer Spear, *Race, Sex, and Social Order in Early New Orleans* (Baltimore: Johns Hopkins University Press, 2009); Emily Landau, *Spectacular Wickedness: Sex, Race, and Memory in Storyville, New Orleans* (Baton Rouge: Louisiana State University Press, 2013); and Emily Clark, *The Strange History of the American Quadroon: Free Women of Color in the Revolutionary World* (Chapel Hill: University of North Carolina Press, 2013).

6. According to the 2010 census, almost 900,000 African immigrants live in the United States. The African countries with the most immigrants are Nigeria, Ghana, Ethiopia, Eritrea, Egypt, Somalia, and South Africa. See also "African Immigrants in the United States Are the Nation's Most Highly Educated Group," *Journal of Blacks in Higher Education*, no. 26 (1999–2000): 60–61.

7. Sociologist Suzanne Model attributes this relative economic success to the "self-selected immigrant status" of black West Indians. See Suzanne Model, *West Indian Immigrants: A Black Success Story?* (New York: Russell Sage Foundation, 2011).

8. In a series of interviews leading up to the 2008 presidential election, journalist Debra Dickerson argued that Barack Obama should not be considered "culturally black" because he is not the descendant of West African slaves. However, a research team from Ancestry.com recently concluded that Obama is the eleventh great-grandson, on his white mother's side, of John Punch, a black person who was enslaved in Virginia in the seventeenth century. See "Ancestry.com Discovers President Obama Related to First Documented Slave in America" (press release, 2012), http://corporate.ancestry.com/press/press-releases/2012/07/ancestry.com-discovers-president-obama-related-to-first-documented-slave-in-america/.

9. Ian F. Haney-Lopez, "The Social Construction of Race," in Richard Delgado and Jean Stefancic, eds., *Critical Race Theory: The Cutting Edge*, 2nd ed. (Philadelphia: Temple University Press, 2000), 165.

10. The history of Louisiana's legal system is a growing field among legal scholars. See, for example, Warren Billings and Mark Fernandez, eds., *A Law unto Itself? Essays in the New Louisiana Legal History* (Baton Rouge: Louisiana State University Press, 2001); and Edward Haas, ed., *Louisiana's Legal Heritage* (Baton Rouge: Louisiana State Museum, 1983). For a brief yet thorough description of the legal status of free people of color in antebellum Louisiana, see Ellen

Holmes Pearson, "Imperfect Equality," in Billings and Fernandez, *A Law unto Itself?*, 191–210.

11. In his research on property ownership among free people of African descent in the antebellum U.S. South, Loren Schweninger has shown that free people of color living in Louisiana were, far and away, the wealthiest; see chapter 1 for a more detailed discussion. For more scholarly studies of the accomplishments and culture of Louisiana's Creoles of color, see, among other works, William Keyse Rudolph, Patricia Brady, and Erin Greenwald, *In Search of Julien Hudson: Free Artist of Color in Pre–Civil War New Orleans* (New Orleans: Historic New Orleans Collection, 2011); Shirley Thompson, *Exiles at Home: The Struggle to Become American in Creole New Orleans* (Cambridge, MA: Harvard University Press, 2009); and Gary Mills, *The Forgotten People: Cane River's Creoles of Color* (Baton Rouge: Louisiana State University Press, 1977). The economic and cultural accomplishments of Louisiana's Creoles of color have become the stuff of legend. The lore surrounding Creoles of color is portrayed in popular culture through, among other things, the Benjamin January mystery series of Barbara Hambly about a free colored detective in antebellum New Orleans. From 1997 to 2004, Hambly published a book a year in the Benjamin January series.

12. With one notable exception, historians of race in early New Orleans agree that free people of color in Louisiana occupied a privileged position in their society relative to free blacks in the rest of the United States. Jennifer Spear argues that Louisiana's "gens de couleur, unlike their counterparts in Charleston and elsewhere in the United States, enjoyed far more security in their legal and economic rights," while Caryn Cosse Bell calls them "the most privileged and articulate free black community in the South." Laura Foner sums up the prevailing view as follows: "Louisiana's free colored community was not only the biggest in the Deep South, but its members had a social, economic, and legal position far superior to that of free Negroes in most other areas of the South, even those in which the free Negro population was substantial." Even Ira Berlin, in his monograph about free blacks in the United States, acknowledges that "in their numbers, origins, traditions, and place in society, the gens de couleur of Louisiana were unlike the free Negro caste of Revolutionary America." Spear, *Race, Sex, and Social Order in Early New Orleans*; Bell, *Revolution, Romanticism, and the Afro-Creole Protest Tradition*; Laura Foner, "The Free People of Color in Louisiana and St. Domingue: A Comparative Portrait of Two Three-Caste Societies," *Journal of Social History* 3 (1970): 407; and Ira Berlin, *Slaves without Masters: The Free Negro in the Antebellum South* (New York: New Press, 1974). Only Thomas Ingersoll disagrees. One of his central arguments in *Mammon and Manon in Early New Orleans* is that the Crescent City was a biracial society, just like every other slave society in the South. According to Ingersoll, the social hierarchy of colonial Louisiana (whose climate and geography were closer to Georgia's than they were to St. Domingue's) was North American rather than Caribbean in character. This position is reflected in the organization

of Ingersoll's book. Each of the book's three sections, dealing with the French, Spanish, and early American periods, respectively, contains, in addition to other chapters, one chapter on the "planter class" and another chapter discussing the "black majority," where he treats slaves and free blacks as if they shared common interests and experiences. Despite Ingersoll's claims to the contrary, however, the general consensus among historians is that antebellum New Orleans was a three-caste society.

13. According to Tannenbaum, the slave law of England and the United States treated slaves as nonpersons (as chattels without legal rights), while Protestantism neglected their spiritual needs. In Latin America, on the other hand, Spanish, Portuguese, and (to a lesser extent) French slave law recognized the fundamental humanity of slaves, and religious institutions, specifically the Roman Catholic Church, administered to their spiritual needs. Most important, Latin American legal institutions and social customs favored manumission, while British and U.S. policy opposed manumission. Frank Tannenbaum, *Slave and Citizen: The Negro in the Americas* (New York: Beacon Press, 1946). Stanley Elkins agreed with this fundamental thesis and expanded on it in his book *Slavery: A Problem in American Institutional and Intellectual Life* (Chicago: University of Chicago Press, 1959). Elkins claimed that the Iberian policy of favoring manumission provided for a smooth transition from slavery to freedom. Free people of color were an accepted part of society in Spanish and Portuguese New World possessions, and color posed no great obstacle to social mobility. Opponents of the Tannenbaum thesis claim that demographic, geographic, and material conditions were more important than legal and religious institutions in determining the type of slave society. See David Brion Davis, *The Problem of Slavery in Western Culture* (Ithaca, NY: Cornell University Press, 1966), and Marvin Harris, *Patterns of Race in the Americas* (New York: Norton, 1964). The important material factors, according to Davis, include the demographic profile (the black-to-white ratio, the sex ratio among whites, and the Afro-Creole mix), the type of crop cultivated, the size of the plantation, the climate, and the distance from the center of authority. Davis also urges that historians should not treat slave law as static, disputing the assumption that "certain humane laws of the late eighteenth and nineteenth centuries were typical of slavery in Latin America throughout its long history." Anthropologist Marvin Harris points to the fundamentally different settlement patterns in Latin America and Anglo America, the former colonized by labor-scarce countries while the latter served as an outlet for surplus population. Historians of slavery and race relations in New Orleans continuously infuse life into these debates. According to Thomas Ingersoll, for example, "Because New Orleans developed under the rule of successive French and Spanish regimes and then came under American republican institutions after 1803, it presents an opportunity to test Tannenbaum's thesis." Ingersoll minimizes the importance of any legal regime in the development of New Orleans's character, holding that socioeconomic factors, such as crop type

and demographics, played a far greater role in the shaping of race relations in colonial New Orleans than did Franco-Spanish legal and religious institutions (Ingersoll, *Mammon and Manon in Early New Orleans*, xviii). After explicitly raising the debates surrounding Tannenbaum's thesis in the introduction to *Bounded Lives, Bounded Places*, Kimberly Hanger asserts that her "own work discerns a combination of cultural-legal traditions and material conditions" that shaped race relations in early New Orleans, "with the latter having the greater influence." However, her use of evidence and her arguments throughout the remainder of the book seem to contradict this assertion. Hanger's work is most interested in the development of a collective identity among free blacks, and she convincingly demonstrates that during the Spanish period in New Orleans, the free black population grew to "assume the 'critical mass' needed to establish a distinct sense of identity." The primary reason for this growth was the Spanish legal institution of *coartacion*, under which slaves had the legal right to purchase their freedom with or without their master's consent. Despite her attempt to downplay the Tannenbaum thesis, Hanger's emphasis on *coartacion* as the primary avenue to freedom confirms the important impact of legal institutions on racial identity and race relations in New World slave societies.

14. In their comparative study of the different ways in which the legal systems of the colonial powers dealt with slavery and freedom, Peabody and Grinberg differentiate between Spain and France more than most adherents of the Tannenbaum thesis. "Both the Spanish and the Portuguese had unified legal codes, based in Roman law, that both regulated slavery and favored individual manumission. . . . By contrast, the French and English had no positive law regarding slavery" (*Slavery, Freedom, and the Law in the Atlantic World*, 24–25).

15. Historian Paul Lachance has written several articles about the French West Indian immigration into Louisiana during and after the Haitian Revolution, demonstrating that, at least in demographic terms, the Caribbean influence on New Orleans was substantial. Lachance shows that by 1820 the racial fluidity of Hanger's Spanish New Orleans had given way to racial endogamy in the city. In seeking to "explain why Louisiana's social and racial pattern was a three-caste system," moreover, Laura Foner compares it to the "three-caste system in the French colony of St. Domingue." See also Donald Everett, "Emigres and Militiamen: Free Persons of Color in New Orleans, 1803–1815," *Journal of Negro History* 38 (1953): 377–402; and Bell, *Revolution, Romanticism, and the Afro-Creole Protest Tradition*. More recently, French historian Nathalie Dessens has done exhaustive archival research in both Aix-en-Provence and New Orleans to reveal the profound impact of French West Indians in New Orleans; see Dessens, *From St. Domingue to Louisiana;* Dessens, "The Saint-Domingue Refugees and the Preservation of Gallic Culture in Early American New Orleans," *French Colonial History* 8 (2007): 53–69.

16. Several legal historians have contributed to this vision of the negative aspects of Americanization when it comes to the legal status of Louisiana's *gens de*

couleur. Judith Schafer's book *Slavery, the Civil Law, and the Supreme Court of Louisiana* examines Louisiana's slave law from the time of the Louisiana Purchase to the adjournment of the Louisiana Supreme Court in 1862. Schafer accepts the view that Spanish slave law was relatively lenient and further argues that the Spanish legal heritage persisted in Louisiana's slave law of the early nineteenth century. Yet, according to Schafer, "a continuous influx of American influence, intensified by the immigration to Louisiana of scores of attorneys trained in the common law, as well as the growing national controversy over the peculiar institution, caused Louisiana slave law to be steadily 'Americanized' to the extent that by the eve of the Civil War, slave law in Louisiana closely resembled the law of slavery in the other states that would soon leave the federal union." For Schafer, therefore, Americanization of Louisiana law represented regression. Ellen Holmes Pearson provides a similar trajectory with regard to laws pertaining to free people of color in Louisiana. She argues that in the decades after the Louisiana Purchase, the legal position of free people of color "grew increasingly tenuous." Nevertheless, Pearson claims, "while the state's politicians undercut incrementally such freedoms as public assembly, education, and travel, they barely touched on other rights. Thus, free blacks managed to cling to a quasi-citizenship down to 1860." Judith Schafer, *Slavery, the Civil Law, and the Supreme Court of Louisiana* (Baton Rouge: Louisiana State University Press, 1994); Ellen Holmes Pearson, "Imperfect Equality," in Billings and Fernandez, *A Law unto Itself?*, 191–210; see also Hans Baade, "The Law of Slavery in Spanish Louisiana," in Haas, *Louisiana's Legal Heritage*, 43–86.

17. This is not to suggest, of course, that these relationships between white males and black enslaved females were "consensual" in the modern sense of the term.

18. Hanger, *Bounded Lives, Bounded Places.* Chapter 2 of this book contains a more detailed discussion of *coartacion.*

19. See Peabody and Grinberg, *Slavery, Freedom, and the Law in the Atlantic World.*

20. Haney-Lopez, "Social Construction of Race," 164.

21. It is not primarily concerned with legal systems and the evolution of laws in a particular society.

22. The analysis in this book is similar to that of Sue Peabody in her essay "'Free upon Higher Ground': Saint-Domingue Slaves' Suits for Freedom in U.S. Courts, 1792–1830," in David Patrick Geggus and Norman Fiering, eds., *The World of the Haitian Revolution* (Bloomington: Indiana University Press, 2009), 261–83, wherein Peabody states her interest in "the ways in which freedom was constructed through judicial institutions in the Age of Revolution." This book analyzes the ways in which race was constructed in the New Orleans courts.

23. This is a larger presence than the numbers alone might suggest. More than half of the cases in the New Orleans City Court were disputes over large commercial transactions involving big corporations. Free people of color were involved in close to 20 percent of the remaining cases.

24. A free person of color would not hesitate to sue another person of color if it was in his or her own personal interest, whatever effect it had on the community of color as a whole.

25. Eugene Genovese's discussion of the "hegemonic function of the law" helps to explain the court's approach to these cases. "In modern societies," Genovese writes, "the theoretical and moral foundations of the legal order and the actual, specific history of its ideas and institutions influence, step by step, the wider social order and system of class rule, for no class in the modern Western world could rule for long without some ability to present itself as the guardian of the interests and sentiments of those being ruled." In territorial New Orleans, as in all early modern Western societies, the appearance of neutrality was essential to the court's authority. Eugene Genovese, *Roll, Jordan, Roll: The World the Slaves Made* (New York: Vintage Press, 1972), 25.

26. *Massant v. Veda*, case no. 3362, August 25, 1812. Records of the New Orleans City/Parish Court, 1806–1813, City Archives, New Orleans Public Library, New Orleans, Louisiana. Hereinafter, all cites to City Court cases will include the case name and date only; for some cases, only the year is recorded, and for a few cases, no date is available.

27. See the cases discussed in chapters 4 through 6.

28. "An Act to Prescribe Certain Formalities Respecting Free Persons of Color" (March 31, 1808), and "An Act Prescribing the Rules and Conduct to Be Observed with Respect to Negroes and Other Slaves of This Territory" (June 7, 1806), in Louis Moreau-Lislet, *General Digest of the Acts of the Legislature of Louisiana: Passed from the Year 1804 to 1827, Inclusive, and in Force at This Last Period* (New Orleans, 1828), 383–91.

29. *Brengle v. Williams and Colcock*, case no. 2932, October 16, 1811.

30. Louis Moreau-Lislet and James Brown, *The Digest of Civil Laws Now in Force in the Territory of Orleans* (1808), www.law.lsu.edu/index.cfm?geaux=digestof1808. home, (hereafter *Civil Digest of 1808*), bk. 1, tit. 8, ch. 1, sec. 8, art. 48.

31. During the nineteenth century, there were three important formative moments in the history of race and the law in New Orleans. In her book *Becoming Free, Remaining Free: Manumission and Enslavement in New Orleans, 1846–1862* (Baton Rouge: Louisiana State University Press, 2003), Judith Schafer uncovers the intersections of law and race in the late antebellum period. Charles Lofgren, among several others, examines another important formative moment in the 1890s with his analysis of the U.S. Supreme Court case of *Plessy v. Ferguson*. See *The Plessy Case: A Legal Historical Interpretation* (New York: Oxford University Press, 1987). *Making Race in the Courtroom* is a close examination of the intersections of race and law in New Orleans during the era of the Louisiana Purchase.

32. Local histories can illustrate the potential for different historical outcomes, serving the purpose of turning "givens" into "contingents." They can refute well-established theses or complicate broad explanatory schemes. Many local studies

of cultural and social historians have examined the daily lives of oppressed groups in local communities to highlight their humanity, dispel the notion that their subjects were passive and helpless victims of oppression, and develop their contributions to the broader society. See, for example, Peter Wood, *Black Majority: Negroes in Colonial South Carolina from 1670 through the Stono Rebellion* (New York: Norton, 1974), which examines the contributions of Africans and African Americans to early colonial South Carolina. Wood successfully refutes the assumptions of many, if not most, early historians of slavery that Africans were an inactive and backward people who made a slow transition from barbarism to civilization and had little, if anything, to contribute to American society and culture. This view of Africans and African Americans was first expressed in a historical work by Ulrich Bonn Phillips in the early twentieth century and was not successfully challenged on any grand scale until the advent of the "new" social history. Ulrich Bonn Phillips, *American Negro Slavery: A Survey of the Supply, Employment, and Control of Negro Labor, as Determined by the Plantation Regime* (1918; Baton Rouge: Louisiana State University Press, 1960).

33. Melvin Ely, *Israel on the Appomattox: A Southern Experiment in Black Freedom from the 1790s through the Civil War* (New York: Vintage Press, 2004). Ely's study is centered on Israel Hill, the 400-acre plot of land along the Appomattox River occupied by Richard Randolph's emancipated former slaves and their descendants, but it encompasses the interactions of free blacks, slaves, and whites throughout Prince Edward County, Virginia, from around 1790 to the eve of the Civil War. Ely's research is impeccable; he sifted through every court record of Prince Edward County for the entire seventy-year period in addition to viewing numerous other sources.

34. Despite its historical significance, very little has been written (in English anyway) about the revolution itself. The seminal work remains C. L. R. James's *The Black Jacobins: Toussaint L'Ouverture and the San Domingo Revolution* (New York: Vintage Press, 1938). Originally published in 1938, this book was expressly intended to "stimulate the coming emancipation of Africa" by telling the heroic story of triumph over the worst form of oppression. Carolyn Fick published *The Making of Haiti: The Saint Domingue Revolution from Below* (Knoxville: University of Tennessee Press, 1990). While previous histories had focused on the more prominent leaders of the revolution (Louverture, Christophe, and Dessalines, for example), Fick devoted her research to "the mass of black slave laborers who participated in this revolution." Laurent Dubois's *Avengers of the New World: The Story of the Haitian Revolution* (Cambridge, MA: Harvard University Press, 2004) is a highly readable synthesis that provides a clear and concise narrative of what was a very complex revolutionary event. Many scholars argue that the Haitian Revolution radicalized the West, inspiring slave revolts and movements for racial equality. See Eugene Genovese, *From Rebellion to Revolution: Afro-American Slave Revolts in the Making of the Modern World* (Baton Rouge: Louisiana State University Press, 1979). The quotation

from David Brion Davis is found in "Impact of the French and Haitian Revolutions," in David Geggus, ed., *The Impact of the Haitian Revolution in the Atlantic World* (Columbia: University of South Carolina Press, 2001), 3; Matt Childs, *The 1812 Aponte Rebellion in Cuba and the Struggle against Atlantic Slavery* (Chapel Hill: University of North Carolina Press, 2006); Laurent Dubois, *A Colony of Citizens: Revolution and Slave Emancipation in the French Caribbean, 1787–1804* (Chapel Hill: University of North Carolina Press, 2004); and Alfred Hunt, *Haiti's Influence on Antebellum America: Slumbering Volcano in the Caribbean* (Baton Rouge: Louisiana State University Press, 1988). All of these works contribute significantly to a growing literature on this important event. Several scholars address the radical impact of the Haitian Revolution in Louisiana. See Hall, *Africans in Colonial Louisiana*; Daniel Rasmussen, *American Uprising: The Untold Story of America's Largest Slave Revolt* (New York: Harper Collins, 2011). Some of the most sweeping claims about the radical impact of the Haitian Revolution in New Orleans, however, are found in Bell, *Revolution, Romanticism, and the Afro-Creole Protest Tradition.*

35. While many scholars credit the Haitian Revolution as a radicalizing influence in the New World, others caution against reading too much into the contagion of St. Domingue's revolution. See David Geggus, "The Enigma of Jamaica in the 1790s: New Light on the Causes of Slave Rebellions," *William and Mary Quarterly*, 3rd ser., 44 (1987): 289, 293, 297. Robin Blackburn's classic book shows that global socioeconomic factors, as much as ideology, shaped the events of the Age of Revolution. Robin Blackburn, *The Overthrow of Colonial Slavery, 1776–1848* (London: Verso Press, 1988); see also Michael Craton, *Testing the Chains: Resistance to Slavery in the British West Indies* (Ithaca, NY: Cornell University Press, 1982).

36. Chapter 6 discusses both (1) the important ways in which the socioracial systems of Spanish colonial New Orleans and antebellum New Orleans differed, and (2) the ways in which French West Indian refugees, acting within the court system, contributed to these differences.

37. Blackburn, *Overthrow of Colonial Slavery*, 19.

NOTES TO CHAPTER 1

1. The quotations in the description of the two routes to New Orleans are taken from C. C. Robin, *Voyages dans l'interieur de la Louisiane, de la Floride occidentale, et dans les isles de la Ma* (Paris, 1807). For the importance of the Mississippi River in the shaping of New Orleans's history, see Ari Kelman, *A River and Its City: The Nature of Landscape in New Orleans* (Berkeley: University of California Press, 2003).

2. Average temperatures in New Orleans are 51 degrees Fahrenheit in January and 82 degrees in July. The annual average is 68 degrees, and the annual average rainfall is 62 inches.

3. Pierce Lewis, *New Orleans: The Making of an Urban Landscape* (Chicago: Center for American Places, 1976). The original city, today known as the "French

Quarter," spreads around a curve of the Mississippi River, giving rise to one of New Orleans's many nicknames, the "Crescent City."

4. Memoir on Louisiana [by Bienville], 1726, in Dunbar Rowland and Albert Godfrey Sanders, eds., *Mississippi Provincial Archives, 1704-1743: French Dominion* (Jackson, MS: J. Little and Ives, 1932), 3:515-16.

5. Pierre François Xavier de Charlevoix, *Journal of a Voyage to North America Undertaken by Order of the French King* (London, 1761), 2:276.

6. François Marie Perrin du Lac, *Travels through the Two Louisianas: 1801, 1802, and 1803* (London, 1807), 87-88.

7. Douglass North, *The Economic Growth of the United States, 1790-1869* (New York: W. W. Norton & Co., 1966), 34; David Lee Sterling, "New Orleans, 1801: An Account by John Pintard," ed. David Lee Sterling, *Louisiana Historical Quarterly* 34 (1951): 217-33; letter from Thomas Jefferson to Robert Livingston, in Paul Leicester Ford, ed., *The Writings of Thomas Jefferson* (New York: Cosimo Classics, 1897), 8:143-47.

8. North, *Economic Growth of the United States*, 52.

9. The progression was as follows: 5,028 in 1785, to 8,056 in 1803, to 12,513 in 1810, and to 27,176 in 1820. In 1820, the top six U.S. cities were New York, Philadelphia, Baltimore, Boston, New Orleans, and Charleston.

10. See Census of New Orleans, 1785, in *American State Papers: Miscellaneous* (Washington, DC, 1832-34), 10:381; Census of the City of New Orleans, Exclusive of Seamen and the Garrison, 1803, in *American State Papers: Miscellaneous*, 10:384; U.S. Bureau of the Census, U.S. census, 1820, Table 5, Population of the 61 Urban Places: 1820, www.census.gov/population/www/documentation/twps0027/tab05.txt (June 15, 1998). By way of comparison, Cap Français, St. Domingue, had a population of just over 18,000 in 1789.

11. See Gabriel Debien and René LeGardeur, "Les Colons de Saint-Domingue réfugiés à la Louisiane (1792-1804)," *Louisiana Review* 10 (1981): 120; and Paul Lachance, "Repercussions of the Haitian Revolution in Louisiana," in David Geggus, ed., *The Impact of the Haitian Revolution in the Atlantic World* (Columbia: University of South Carolina Press, 2001), 209-30.

12. René J. LeGardeur Jr., "The Origins of the Sugar Industry in Louisiana," in *Green Fields: Two Hundred Years of Louisiana Sugar* (Layfayette: Center for Louisiana Studies, University of Southwestern Louisiana, 1980), 1-28.

13. William Claiborne, the newly appointed American governor of Louisiana, took precautions to screen those refugees seeking admittance into New Orleans but fell short of the Spanish policy of prohibiting the entry of refugees with slaves. Americans, at least those who controlled the government of Louisiana, were more committed to plantation slavery than the Spanish had been.

14. The life of Moreau-Lislet is discussed in greater detail in the next chapter. The best work to date on the economic influence of the refugees is Nathalie Dessens's *From St. Domingue to New Orleans: Migration and Influences* (Gainesville: University of Florida Press, 2007), esp. ch. 4. Dessens's thorough research

identifies scores of individual free refugees of color, where they lived, and what they did for a living. She shows that they rapidly fit into New Orleans's occupational pattern. See also Dessens, "The Saint-Domingue Refugees and the Preservation of Gallic Culture in Early New Orleans," *French Colonial History* 8 (2007): 53–69; Carl A. Brasseaux and Glenn R. Conrad, eds., *The Road to Louisiana: The Saint-domingue Refugees, 1792–1809* (Lafayette: Center for Louisiana Studies, University of Southwestern Louisiana, 1992), introduction.

15. See passenger ship lists from the 1809–10 immigration.

16. Using sacramental records and census data, Paul Lachance estimated that 7,000 to 8,000 refugees remained in New Orleans as opposed to leaving the city for the Louisiana countryside or other parts of the United States. See his essay "Repercussions of the Haitian Revolution in Louisiana."

17. Letter from Claiborne to Savage, November 10, 1809, in Dunbar Rowland, ed., *Official Letter Books of W. C. C. Claiborne, 1801–1816*, 6 vols. (Jackson, MS: J. Little and Ives, 1917), 5:4.

18. Gwendolyn Midlo Hall, *Africans in Colonial Louisiana: The Development of Afro-Creole Culture in the Eighteenth Century* (Baton Rouge: Louisiana State University Press, 1992), appendix A; and Kevin Roberts, "Slaves and Slavery in Louisiana: The Evolution of Atlantic World Identities, 1791–1831" (PhD diss., University of Texas, 2003).

19. Compared with port cities on the Eastern Seaboard, those in Virginia in the seventeenth century and Charleston in the eighteenth century, the port of New Orleans saw very few slaves come directly from Africa.

20. See William Lewis Newton, *The Americanization of French Louisiana: A Study of the Process of Re-adjustment between the French and the Anglo-American Populations of Louisiana, 1803–1860* (New York: Arno Press, 1980).

21. The term "creole" in this context refers to slaves born in Louisiana, while the term "saltwater" slaves refers to slaves born on the continent of Africa. The latter were mostly Congolese, as shown by Roberts in "Slaves and Slavery in Louisiana." The ethnicity of the former group is less certain. Hall argued in *Africans in Colonial Louisiana* that they were primarily Bambaran. Yet Peter Caron ("'Of a Nation Which the Others Do Not Understand': Bambara Slaves and African Ethnicity in Colonial Louisiana, 1718–60," *Slavery and Abolition* 18, no. 1 [1997]: 98–121) and Alexander Byrd (review of Hall, Gwendolyn Midlo, *Slavery and African Ethnicities in the Americas: Restoring the Links*, H-Atlantic, H-Net Reviews, August 2006) have criticized Hall for her analysis of Bambara and reification of African ethnicities.

22. See Daniel Usner, *Indians, Settlers, and Slaves in a Frontier Exchange Economy* (Chapel Hill: University of North Carolina Press, 1992).

23. Thomas Ashe, *Travels in America Performed in 1806 for the Purposes of Exploring the Rivers Alleghany, Monogahela, Ohio, and Mississippi, and Ascertaining the Produce and Condition of Their Banks and Vicinity* (London, 1808), 263–64.

24. Ibid., 266–70.

25. Ibid., 274.
26. See, for example, Pierre-Louis Berquin-Duvallon, *Vue de la Colonie Espagnole du Mississippi ou des provinces de Louisiane et Floride occidentale, en annee 1802, par un observateur resident sure les lieux* (Paris, 1803); Christian Schultz, *Travels on an Inland Voyage in the Years 1807–1808*, 2 vols. (New York, 1810); and Amos Stoddard, *Sketches, Historical and Descriptive of Louisiana* (Philadelphia, 1812).
27. Du Lac, *Travels through the Two Louisianas*, 94.
28. Ibid., 94–95.
29. In addition, the use of the term "free people of color" as opposed to "free blacks" suggests the influence of the French Caribbean, especially St. Domingue, where the term *gens de couleur* identified people of African descent who were not enslaved. Nevertheless, the combined considerations of race and status that form the basis of the categories resemble what the Spanish called *calidad*. The difference between *calidad* of Spanish colonial New Orleans and the three-race society of antebellum American New Orleans is discussed in chapter 6.
30. See Rebecca Scott, "Paper Thin: Freedom and Re-enslavement in the Diaspora of the Haitian Revolution," *Law and History Review* 29 (2011): 1061–87; Scott, "'She . . . Refuses to Deliver Up Herself as a Slave to Your Petitioner': Émigrés, Enslavement, and the 1808 Louisiana Digest of the Civil Laws," *Tulane European and Civil Law Forum* 24 (2009): 115–36.
31. These lawsuits, and other freedom suits, are the subject of chapter 6 of this book.
32. The numbers in this table come from Paul Lachance's essay "Repercussions of the Haitian Revolution in Louisiana."
33. Secretary Thomas B. Robertson wrote to Secretary of State Robert Smith on May 24, 1809: "At this moment an event occurs which will be attended with moral and political consequences much to be deprecated, which will rivet upon us a decided and irresistible preponderance of French influence—and thus prevent us for many years to come from considering this in heart and in sentiment as an American country—Many of the unfortunate French are arriving daily from Cuba about two thousand are expected they bring with them negro slaves & free people of colour. I pity their distresses and would relieve them to the utmost of my ability but I sincerely wish that they had gone to some other part of our extensive continent." Clarence C. Carter, ed., *The Territorial Papers of the United States*, vol. 9, *The Territory of Orleans, 1803–1812* (Washington, DC: Nabu Press, 1940), 842.
34. See Paul Lachance, "The 1809 Immigration of Saint-Domingue Refugees to New Orleans: Reception, Integration, and Impact," *Louisiana History* 29 (1998): 6, 13. In 1785 there were 563 free people of color living in the city with a total population of 5,028; in 1803 they accounted for 1,335 out of a population of 8,056; and in 1810 they accounted for 3,351 out of a population of 12,513. New Orleans's free black population reached its antebellum peak, in terms of numbers, in

1840, when almost 20,000 free people of color lived in the city, out of a total New Orleans population of slightly over 100,000. A growing slave and white immigrant population in the 1830s reduced the proportion of free blacks in the total populace. Free blacks composed about 40 percent of the African American population in New Orleans, reaching a high of 46 percent in 1820.

35. Some of the implications of this are discussed in chapters 4 and 6.

36. Throughout the period in question, slaves were the only one of the three groups with an even sex ratio.

37. "An Act to Prevent the Introduction of Free People of Color, from Hispaniola and the Other French Islands of America, into the Territory of Orleans" (June 7, 1806), and "An Act to Prevent the Emigration of Free Negroes and Mulattoes into the Territory of Orleans" (April 14, 1807), in Louis Moreau-Lislet, *General Digest of the Acts of the Legislature of Louisiana: Passed from the Year 1804 to 1827, Inclusive, and in Force at This Last Period* (New Orleans, 1828), 498–501.

38. Letter from Claiborne to Maurice Rogers, American consul at St. Iago de Cuba, August 9, 1809, in Rowland, *Official Letter Books of W. C. C. Claiborne*, 5:402; and letter from Claiborne to William Savage, consulate to Jamaica, November 10, 1809, in Rowland, *Official Letter Books of W. C. C. Claiborne*, 6:3–4.

39. Letter from Mather to Claiborne, July 18, 1809, in Carter, *Territorial Papers*, 9:387–88.

40. The bill banning the importation of slaves from outside the United States had been signed into law on March 3, 1807, and anticipated in Article I, Section 9, of the Constitution.

41. "An Act Respecting Slaves Imported into This Territory in Violation of the Act of Congress of March the Second Eighteen Hundred and Seven and for Other Purposes," in Moreau-Lislet, *General Digest*, 383–91; letter from Mather to Claiborne, in Rowland, *Official Letter Books of W. C. C. Claiborne*, 5:387–88; letter from Claiborne to Julien Poydras, June 4, 1809, in Carter, *Territorial Papers*, 9:843; 2 STAT 549–50. For a discussion of the way in which Maryland dealt with the importation of refugee "slaves" from St. Domingue, see Sue Peabody, "'Free upon Higher Ground': Saint-Domingue Slaves' Suits for Freedom in U.S. Courts, 1792–1830," in David Patrick Geggus and Norman Fiering, eds., *The World of the Haitian Revolution* (Bloomington: University of Indiana Press, 2009), 261–83.

42. The best examination of the social and economic structure of Louisiana from its founding until 1783 is Usner, *Indians, Settlers, and Slaves in a Frontier Exchange Economy*.

43. Kelman, *A River and Its City*, 34.

44. LeGardeur, "Origins of the Sugar Industry in Louisiana."

45. By 1820, the port of New Orleans had become one of the largest ports in North America in terms of the value of products it received, exceeding both the port of Boston ($12 million in 1820) and the port of New York ($13 million in 1820). See James E. Winston, "Notes on the Economic History of New Orleans, 1803–1836," *Mississippi Valley Historical Review* 11 (1924): 200–226.

46. North, *Economic Growth of the United States*, 34–35. Antebellum New Orleans was the transfer point for American and foreign goods. These products were offloaded and stored in warehouses or transferred directly to oceangoing vessels, and then shipped to the Northeast, Europe, and the Caribbean. In the territorial period, trade was primarily one-way, since steamboats were not yet in use, and movement upriver was slow and freight charges high. The first steamboat to come down the Mississippi arrived in the Crescent City in 1812. By the 1850s, around 3,000 steamboats docked at New Orleans each year.

47. See John G. Clark, *Economic History of New Orleans* (Baton Rouge: Louisiana State University Press, 1970), 342.

48. Junius Rodriguez, *The Louisiana Purchase: A Historical and Geographical Encyclopedia* (Santa Barbara, CA: ABC-CLIO, 2002), 292.

49. Clark, *Economic History of New Orleans*, 287.

50. Ibid., 357–58; du Lac, *Travels through the Two Louisianas*, 91; and North, *Economic Growth of the United States*, 34–35.

51. See Kimberly Hanger, *Bounded Lives, Bounded Places: Free Black Society in Colonial New Orleans, 1769–1803* (Durham, NC: Duke University Press, 1997), 59.

52. Again, most of these "slaves" had been freed by the revolutionary events in the West Indies and then reenslaved in Cuba and/or Louisiana.

53. Hanger, *Bounded Lives, Bounded Places*, 59. See also the following cases of the New Orleans City Court: *Marcellin Gilleau v. Anfoux and Marigny*, case no. 108, 1812; *Callender v. Ash*, case no. 1757, July 25, 1809; and *Brulet v. Gonzalez*, case no. 2921, October 3, 1811; and letter from Mather to Claiborne, July 18, 1809, in Carter, *Territorial Papers*, 9:387–88.

54. See Dessens, *From St. Domingue to New Orleans*, 75–78.

55. Bernabee was one of several free black artisans who helped construct the Cabildo building, completed in 1799, which housed the city government and still stands today.

56. Bernabee, Rafael, free Negro, by Santiago Villére, Sale of Property with Mortgage, June 10, 1795, New Orleans Notarial Archives (NONA), vol. 25 p. 491; Bernabee, Rafael, to Jose Zamora, Obligation with Mortgage, January 8, 1808, NONA, vol. 56, p. 6; Bernabee, Rafael, to P. R. Delongy, Obligation with Mortgage, April 7, 1808, NONA, vol. 56, p. 150; Bernabee, Rafael, to M. de Laura, Mortgage, September 24, 1808, NONA, vol. 57, p. 387; and Bernabee, Rafael, to Antoine Fromentin, Sale, February 2, 1811, NONA, vol. 62, p. 53.

57. Kearsey died in 1776, after which West purchased Durham. West sold Durham to Dow when the two encountered each other in Pensacola during the American Revolution.

58. Betty L. Plummer, ed., "Letters of James Durham to Benjamin Rush," *Journal of Negro History* 65 (Summer 1980): 261–69.

59. Dessens, *From St. Domingue to New Orleans*, 75–78.

60. Hanger, *Bounded Lives, Bounded Places,* 58. See also *Brengle v. Williams and Colcock,* case no. 2932, October 16, 1811; *Marie Louise v. Saignal and Delinau,* case no. 2087, March 14, 1810.

61. See Kenneth Aslakson, "The Quadroon-*Plaçage* Myth: Anglo-American (Mis) interpretations of a French-Caribbean Phenomenon," *Journal of Social History* 45 (2012): 709–34. The intimate relationships between white men and women of color in early New Orleans as well as the efforts of women of color to establish themselves in business and accumulate and protect their property are covered in greater detail in chapters 4 and 5 of this book.

62. For perspective on the wealth of free people of color in New Orleans compared with the rest of the U.S. South, see the following works of Loren Schweninger: *Black Property Owners in the South, 1790–1915* (Champaign-Urbana: University of Illinois Press, 1990); "Property-Owning Free African-American Women in the South, 1800–70," *Journal of Women's History* 1, no. 3 (1990): 13–44; and "Prosperous Blacks in the South, 1790–1880," *American Historical Review* 95 (1990): 31–56.

63. U.S. census, 1810.

64. James E. Winston, "Notes on the Economic History of New Orleans, 1803–1836," 201.

65. The river itself flows through the city at four feet above sea level.

66. "Cabildo" is the term both for the city's governing body under the Spanish and for the building in the city center where this body met to conduct official business. The building, constructed in 1799, still stands today and is located next to St. Louis Cathedral in the French Quarter. The Place d'Armes was called the Plaza de Armas by the Spanish and is today known as Jackson Square.

67. Sterling, "Account by John Pintard," 226.

68. Ibid., 224. The architecture of the "French Quarter," therefore, is largely Spanish, constructed, as it was, by Spanish artisans around the turn of the nineteenth century.

69. *New Orleans in 1805, a Directory and a Census, Together with Resolutions Authorizing Same Now Printed for the First Time from the Original Manuscript, with an Introduction by Charles Thompson* (New Orleans, 1936). See also Clark, *Economic History of New Orleans,* 358.

70. *New Orleans in 1805.*

71. See Moreau-Lislet, *General Digest,* 422–23.

72. The streets in the Marigny are crooked extensions of French Quarter streets such as Bourbon, Chartres, Dauphine, and Royal. Bernard Marigny was the petitioner in dozens of foreclosure suits in the New Orleans City Court against defendants who had defaulted on their mortgages to him.

73. Scott Ellis, author of *Madame Vieux Carré: The French Quarter in the Twentieth Century* (Oxford: University of Mississippi Press, 2010), is currently working on a book about the history of Faubourg Marigny. I thank him for conversations we have had on the topic of early purchasers of property in the suburb.

74. For an entertaining, if somewhat romanticized, depiction of this rivalry, see Grace King, *New Orleans: The Place and the People* (New York, 1895).

75. Samuel Wilson, Marie Louise Christovich, and Roulhac Toledano, *New Orleans Architecture: Faubourg Tremé and the Bayou Road: North Rampart Street to North Broad Street, Canal Street to St. Bernard Avenue* (Gretna, LA: Pelican, 1997).

76. *Niles Weekly Register* 49 (1814): 187.

77. For the policies of Carondolet, see Hanger, *Bounded Lives, Bounded Places;* Thomas Ingersoll, *Mammon and Manon in Early New Orleans: The First Slave Society in the Deep South, 1718–1819* (Knoxville: University of Tennessee Press, 1999). See also Emily Clark and Virginia Gould, "The Feminine Face of Afro-Catholicism in New Orleans, 1727–1852," *William and Mary Quarterly*, 3rd ser., 59 (2002): 59.

78. King, *New Orleans.*

79. Within a few years of statehood, New Orleans would have several slave markets

80. Sterling, "Account by John Pintard," 228.

NOTES TO CHAPTER 2

1. The value of the peso was roughly equivalent to that of both the piastre and the dollar.

2. The petition arrives at the figure of 284 piastres by dividing 2,400 by the number of children (4) and then subtracting 316, which is what Coffi had paid, from the remaining 600. It is not clear what happened to Coffi's three other children.

3. *Jean Baptiste v. Delaronde and Castillon,* case no. 2967, December 16, 1811.

4. The full text of the Louisiana Purchase treaty is reprinted in the *Connecticut Courant,* November 2, 1803. France had reacquired the Louisiana Territory from Spain in 1800 by virtue of the Treaty of San Ildefonszo. According to the terms of this treaty, France had promised Spain that it would never alienate the territory to a third party. The formal transfer from Spain to France took place on November 20, 1803, and the formal transfer from France to the United States took place on December 20, 1803. The quotation is found in a letter from Thomas Jefferson to Pierre Samual de Nemours, January 18, 1802, in Dumas Malone, ed., *Correspondence between Thomas Jefferson and Pierre Samual de Nemours, 1798–1817* (New York: Ulan Press, 1970), 40.

5. Peter Kastor's *The Nation's Crucible: The Louisiana Purchase and the Creation of America* (New Haven, CT: Yale University Press, 2004) deals with all of these issues and more. More than any other scholar of the Louisiana Purchase, Kastor delves into the practical, rather than the theoretical, problems of "incorporating" Louisiana into the new nation. He argues, as the title suggests, that Louisiana shaped America as much as vice versa. He explicitly rejects two common understandings of the Louisiana Purchase: that it was perceived among Americans to be part of the nation's "manifest destiny," and that American leaders sought to spread liberty and republicanism to a region reared in despotism and monarchy.

6. "An Act Erecting Louisiana into Two Territories and Providing for the Temporary Government Thereof," Statutes at Large, 8th Cong., 1st sess., ch. 38, Library of Congress, Washington, DC. Article IV, Section 3, of the Constitution gave Congress the power to "make all needful rules and regulations respecting the territory or other property of the United States."

7. For academic studies of Louisiana's legal history and current legal system, see Edward F. Haas, ed., *Louisiana's Legal Heritage* (Baton Rouge: Louisiana State Museum, 1983); George Dargo, *Jefferson's Louisiana: Politics and the Clash of Legal Traditions* (Cambridge, MA: Harvard University Press, 1975); and Warren Billings and Mark Fernandez, eds., *A Law unto Itself: Essays in the New Louisiana Legal History* (Baton Rouge: Louisiana State University Press, 2001). Historians and legal scholars have long presented the state of Louisiana's legal system as unique within the United States. According to Haas in his introduction to *Louisiana's Legal Heritage*, "Louisiana is the sole solid enclave of civil law in the United States. In a nation that reveres the Anglo-American tradition of common law, Louisiana stands alone. Its unique legal system, based fundamentally on Roman law, derives from the lengthy colonial rule of France and Spain" (1). While this claim captures the singularity of Louisiana's legal system, it is only partially true. Many aspects of the common law tradition made their way into the Louisiana legal system. Moreover, to the extent the civil law did remain after the Great Purchase, its survival owes as much to immigration from the Caribbean in the first decade of the nineteenth century as it does to "the lengthy colonial rule of France and Spain."

8. For a good overview of the similarities and differences between common law and civil law, see John Henry Merryman, *The Civil Law Tradition: An Introduction into the Legal Systems of Europe and Latin America*, 3rd ed. (Palo Alto, CA: Stanford University Press, 2007).

9. Ibid., 1–2.

10. Ibid., 22.

11. Ibid., 21.

12. Contrary to popular belief, the difference between civilian law and common law is not based on the amount or degree of authority of legislation. The number of statutes varies a great deal within legal traditions rather than between them, and all statutes are, of course, binding in all legal traditions. Rather, the differences between the two traditions center on their different visions of the source of law. Ibid., 60.

13. Ibid., 18.

14. According to Merryman, "State positivism was much more sharply and consciously emphasized on the European continent than it was in England during this period of revolutionary change. One reason, of course, was the milder, more gradual, and more evolutionary nature of the English revolution. In England many of the forms of feudalism were retained, while their substance was transformed" (ibid., 21).

15. Letter from Jefferson to Monroe, November 24, 1801, in Paul L. Ford, ed., *The Works of Thomas Jefferson*, 12 vols. (New York: Cosimo Classics, 1904–5), 10:317.
16. Dargo, *Jefferson's Louisiana*, ch. 5; letter from Jefferson to Horatio Gates, July 11, 1803, in Paul Leicester Ford, ed, *The Writings of Thomas Jefferson*, 10 vols. (New York: Cosimo Classics, 1892–99), 8:249.
17. See Dunbar Rowland, ed., *Official Letter Books of W. C. C. Claiborne, 1801–1816*, 6 vols. (Jackson, MS: J. Little and Ives, 1917); Joseph T. Hatfield, "Governor William Claiborne, Indians and Outlaws in Frontier Mississippi, 1801–1803," *Journal of Mississippi History* 27 (1965): 323–50; and Hatfield, "William C. C. Claiborne, Congress, and Republicanism, 1797–1804," *Tennessee Historical Quarterly* 24 (1965): 156–80.
18. James Brown later served as a U.S. senator from Louisiana from 1813 to 1817. See Biographical Directory of the United States Congress, http://bioguide.congress.gov/scripts/biodisplay.pl?index=B000921.
19. "A Short Letter to a Member of Congress Concerning the Territory of Orleans" (Washington, DC, 1806), in Dargo, *Jefferson's Louisiana*, 149–53.
20. Aaron Burr, Alexander Hamilton, and James Kent also studied law under Lansing.
21. While Edward Livingston was U.S. attorney, a confidential clerk lost or stole some funds belonging to the national government. Livingston was responsible for and assumed this debt, but his relationship with his onetime friend and mentor Thomas Jefferson had been irreparably damaged. For a good discussion of Edward Livingston's life, education, legal training, and contribution to Louisiana's legal system, see Mark Fernandez, "Edward Livingston and the Problem of Law," in Peter Kastor, ed., *The Louisiana Purchase: Emergence of an American Nation* (Washington, DC: CQ Press, 2002), 90–104. See also William B. Hatcher, *Edward Livingston: Jeffersonian Republican and Jacksonian Democrat* (Baton Rouge: Louisiana State University Press, 1940).
22. Derbigny was the sixth governor of Louisiana. He was born in 1769, at Laon near Lille, France, the eldest son of Augustin Bourguignon d'Herbigny, who was president of the Directoire de l'Aisne and mayor of Laon, and Louise Angelique Blondela. Derbigny studied law at St. Geneviéve but fled France in 1791 during the French Revolution. He arrived in Pittsburgh, Pennsylvania, and married Félicité Odile de Hault de Lassus, with whom he would have five daughters and two sons. He arrived in New Orleans, then a Spanish colony, in 1797 and by 1803 had been appointed secretary of the legislative council. In 1804, he became a representative from Louisiana in Congress. From 1814 to 1820, Derbigny served as a justice of the Louisiana Supreme Court. In 1821, Derbigny resigned from the Supreme Court of Louisiana to run unsuccessfully for governor against Jean N. Destrehan, Abner Duncan, and Thomas B. Robertson. Despite his loss to Robertson, Derbigny was appointed secretary of state of Louisiana and served from 1821 to 1828. In 1828, he ran for governor again and this time defeated Thomas Butler, his former supporter, Bernard Marginy, and Congressman

Philemon Thomas. Derbigny was affiliated with the nascent National Republican Party, an anti-Jackson group. See Biography of Louisiana Governors, 1812–1861, Pierre Auguste Bourguignon Derbigny, 1818–29, Louisiana Secretary of State's Office, www.sos.louisiana.gov.

23. Letter to an unknown correspondent, June 2, 1804, Joseph Dubreuil de Villars Papers, Duke University.

24. Dargo, *Jefferson's Louisiana*, 126.

25. Fernandez, "Edward Livingston and the Problem of Law," 95.

26. "Instructions from the Inhabitants of the Territory of Orleans to Their Representatives in the Legislature" (New Orleans, 1805), in Dargo, *Jefferson's Louisiana*, 133.

27. Clarence Carter, ed., *Territorial Papers of the United States*, vol. 9, *The Territory of Orleans, 1803-1812* (Washington, DC: Nabu Press, 1940), 643–57. This manifesto was published in *Le Telegraphe* on June 3, 1806. The manifesto was signed and endorsed by ten members: Étienne Boré, D. Bouligny, J. Arnould, M. Landry, Felix Bernard, J. Sorrel, Prudhomme, Isaac Hebert, Hazeur Delorme, and Joseph Landry.

28. In addition to his work as a jurist, he was one of the founders and one of the regents of the first university in Louisiana, called the University of Orleans, a member of the state House of Representatives, and, finally, a state senator. He died in New Orleans on December 4, 1832. Most of the biographical information in this sketch comes from Alain A. Levasseur, *Moreau-Lislet: The Man behind the Digest of 1808* (Baton Rouge: Louisiana State University Press, 2008). See also Gabriel Debien and René LeGardeur, "Les Colons de Saint-Domingue réfugiés à la Louisiane, 1792–1804," *Louisiana Review* 10 (1981): 120.

29. "Batture" comes from the French verb for "to beat" and refers to the land beaten by the river.

30. Several works on Louisiana history discuss the batture case. While George Dargo highlights the legal implications of the case in his book *Jefferson's Louisiana*, Ari Kelman examines the case from an environmental perspective in *A River and Its City: The Nature of Landscape in New Orleans* (Berkeley: University of California Press, 2003).

31. While George Dargo would likely agree with this point, he nevertheless argues that "the controversy over the Batture of the Faubourg St. Marie dramatized the confrontation between diverse legal cultures. The political, social, and legal issues raised in the course of the Batture fight impinged with unparalleled immediacy upon larger questions of law and the overall problem of the conflict of legal traditions. Indeed, it seems to be an inescapable conclusion that the Batture controversy solidified local realignments which the Burr conspiracy had precipitated. At the same time it prepared the ground at the territorial and national levels of government for the adoption of the *Digest of the Laws in Force* on March 31, 1808, a moment when the clamor over the New Orleans Batture was still at its height" (*Jefferson's Louisiana*, 101). Thus, according to Dargo, the

batture controversy influenced the state's civil law doctrine in a roundabout way.

32. Edward Livingston to Robert Livingston, May 6, 1804, Robert R. Livingston Papers, New York Historical Society.

33. See Dargo, *Jefferson's Louisiana*, 48, 132, 141; Levasseur, *Moreau-Lislet*.

34. For an in-depth analysis of the important differences between digests and codes in common law and civil law traditions and their application to Louisiana's legal history, see Vernon Palmer, "The Death of a Code, the Birth of a Digest," *Tulane Law Review* 63 (1988): 221.

35. François Xavier Martin, one of the justices of the Louisiana Supreme Court, also contributed to this effort.

36. The adversarial system is one in which two advocates represent their parties' positions before an impartial judge or jury. Civil law courts, generally speaking, use an inquisitorial system in which a judge or group of judges work together to investigate the case. Under the Spanish system in Louisiana, each parish had a commandant who decided the disputes and whose decision could be appealed to the governor.

37. "Private" law is contrasted with both criminal law and administrative law, both of which involve the government as parties. "Substantive" law is contrasted with the rules governing procedure—such as how lawsuits are initiated and when and in what form evidence is admitted. Chapter 4 deals in depth with the domestic and inheritance laws of early Louisiana; chapter 5 deals with its law of contracts.

38. See Dargo, *Jefferson's Louisiana*; Levasseur, *Moreau-Lislet*.

39. See Fernandez, "Edward Livingston and the Problem of Law," 98; *Barran v. Maussuy*, case no. 1277, 1808, and *Sauzenau v. Jones*, case no. 3013, February 1812.

40. Letter from Claiborne to Madison, October 7, 1808, in Carter, *Territorial Papers*, 9:802.

41. See letter from Claiborne to Madison, October 27, 1804, in Carter, *Territorial Papers*, 9:312. In this letter Claiborne identifies Derbigny as the author of *Esquisse de la situation politique et civile de la Louisiane, depuis le 30 Novembre, 1803 jusq'au 1er Octobre, 1804*, an anonymous pamphlet that is very critical of early U.S. policies in the Orleans Territory. See also letter from Claiborne to Jefferson, July 1, 1804, in Carter, *Territorial Papers*, 9:246; and letter from Claiborne to Madison, July 13, 1804, in Carter, *Territorial Papers*, 9:261. In these letters Claiborne refers to Clark, Jones, and Livingston as the allies of the francophone Derbigny, Detrion, and Suave.

42. This is the common socialist law critique of both traditions.

43. The implications of this emphasis on private property rights for free people of color in racially based slave societies are discussed more fully in chapter 5.

44. To be sure, the 1685 Code Noir required that former slaves show respect to their former masters and allowed for reenslavement as punishment for certain

crimes. But these provisions applied only to former slaves, not to people of African ancestry who had been born free.

45. *Edit du roi, touchant la police des isles de l'Amerique français* (Paris, 1687), 28–58; B. F. French, *Historical Collections of Louisiana: Embracing Translations of Many Rare and Valuable Documents Relating to the Natural, Civil, and Political History of That State* (New York, 1851).

46. See Laura Foner, "The Free People of Color in Louisiana and St. Domingue: A Comparative Portrait of Two Three-Caste Societies," *Journal of Social History* 3 (1970): 406; and Daniel Usner, *Indians, Settlers, and Slaves in a Frontier Exchange Economy* (Chapel Hill: University of North Carolina Press, 1992).

47. Governor Alejandro O'Reilly, who took control of Louisiana in 1769, formally "reenacted" the Code Noir in that year as part of his effort to restore order and security after the French rebellion against the Spanish government in Louisiana. But this was simply a show of force, and the French Code never truly governed Spanish Louisiana.

48. Hans Baade, "The Law of Slavery in Spanish Louisiana," in Edward F. Haas, ed., *Louisiana's Legal Heritage*, 43–86.

49. See Gwendolyn Midlo Hall, "Louisiana Free Database, 1719–1820," in *Databases for the Study of Afro-Louisiana History and Genealogy, 1699–1860: Computerized Information from Original Manuscript Sources*, 2000, www.ibiblio.org/laslave/introduction.php.; Baade, "Law of Slavery in Spanish Louisiana," 46–47; and Kimberly Hanger, *Bounded Lives, Bounded Places: Free Black Society in Colonial New Orleans, 1769–1803* (Durham, NC: Duke University Press, 1997), 27.

50. See Gwendolyn Midlo Hall, *Africans in Colonial Louisiana: The Development of Afro-Creole Culture in the Eighteenth Century* (Baton Rouge: Louisiana State University Press, 1992), ch. 5; Hanger, *Bounded Lives, Bounded Places*, ch. 1; and Jennifer Spear, *Race, Sex, and Social Order in Early New Orleans* (Baltimore: Johns Hopkins University Press, 2009), ch. 4.

51. *Catherina v. Estate of Juan Bautista Destrehan, Louisiana Historical Quarterly* 9 (1926): 556–58. For an in-depth discussion of Catherina's case and *coartacion* in general, see Spear, *Race, Sex, and Social Order in Early New Orleans*, ch. 4.

52. See Sue Peabody and Keila Grinberg, *Slavery, Freedom, and the Law in the Atlantic World: A Brief History with Documents* (Boston and New York: Bedford/St. Martin's Press, 2007), 3; and James Thomas McGowan, *Creation of a Slave Society* (Rochester, NY: University of Rochester Press, 1976), 194.

53. Spear, *Race, Sex, and Social Order in Early New Orleans*, 121.

54. *Jean Baptiste v. Delaronde and Castillon*, case no. 2967, December 16, 1811; Hanger, *Bounded Lives, Bounded Places*, 31. Jennifer Spear shows that some slaves, in an appeal to the financial interests of their masters, offered to purchase their freedom at much higher prices than their market value. See the case of the slave Nicholas in *Race, Sex, and Social Order in Early New Orleans*, 120.

55. "An Act Erecting Louisiana into Two Territories," *Annals of Congress*, 8th Cong., 1st sess., p. 1186; "Remonstrance of the People of Louisiana," in

American State Papers: Class X, Misc. (Washington, DC, 1832–34), 1:399; letter from James Brown to the Secretary of the Treasury, December 11, 1805, in Carter, *Territorial Papers*, 9:548; and "An Act for the Government of Orleans Territory," March 2, 1805, in Carter, *Territorial Papers*, 9:406. For a detailed and thoughtful discussion of Congress's regulation of slavery in the Orleans Territory immediately after the Louisiana Purchase, see John Craig Hammond, "'They Are Very Much Interested in Obtaining Slavery': Rethinking the Expansion of Slavery in the Louisiana Purchase Territories, 1803–1805," *Journal of the Early Republic* 23 (2003): 353–80. Hammond refers to the collective action of some members of Congress in 1804 as "a bold measure designed to destroy the plantation revolution in the lower Mississippi Valley" (256). Hammond is one of several historians who have recently done a good job of historicizing the spread of slavery to what became the Deep South, showing that it was not an inevitable process. See also Adam Rothman, *Slave Country: American Expansion and the Origins of the Deep South* (Cambridge, MA: Harvard University Press, 2005).

56. See Hammond, "'They Are Very Much Interested in Obtaining Slavery,'" 370. The Breckinridge Bill would have ended slavery in all of the Louisiana Purchase territories.

57. Whether or not Louisianans would have followed through on their threats to secede is in question. Gary Nash has argued that, in a similar situation at the time of the American Revolution, the founding fathers missed a golden opportunity to put America on a path to ending slavery, but they failed to do so because they feared losing Georgia and South Carolina. Nash contends that these two states would have joined the Union even if the Constitution had been framed in such a way to end slavery because they needed the other states more than vice versa. This could have been true in Louisiana at the time as well. See Gary Nash, *Race and Revolution* (Lanham, MD: Rowman and Littlefield, 1990).

58. Letter from James Brown to the Secretary of the Treasury, December 11, 1805, in Carter, *Territorial Papers*, 9:548.

59. Letter from Claiborne to Jefferson, October 27, 1804, in Carter, *Territorial Papers*, 9:314; letter from Claiborne to Madison, November 5, 1804, in Carter, *Territorial Papers*, 9:320.

60. "An Act for the Government of Orleans Territory," March 2, 1805, in Carter, *Territorial Papers*, 9:406; Dargo, *Jefferson's Louisiana*, 48.

61. "Acts Passed at the First Session of the First Legislature of the Territory of Orleans" (1806); "An Act Prescribing the Rules and Conduct to Be Observed with Respect to Negroes and Other Slaves of This Territory" (June 7, 1806); and "An Act to Regulate the Conditions and Forms of the Emancipation of Slaves" (March 9, 1807). These acts are found in Louis Moreau-Lislet, *General Digest of the Acts of the Legislature of Louisiana: Passed from the Year 1804 to 1827,*

Inclusive, and in Force at This Last Period (New Orleans, 1828). Almost 200 manumissions were exercised between 1804 and 1807, and many of these were the result of self-purchase arrangements. In 1806, Justice Prevost upheld the legitimacy of *coartacion* in a freedom purchase suit. The legislature responded with the law stating that "no person shall be compelled to emancipate his or her slave except when made in the name of and at the expense of the territory." For an excellent discussion of the ways in which the *Civil Digest* dealt with slavery, see Vernon V. Palmer, "The Strange Science of Codifying Slavery—Moreau Lislet and the Louisiana Digest of 1808," *Tulane European and Civil Law Forum* 24 (2009): 83–113.

62. See Ellen Holmes Pearson, "Imperfect Equality: The Legal Status of Free People of Color in New Orleans, 1801–1860," in Warren Billings and Mark Fernandez, eds., *A Law unto Itself?*, 191–210.

63. See *Civil Digest of 1808*, tit. 4, ch. 2, art. 8. See also "An Act to Prescribe Certain Formalities Respecting Free Persons of Color" (March 31, 1808); "An Act Prescribing the Rules and Conduct to Be Observed with Respect to Negroes and Other Slaves of This Territory" (June 7, 1806); and "An Act Supplementary to an Act Prescribing the Rules and Conduct with Respect to Negroes and Other Slaves of This Territory" (February 16, 1818). These acts are found in Louis Moreau-Lislet, *General Digest of the Acts of the Legislature of Louisiana: Passed from the Year 1804 to 1827, Inclusive, and in Force at This Last Period* (New Orleans, 1828). Specifically, the act clarifying rape states that "if any slave, free negro, mulatto, Indian or mustee, shall attempt to commit a rape on the body of any white woman or girl, the said slave, free negro, mulatto, Indian or mustee, shall, on conviction thereof, suffer death." In addition, the 1812 Louisiana Constitution, and all subsequent state constitutions before the Civil War, limited suffrage to white males.

64. There were other colony-wide laws and local ordinances that discriminated against the *gens de couleur*. See Laurent Dubois, *Avengers of the New World: The Story of the Haitian Revolution* (Cambridge, MA: Harvard University Press, 2004), 62 and sources cited therein. For a comparison of colonial St. Domingue and Louisiana, see Foner, "Free People of Color in Louisiana and St. Domingue."

65. For laws restricting the rights and privileges of free people of African descent in the various states, see John C. Hurd, *The Law of Freedom and Bondage in the United States* (Ithaca, NY: Cornell University Press, 2009); and Digital Library on American Slavery, University of North Carolina at Greensboro (2000–2009), https://library.uncg.edu/slavery/.

66. Eugene Genovese, *Roll, Jordan, Roll: The World the Slaves Made* (New York: Vintage Press, 1972), 25.

67. The Seventh Amendment to the Constitution guarantees the right to trial by jury in all suits "where the value in controversy exceeds twenty dollars."

NOTES TO CHAPTER 3

1. The Cabildo building was (and is) right next to—on the downriver side—St. Louis Cathedral, which is the centerpiece of the Place d'Armes, now known as Jackson Square. As was the case with the community of free people of African descent as a whole, most, though not all, free militiamen of African descent were of mixed ancestry. During the Spanish period, the terms *pardo* and *moreno* referred to a "person of color" and a "Negro," respectively. Two *pardo* battalions and one *moreno* battalion of 100 persons each mustered at the Louisiana Purchase ceremony. When I discuss the militia as a whole, I will refer to them the "free colored militia" even though some of the militiamen were "blacks" or "Negroes."

2. Letter from Claiborne to Madison, December 20, 1803, in Dunbar Rowland, ed., *Official Letter Books of W. C. C. Claiborne, 1801–1816*, 6 vols. (Jackson, MS: J. Little and Ives, 1917), 2:307–8. *Ancienne population,* like *ancienne habitants,* is a term used to describe the population of (white) French- and Spanish-speaking creoles who lived in Louisiana prior to the Louisiana Purchase.

3. Clarence C. Carter, ed., *The Territorial Papers of the United States,* vol. 9, *The Territory of Orleans, 1803–1812* (Washington, DC: Nabu Press, 1940), 174.

4. Sue Peabody speaks to the dilemma of racially based slavery in a republic when she writes, "The problem of social hierarchies in a world where all people are to be considered 'free' (i.e. not subject to others' domination) has yielded, on one hand, a commitment to an ideology of absolute social equality and, on the other, a system of justification for why some classes of individuals are entitled to more privileges than others." Sue Peabody, *"There Are No Slaves in France": The Political Culture of Race and Slavery in the Ancien Regime* (New York: Oxford University Press, 1996), 8.

5. Herbert S. Klein, "The Colored Militia of Cuba: 1568–1868," *Caribbean Studies* 6 (July 1966): 17–27; David Geggus, "The Enigma of Jamaica in the 1790s: New Light on the Causes of Slave Rebellions," *William and Mary Quarterly,* 3rd ser., 44 (1987): 274–99; John Garrigus, "Catalyst or Catastrophe? Saint Domingue's Free Men of Color and the Battle of Savanah, 1779–1782," *Revista/ Review Interamericana* 22 (1992): 109–25. According to Klein, in 1779, Cuba's military forces totaled 11,667 men, including 4,645 white militiamen, 3,413 free colored militiamen, and 3,609 royal troops.

6. For a discussion of the militia in colonial Cuba, see Klein, "Colored Militia of Cuba," 17–26. The quotation "especially so in this age before the creation of mass conscript citizen armies" is found in ibid., 22. The free colored militia was so valuable to defense of Spain's possessions that in 1714 the king ordered colonial officials in Cuba to see that free colored militiamen were treated with respect. The crown recognized their value even if the colonial officials did not. In Cuba, free colored militias offered especially good opportunities for social advancement and for breaking down the color barrier. In the 1770s, the free colored Cuban Antonio Flores demanded from the crown that any color barriers

be lifted from his sons pursuing the professions. In the 1790s the mulatto militiaman attended university, became a doctor of civil law, a practicing lawyer, and a high government official; ibid., 26. For a discussion of the militia in St. Domingue, see Garrigus, "Catalyst or Catastrophe?" In St. Domingue, Vincent Olivier, a free black man reported to be 119 years old in 1779, had been a slave but gained his freedom after a raid on Cartagena in 1697. In 1716, Olivier was named Captain General of the free colored militia in Cap Français. Garrigus, "Catalyst or Catastrophe?," 114. The quotation "employed by free families of color . . . to maintain and reinforce their status in local society" is found in Garrigus, "Catalyst or Catastrophe?," 109.

7. Klein, "Colored Militia of Cuba," 19; Kimberly Hanger, *Bounded Lives, Bounded Places: Free Black Society in Colonial New Orleans, 1769–1803* (Durham, NC: Duke University Press, 1997), 113.

8. Yet, in a pattern that was to repeat itself into the eighteenth century, both sides armed slaves and promised them freedom in exchange for military service in 1676 during Bacon's Rebellion. See Sylvia Frey, *Water from the Rock: Black Resistance in a Revolutionary Age* (Princeton, NJ: Princeton University Press, 1991).

9. Laura Foner, "The Free People of Color in Louisiana and St. Domingue: A Comparative Portrait of Two Three-Caste Slave Societies," *Journal of Social History* 3 (1970): 410.

10. While Hanger argues that demographic and social realities caused the government to turn to free blacks for defense in the circum-Caribbean region, claiming there were simply not enough whites in the region, Louisiana's demographics were not similar to most Caribbean slave societies.

11. Klein, "Colored Militia of Cuba," 20.

12. Foner, "Free People of Color in Louisiana and St. Domingue," 415.

13. Hanger, *Bounded Lives, Bounded Places*, 114.

14. Several historians see the *feuro militar* as crucial to the collective advancement of free blacks and the most important contributor to a collective free black identity in the Spanish New World. For broader discussions of the *feuro militar,* see Hanger, *Bounded Lives, Bounded Places*, and, especially, Joseph Sanchez, "African Freedmen and the Fuero Militar: A Historical Overview of Pardo and Moreno Militiamen in the Late Spanish Empire," *Colonial Latin American Historical Review* 3 (1994): 165–84. Kimberly Hanger argues that the *feuro militar* "separated libres from slaves and associated them with whites", while Joseph Sanchez claims that it accorded privileges that set militia members apart from the rest of society and hence constituted a social elite.

For the quotation "exemption from paying tribute, opportunities to receive retirement and death benefits, and the right to bear arms and wear uniforms," see Hanger, *Bounded Lives, Bounded Places*, 111.

15. Many officers in the militia owned substantial amounts of property. Carlos Brulet, a free *pardo* officer, possessed three slaves in 1795 and in 1801 held the

rank of grenadier captain. Vincent Cupidon was a mason and lieutenant in the free *moreno* militia. Brulet's brother-in-law, Raymundo Gaillard, was a free *pardo* silversmith and grenadier married to Maria Isabel Destrehan, whose brother Honorato was second lieutenant of the grenadiers. The free *pardo* butcher Carlos Montreuil owned two slaves and served as a first corporal. The battalion commander Mañuel Noel Carriere plied his trade as a cooper and in 1795 owned five slaves. Cupidon Caresse, a *moreno* sergeant in 1779, hunted to earn his keep; in 1795 he owned five slaves, who helped to support him. See the 1795 census and the 1798 census of Faubourg St. Marie, Archivo General de Indias (AGI), Seville, Spain, AGI PC 215-A.

16. For a detailed discussion of the Pointe Coupee revolt, see Jack Holmes, "The Abortive Slave Revolt at Pointe Coupee," *Louisiana History* 11 (1970): 353; see also Ernest R. Liljegren, "Jacobinism in Spanish Louisiana: 1792–1797," *Louisiana Historical Quarterly* 22 (1939): 47–97; and Gwendolyn Midlo Hall, *Africans in Colonial Louisiana: The Development of Afro-Creole Culture in the Eighteenth Century* (Baton Rouge: Louisiana State University Press, 1992), ch. 5.

17. Hall, *Africans in Colonial Louisiana*, 349–50; Geggus, "Enigma of Jamaica in the 1790s," 290.

18. Hanger, *Bounded Lives, Bounded Places*, 125.

19. Bailly fought in the Baton Rouge, Mobile, and Pensacola campaigns under Governor Galvez during the American Revolution.

20. First trial: "Criminales seguidos de oficio contra el Pardo Libre Pedro Bahy," October 7, 1791, Spanish Judicial Records, Louisiana State Museum, New Orleans; second trial: "Testimonio de la Sumaria contra el Muprorrumpido especies contra el Govierno Espanol, y haverse manifestado adicto las maximas de los Franceses rebeldes," AGI Estado 14, n. 60, February 11, 1794. Unless otherwise indicated, all quotations are taken from these trial summaries.

21. Hanger, *Bounded Lives, Bounded Places*, 156; "Criminales seguidos de oficio contra el Pardo Libre Pedro Bahy."

22. The petition is found in Actas Originales del Cabildo de Nueva Orleans, 1769–1803 (Cabildo Records), bk. 4088, doc. 367.

23. For a sound discussion of feminine virtue, see Carroll Smith-Rosenberg, *Disorderly Conduct: Visions of Gender in Victorian America* (New York: Oxford University Press, 1986), 165.

24. "Free Citizens of Color Address to the National Assembly, October 22, 1789," in Laurent Dubois and John D. Garrigus, eds., *Slave Revolution in the Caribbean, 1789–1804: A Brief History with Documents* (Boston: Bedford/St. Martin's Press, 2006), 67–70.

25. "Letters from the Uprising of Vincent Ogé, October 1790," in Dubois and Garrigus, *Slave Revolution in the Caribbean*, 75–78; "Julien Raimond, Observations on the Origin and Progression of the White Colonists' Prejudice against Men of Color, 1791," in Dubois and Garrigus, *Slave Revolution in the Caribbean*, 78–82.

26. Juan Bautista Saraza (Scarasse) and Pedro Galfate (Calpha) identified themselves as octoroons, while Pedro José Tomas and Juan Bautista Bacusa (Bacuse) identified themselves as quadroons.

27. Cabildo Records, bk. 4088, doc. 367.

28. "Free Citizens of Color Address to the National Assembly," 69.

29. Stewart King, Blue Coat or Powdered Wig: Free People of Color in Pre-revolutionary St. Domingue (Athens: University of Georgia Press, 2001).

30. "Letters from the Uprising of Vincent Ogé, October, 1790," 79.

31. In St. Domingue about 60 percent of free people of African descent were born free and about the same were of mixed ancestry. In Louisiana, about two-thirds were of mixed ancestry.

32. The other two petitioners were Pedro Galfate and Pedro Tomas. Galfate joined the New Orleans Mulatto Militia in the early 1790s. He became corporal first class in 1793, and by 1800 he had become a second lieutenant. His uncle was the captain and commandant of the Mulatto Militia. In the War of 1812, he was corporal in the Third Regiment of the Louisiana Militia. He established his residence at 67 Toulouse Street and was employed as a lamplighter for the city. Tomas was born in 1767. When he came to Louisiana, he established his residence at 41 Rue St. Ann. In 1800, he was a captain in the free black militia.

33. See Louisiana Purchase treaty as reprinted in the Connecticut Courant, November 2, 1803.

34. Thomas Ingersoll, Mammon and Manon in Early New Orleans: The First Slave Society in the Deep South, 1718–1819 (Knoxville: University of Tennessee Press, 1999), 244. When Louisiana was a colony of monarchical France and Spain, slavery and race relations were regulated by royal decrees, such as the French Code Noir of 1715 and the Spanish Black Code of 1777.

35. Carter, Territorial Papers, 9:174.

36. In New Orleans, as in much of the colonized circum-Caribbean, free people of African descent more strongly identified with their colony than did most Spanish or French whites. As natives of the colony who planned to remain, free people of color did not share the same dream as most whites, which was to get rich quick and return home to Europe. For a discussion of the free colored militia in colonial St. Domingue, see King, Blue Coat or Powdered Wig.

37. Although there is no overlap between the subscribers of the 1800 petition and the 1804 address, all who signed the address had served in the militia under the Spanish. Moreover, Bailly and his son are two of the subscribers along with Francisco Dorville and possibly another accuser of Bailly.

38. In the years 1804–6, rumors abounded in New Orleans that the Spanish government had amassed troops in Florida with plans to attack Louisiana from land and sea.

39. Rowland, Official Letter Books of W. C. C. Claiborne, 2:248.

40. Ibid., 233.

41. The primary sources do not specifically refer to the free men of color as militia-men. But in Claiborne's letters about the event he refers to influential men of color, and in later correspondence he identifies some of them as militia officers.

42. Rowland, *Official Letter Books of W. C. C. Claiborne*, 2:233–45. The quotations are taken from a letter Claiborne wrote to Secretary of State James Madison.

43. In December 1803, Louisiana's militia numbered 5,440 men in all. In New Orleans and surrounding areas this number was around 800, including 300 free men of color enrolled in one *moreno* and two *pardo* companies. These numbers are from a report issued by the Baron de Carondelet. Carter, *Territorial Papers*, 9:33, 139; Rowland, *Official Letter Books of W. C. C. Claiborne*, 2:244–45.

44. Rowland, *Official Letter Books of W. C. C. Claiborne*, 1:314.

45. Ibid., 2:54.

46. Ibid., 104. For Claiborne's praise of Dearborn's decision, see ibid., 218.

47. Ibid., 215–16.

48. *Louisiana Gazette*, January 29, 1805. Daniel Clark publicly criticized Claiborne for "putting up with their disrespectful refusal of the officers whom he had appointed as their adjutants."

49. Carter, *Territorial Papers*, 9:738.

50. On March 26, 1804, Congress passed a law establishing a legislative council in Orleans of thirteen "notables." However, the territorial legislature did not meet until the following year. Chapter 2 presents the more detailed discussion.

51. Carter, *Territorial Papers*, 9:559.

52. Ibid., 576.

53. Libro primero de matrimonios de negros y mulattos, 22 A, No. 3, December 12, 1805, MS in St. Louis Cathedral, New Orleans.

54. Letter from Claiborne to Madison, January 29, 1806, in Rowland, *Official Letter Books of W. C. C. Claiborne*, 3:252–53.

55. Carter, *Territorial Papers*, 9:717.

56. Rowland, *Official Letter Books of W. C. C. Claiborne*, 4:92–93.

57. See chapter 1 for the numbers on this immigration.

58. Charles Gayarre, *History of Louisiana*, 4 vols. (New York: William J. Widdleton, 1866), 4:226–27.

59. King, *Blue Coat or Powdered Wig*, 75.

60. It was the largest in terms of the number of slaves involved.

61. Few scholars have studied the German Coast rebellion in detail. For accounts of the rebellion, see James Dormon, "The Persistent Specter: Slave Rebellion in Territorial Louisiana," *Louisiana History* 18 (1977): 389–404; and Daniel Rasmussen, *American Uprising: The Untold Story of America's Largest Slave Revolt* (New York: Harper Perennial, 2011).

62. However, all of the slaves identified as leaders of the rebellion, including Charles Deslondres, had been born in Louisiana.

63. There is some scholarly discussion on the role of the free colored militia in the event. While Rasmussen suggests that free men of color stood ready to join

the rebellion should it achieve a certain amount of success, Ira Berlin, in *Slaves without Masters: The Free Negro in the Antebellum South* (New York: New Press, 1974), claims that the free colored militia helped put down the rebellion.

64. Rowland, *Official Letter Books of W. C. C. Claiborne*, 5:100.

65. "Jackson's Address to the Men of Colour, December 18, 1814," in John Spencer Bassett, ed., *Correspondence of Andrew Jackson* (Washington, DC, 1926–33), 2:57–58.

66. See Roland McConnell, *Negro Troops in Antebellum Louisiana: A History of the Battalion of Free Men of Color* (Baton Rouge: Louisiana State University Press, 1968), 91.

67. Historians have interpreted Andrew Jackson's praise of the efforts of the free colored battalion as the realization of the efforts of free men of African descent to receive recognition as citizen-soldiers. To be sure, Jackson's praise of the free men of color is remarkable coming from a man who, as president, was certainly no friend of America's nonwhite population, but his use of these soldiers both during and after the battle comes closer to exploitation than honor. After the battle, Jackson ordered the troops to remain alert, refusing to commit to a date of dismissal.

68. "Claiborne to Jackson, August 24, 1814," in Bassett, *Correspondence of Andrew Jackson*, 2:29–30.

69. "Jackson to Claiborne, September 21, 1814," in Bassett, *Correspondence of Andrew Jackson*, 2:56–57.

70. The address begins with a recognition that free colored militiamen had been mistreated in the past. "Through a mistaken policy, my brave fellow Citizens, you have heretofore been deprived of a participation in the Glorious struggle for National rights, in which our Country is engaged. This shall no longer exist, as sons of freedom, you are now called upon to defend our most estimable blessing. As Americans, your Country looks with confidence to her adopted Children, for a valorous support, as a partial return for the advantages enjoyed under her mild and equitable government. . . . Your love of honor would cause you to despise the Man who should attempt to deceive you. I shall not attempt it. In the sincerity of a Soldier, and the language of truth I address you. Your country, altho' calling for your exertions does not wish you to engage in her cause, without amply remunicating [*sic*] you, for the services rendered."

71. "Claiborne to Jackson, October 17, 1814," in Bassett, *Correspondence of Andrew Jackson*, 2:75–76.

72. Ibid.

73. See "Acts Passed at the First Session of the First Legislature of the State of Louisiana" (1812), found in Louis Moreau-Lislet, *General Digest of the Acts of the Legislature of Louisiana: Passed from the Year 1804 to 1827, Inclusive, and in Force at This Last Period* (New Orleans, 1828), 335.

74. Ibid., 72.

75. McConnell, *Negro Troops in Antebellum Louisiana*, 98.

76. Ibid.

NOTES TO CHAPTER 4

1. Tessier, August, to Eleanore, mistise, Donation, June 21, 1808, NONA, vol. 56, p. 249; *Bechillon v. Tessier*, case no. 2647, April 16, 1811.

2. By domestic law I mean the laws governing domestic relationships in early New Orleans. These included laws regulating the relationship between husband and wife and between parent and child. The chapter also includes a discussion of how the property of a deceased person was to be distributed.

3. In medieval Europe, marriage came under the jurisdiction of canon law, which recognized as a valid marriage one where the parties stated that they took one another as wife and husband, even in absence of any witnesses. But the Protestant Reformation, in rejecting many Catholic doctrines, treated marriage as a secular contract rather than a religious sacrament. The Puritans brought this latter concept of marriage to the English colonies of North America, where it survived. Moreover, the French Revolution in 1792 introduced the concept of compulsory civil marriage to France. See John Witte Jr., *From Sacrament to Contract: Marriage, Religion, and Law in the Western Tradition* (Louisville, KY: Westminster John Knox Press, 1997), 39–40. The Catholic churches of the Diocese of New Orleans performed dozens of weddings a year in the early nineteenth century and the Protestant churches a lesser number. For the legal definition of marriage in early New Orleans, see the *Civil Digest of 1808*, tit. 4, ch. 1, art. 1.

4. For a study of the political, moral, and economic purposes of marriage in what is now the United States from colonial times to the present, see Nancy F. Cott, *Public Vows: A History of Marriage and the Nation* (Cambridge, MA: Harvard University Press, 2000). Cott shows how marriage laws have played a role in defining citizenship along racial and gender lines.

5. *Civil Digest of 1808*, bk. 1, tit. 4, ch. 2, art. 8. The Louisiana Code Noir of 1724 had banned the marriage of Catholics and non-Catholics but was silent on interracial marriages.

6. Pennsylvania repealed its antimiscegenation law in 1780, together with some of the other restrictions placed on free blacks, when it enacted a bill for the gradual abolition of slavery in the state. Later, in 1843, Massachusetts repealed its anti-miscegenation law after abolitionists protested against it. Things changed briefly after the Civil War, but laws preventing interracial mixing were the heart of legally mandated segregation in the Jim Crow era. These laws still existed in many states until the U.S. Supreme Court declared them to be unconstitutional in the decision in *Loving v. Virginia* (1967). See Frank W. Sweet, *The Legal History of the Color Line* (Palm Coast, FL: Backintyme Press, 2005); Peggy Pascoe, *What Comes Naturally: Miscegenation Law and the Making of Race in America* (New York: Oxford University Press, 2009). Pascoe's book focuses on the postbellum period when laws regulating sex and marriage, and the discourse surrounding it, served to maintain social distinctions based on race after the end of slavery. Still, the first chapter of her book shows that while laws banning interracial marriage may have taken on new meaning during and after the Civil War, they were not new to the period.

7. The *Civil Digest of 1808* states, "Free persons and slaves are incapable of contracting marriage together; the celebration of such marriages is forbidden, and the marriage is void; it is the same with respect to the marriages contracted by free white persons with free people of color" (bk. 1, tit. 4, ch. 2, art. 8). Louisiana's ban on interracial marriage was clearly not unique, but its prohibition of free and enslaved blacks from marrying did make it exceptional. The significance of this as it relates to both the Spanish system of *calidad* and the similar but different emergence of racial categories is discussed more fully in chapter 6.

8. Coverture persisted in the colonies and former colonies of England until the mid-nineteenth century, when many jurisdictions passed married women's property acts. For the history of coverture in early America, see Linda Kerber, *No Constitutional Right to Be Ladies: Women and the Obligations of Citizenship* (New York: Hill and Wang, 1999).

9. For a comparative study of the impact of the different legal traditions on women's property and legal rights, see Deborah A. Rosen, "Women and Property across Colonial America: A Comparison of Legal Systems in New Mexico and New York," *William and Mary Quarterly*, 3rd ser., 60 (2003): 355–81.

10. The *Civil Digest of 1808*, bk. 1, tit. 4, ch. 4 lays out the rights and obligations of husband and wife.

11. There was no such thing as a divorce as we know it today, much less a no-fault divorce.

12. See *Civil Digest of 1808*, bk. 1, tit. 5, ch. 1.

13. The seventeen legal separation cases are *Wiltz v. Trudeau*, case no. 593, May 21, 1807; *Fleurian v. Charbonne*, case no. 1493 (date unknown); *Anthony v. Anthony*, case no. 1698, June 28, 1809; *St. Hilain v. Turcotty*, case no. 1730, August 23, 1809; *Wilde v. Wilde*, case no. 1826, 1809; *Durcy v. Clermont*, case no. 1885, October 6, 1809; *Barbin v. Bellevue*, case no. 1890, October 9, 1809; *Bacchus v. Cassepare*, case no. 2171, April 12, 1810; *Blaise v. Jean*, case no. 2192, April 25, 1810; *Smith v. Smith*, case no. 2236, June 5, 1810; *Cadou v. Dury*, case no. 2255, June 16, 1810; *Hernandez v. Del Puerto*, case no. 2365, September 12, 1810; *Hareng v. Zerinque*, case no. 2396, October 17, 1810; *Dupon v. Survine*, case no. 2454, January 9, 1811; *Caraby v. Nice*, case no. 2654, April 29, 1811; *Bougaud v. Bougaud*, case no. 2835, August 31, 1811; and *Crousot v. Brainpain*, case no. 673, July 13, 1807.

14. This is not to suggest that the outcome would have been different had the married couples been of color instead of white.

15. *Lucie Bardon v. Louis Durand, Her Husband*, New Orleans District Court, 1816; *Crousot v. Brainpain*, case no. 673, July 13, 1807.

16. *Hannah Smith v. John Smith*, case no. 2236, June 5, 1810.

17. Bertram Wyatt-Brown, *Honor and Violence in the Old South* (New York: Oxford University Press, 1986), 97.

18. *Bacchus v. Cassepare*, case no. 2171, April 12, 1810; *Euphrosine Wiltz v. Valfroy Trudeau*, case no. 593, May 21, 1807; *Euphrosine Wiltz v. Honoré Valfroy Trudeau*, case no. 1214, 1808.

19. *Mathieu v. Mathieu,* case no. 1690, June 13, 1809.
20. These laws are scattered among the various chapters of the *Civil Digest of 1808,* bk. 3, tit. 2.
21. The enslaved population was the only group with a natural ratio. See chapter 1 for a discussion of the demographics of early American New Orleans.
22. While it is impossible to know exactly how many interracial relationships developed in early New Orleans, one can get a sense from examining a combination of sources, including sacramental records, court documents, wills, and census data. These sources reveal more than 330 white male–colored female relationships in the years between 1780 and 1860 and do not reveal any relationships between white women and men of African descent in the same time period.
23. For an excellent examination of the history of interracial sex in New Orleans during the first century of its existence, see Jennifer Spear, *Race, Sex, and Social Order in Early New Orleans* (Baltimore: Johns Hopkins University Press, 2009). According to Spear, "regulating sex was the principal way in which officials tried to define and maintain discrete racial groups." She convincingly argues that Anglo-Americans had a different concept of acceptable sexual behavior than did French or Spanish colonials in Louisiana. Yet Anglo-American "desires for racial endogamy were slow to be accepted by all New Orleanians, who continued to form families across the color lines well into the antebellum period" (4–5). This chapter builds on Spear's analysis by arguing the imbalanced sex demographics among the white and free colored populations was one of the important reasons for this continuity.
24. Joseph Eysallene, a native of Marseilles, France, and former resident of St. Domingue, and Marie Magdeleine Poisson (aka "Fillette"), a "quadroon libre" and native of Croix des Bouquets, St. Domingue, had three children together. Adéle Eyssalene was born in 1804, and Laurent Pierre Louis in April 1809, both in Santiago de Cuba. The couple had a third child, Anne Louise Eyssalene, on January 18, 1811, after they had arrived in New Orleans. The godparents for all three children were themselves refugees of the Haitian Revolution who had come to New Orleans via Cuba. Another couple, Jean Baptiste Noel, a native of Port-au-Prince, and Marie Elizabeth Delatte, a "femme de couleur libre" and native of Croix de Bouquets, St. Domingue, had four children together. The first two, Joseph Guillaume Elisée (1806) and Marie Elizabeth (1808), were born in Santiago; the two youngest, Marie Magdeleine (1811) and Noel Catherine (1815), were born in New Orleans.
25. The term *plaçage* comes from the French verb *placer,* meaning "to place." It was rarely used in the antebellum period. None of the travelers' accounts discussing interracial relationships use the term. *Plaçage* appears in the antebellum probate records, but it is referring to a relationship between two free people of color. It was later used to apply to white male–colored female relationships by popular historians in the early twentieth century. The term is loaded with meaning and goes a long way in perpetuating the myth in that it implies that women of color are placed (as objects) with white male protectors and providers.

26. For example, after attending both the quadroon balls and the fashionable white subscription masked balls, the Duke of Saxe-Weimer "could not refrain from making comparisons, which in no wise redounded to the advantage of the white assembly." Although the price of admission at the subscription balls was fixed "so that only persons of the better class can appear there," the duke still found the quadroon balls "much more decently conducted than the white affairs." His Highness Bernard, Duke of Saxe-Weimar Eisnach, *Travels through North America during the Years 1825 and 1826*, 2 vols. (Philadelphia, 1828), 1:62. Louis Tasistro, speaking of the three different types of balls offered each week (the "white ball," the "quadroon ball," and the "colored ball"), stated, "With the exception of the Quadroon ball, which is really a respectable affair, the others are of very low character, being, in fact, mere chances of rendezvous for all the gay females of the town." Louis Fitzgerald Tasistro, *Random Shots and Southern Breezes* (New York, 1842), 2:18. An English traveler named James Silk Buckingham opined that the balls "furnish[ed] some of the most beautiful women that can be seen, resembling in many respects, the higher orders of women among the high-class Hindoos; lovely countenances, full, dark, liquid eyes, lips of coral, teeth of pearl, sylphlike figures; their beautifully rounded limbs, exquisite gait, and ease of manner might furnish models for Venus or Hebe." James Silk Buckingham, *The Slave States of America* (London and Paris, 1842), 1:357. Harriet Martineau commented, "The [quadroon] girls are probably as beautiful and accomplished a set of women as can be found." Harriet Martineau, *Society in America* (London, 1837), 117.

27. Annie Lee Stahl, "The Free Negro in Ante-Bellum Louisiana," *Louisiana Historical Quarterly* 25 (1942): 308–10; Herbert Asbury, *The French Quarter* (New York: Basic Books, 1936), 131.

28. See Will Books, vol. 3, p. 25, New Orleans Public Library; *Moniteur de la Louisiane*, November 23, 1805; *Bechillon v. Tessier*, case no. 2647, April 26, 1811; Sacramental Records of the St. Louis Cathedral (SLC), Baptisms 24, p. 144.

29. Tessier never called these balls "quadroon balls"; rather, he advertised them as balls given for free women of color. The advertisements became increasingly specific as to who would be allowed to attend. The first ad announced balls for "femmes de couleur libres," the second for "femmes de couleur libres seulement," and then finally "pour les blancs et les femmes de couleur libres." The advertisements in the *Moniteur de la Louisiane* specifically stated that free men of color would not be admitted.

30. In 1803, Don Francisco La Rosa, suffering from a decline in attendance at his white public balls, pleaded with the "families of distinction" in the city to hold their society balls at La Salle de Conde rather than in private homes. After opening the Grand Ball Room on Conti Street in 1806, Antonio Boniquet, moreover, began hosting society balls there. In the November 23, 1810, edition of the *Courrier*, Boniquet announced "to the inhabitants of Louisiana that he will give ten balls in his hall on Conti Street. The price will be sixteen dollars.

Each subscriber will have the privilege of introducing to society those young women that he judges to be respectable and he believes eligible." Actas Originales del Cabildo de Nueva Orleans, 1769–1803 (Cabildo Records), bk. 4, doc. 415.

31. Cabildo Records, bk. 3, vol. 2, p. 196, February 2, 1792; bk. 4, vol. 1, p. 95, March 11, 1796; bk. 4, vol. 1, p. 102, April 1, 1796; bk. 4, vol. 1, p. 107, April 22, 1796; bk. 4, doc. 338, February 1799.

32. Pierre-Louis Berquin-Duvallon, *Travels in Louisiana and the Floridas in the Year 1802*, trans. John Davis (New York, 1806), 54.

33. For a more detailed discussion of the myth and reality of white male–colored female relationships in New Orleans throughout the antebellum period, see Kenneth Aslakson, "The Quadroon-*Plaçage* Myth: Anglo-American (Mis) interpretations of a French-Caribbean Phenomenon," *Journal of Social History* 45 (2012): 709–34.

34. The property of a "minor female who ha[d] not arrived at the full age of twelve years" was placed under the authority of a tutor, in this case, the child's mother. *Civil Digest of 1808*, bk. 1, tit. 8, ch. 1, sec. 1.

35. For example, in his will, probated more than ten years after his lawsuit with Bechillon, Tessier left 500 piastres to another woman of color named Françoise Godefroy "for two years of service to [him] as [his] personal manager."

36. *Marie Louise v. Saignal and Delinau*, case no. 2087, March 14, 1810.

37. *Jung v. Doriocourt*, 4 La. 181 (1832).

38. *Civil Digest of 1808*, bk. 1, tit. 7, ch. 2, sec. 2.

39. See *Civil Digest of 1808*, bk. 2, tit. 2, arts. 44–47.

40. In her comparison of the legal systems of colonial New Mexico and colonial New York, Deborah Rosen argues that "civil law systems were far more protective of women's property rights than the common law system was" ("Women and Property across Colonial America," 355). While this may be true generally, the inheritance laws of civil law systems placed many restrictions on to whom one could bequeath his or her property in a will. So, for example, in common law jurisdictions a husband could, should he so desire, leave all his property to his wife, his children, or anyone he cared to. Such is not the case in civil inheritance law.

41. *Civil Digest of 1808*, bk. 3, tit. 2, arts. 12–14, 19–20.

42. The case is *Sennet v. Sennet's Legatees*, Supreme Court of the State of Louisiana, Western District 3 Mart. (o.s.) 411 (La. 1814), decided August 1814; will of Pierre Lardy, Will Books, vol. 1, p. 517; *Darby v. Darby*, Superior Court case no. 532, 1805.

43. Duquery had died intestate (without a will) on December 20, 1809.

44. Of course $500 was not a "measly" sum in 1810. It would have been enough money to purchase a young slave skilled in one of the trades or a small plot of land in one of New Orleans's burgeoning suburbs.

45. *Marie Louise v. Saignal and Delinau*, case no. 2087, March 14, 1810.

46. See *François Morin (Husband of Marie Françoise Fiset) v. Marie Louise, aka Quinones*, December 4, 1811. The battle on appeal of the *Dupre* case reveals

the impact of a variety of laws in the context of New Orleans's race and sex demographics: (1) Duqery and Dupre were prevented by law from marrying; (2) Fiset, Duquery's cousin, was preferred in the inheritance laws to Dupre, his black lover; and (3) the laws regulating marriage required that Fiset's husband be a party to the lawsuit.

47. Moreover, Jean Gabriel Fazende, a native of New Orleans and scribe, moved up the social ladder when he combined his resources with those of Constance Larche, a "mulatress libre" and plantation owner in Plaquemines Parish. And Louis Boisdoré, who worked as both a foreman and a collector, combined resources with Charlotte Morand, the quadroon daughter of landowners on Bayou Road, to purchase land in St. Tammany Parish on the north shore of Lake Ponchartrain. See SLC, bk. 12, p. 15; SLC, Baptisms 18, p. 39; Will Books, vol. 5, p. 9; SLC, Baptisms 21, p. 128; SLC, Baptisms 27, p. 45; SLC, Baptisms 4, p. 109; New Orleans City Directory 1822, New Orleans Public Library, Louisiana Division; New Orleans City Directory 1832; SLC, Funerals 16, p. 88; SLC, Baptisms 16, p. 75; SLC, Baptisms 16, p. 230; SLC, Baptisms 18, p. 85; SLC, Funerals 16, p. 201; SLC, Baptisms 24, p. 95; SLC, Baptisms 27, p. 94; SLC, Baptisms 29, p. 111; SLC, Funerals 14, p. 302; *Marie Louise Dupre v. Saignal and Delinau,* case no. 2087, March 14, 1810.

48. See Aslakson, "The Quadroon-*Plaçage* Myth." Alecia Long comes to the same conclusions about interracial relationships in New Orleans in the late nineteenth and early twentieth centuries. See Alecia Long, *Great Southern Babylon: Sex, Race, and Respectability in New Orleans, 1865–1920* (Baton Rouge: Louisiana State University Press, 2004).

49. Diana Williams, "'They Call It Marriage': The Interracial Louisiana Family and the Making of American Legitimacy" (PhD diss., Harvard University, 2007).

50. New Orleans Death Records, vol. 11, p. 1484, New Orleans Public Library, Louisiana Division; SLC, M3, p. 43, March 29, 1812; Will Books, vol. 10, pp. 481–83.

51. *Smith v. Smith,* case no. 2236, June 5, 1810.

52. Moreau-Lislet, *General Digest,* 1804–27, Black Code sec. 12 and "An Act for the Punishment of Crimes and Misdemeanors" (May 4, 1805), sec. 2.

53. *Raby v. Forstall,* case no. 742, August 1807.

54. *Massant v. Veda,* case no. 3362, August 25, 1812.

55. In cases based on other areas of the law, such as property disputes, whether the case was tried before a jury or a judge only seems to have had little impact on its outcome. Nevertheless, it may have mattered more in cases involving the alleged insubordination of free women of African descent.

56. *The State v. Jose Fuentes,* 5 La. Ann. 427 (May 1850).

57. *Durand v. Durand and Foucher,* case no. 3255, May 29, 1812.

58. It is difficult to generalize about responses to the perceived insubordination of women of color in New Orleans based on three cases. Court intervention in white male "correction" of women of color may have been the rare exception. The available sources simply do not provide sufficient information to make such

a determination. Nevertheless, these cases do indicate that the courts offered an avenue of recompense for women of color with knowledge and/or resources.

59. Cabildo Records, bk. 4, doc. 338. In another petition filed in February 1800, petitioner Barran complained also about selling strong drink to slaves and the inferior orders of society. The taverns, according to Barran, were always full of soldiers, sailors, laborers, and slaves when these people should be in barracks, boats, offices, and houses of their masters. In December 1800, Barran petitioned the Cabildo to close down all gaming parlors in the city.

60. Cabildo Records, bk. 4, doc. 341.

61. The petition is found in Cabildo Records, bk. 4088, doc. 367. In *Revolution, Romanticism, and the Afro-Creole Protest Tradition in Louisiana, 1718–1868,* Caryn Cosse Bell also argues that free men of color opposed tricolor/quadroon dances for gendered reasons.

62. *Moniteur de la Louisiane,* November 20, 23, 1805; *Courrier,* August 25, 1807; Asbury, *French Quarter,* 134.

63. *Moniteur de la Louisiane,* April 12, 1806; NONA, April 5, 1810, vol. 60, p. 164; Ronald Morazan, "Quadroon Balls in the Spanish Period," *Louisiana History* 14 (1973): 312. In 1832, the St. Phillip Street Theatre was renamed the Washington Ballroom. Several other ballrooms offering quadroon balls opened over the course of the next couple of decades. By 1826, a man named Laignal was offering, among other events, a "dinner and ball" on the second Sunday of each month "for white gentlemen and free women of color." Laignal announced in April 1826 that he would keep this schedule throughout the year, not just during the extended carnival season. His ballroom, which he called "Laignal's Pleasure Palace," was located in the upriver suburb of de la Course. At least three other ballrooms were offering quadroon balls by the 1830s: the Chartres Street Ballroom, the Globe Ballroom, and the Louisiana Ballroom. Thus, through the course of the antebellum period, at least seven different ballrooms hosted quadroon balls. NONA, vol. 60, p. 164; *Courrier,* April 11, 1826; Henry Kmen, *Music in New Orleans: The Formative Years, 1791–1841* (Baton Rouge: Louisiana State University Press, 1966).

64. *Courrier,* February 4, 1806; *New Orleans Bee,* November 28 and 30, 1835. Anxiety over intimate interracial contact produced, in addition to proposed legislation, periodic outcries from "concerned citizens." See Roger A. Fischer, "Racial Segregation in Ante Bellum New Orleans," *American Historical Review* 74 (1969): 931–933.

65. See Reid Mitchell, *All in a Mardi Gras Day: Episodes in the History of New Orleans Carnival* (Cambridge, MA: Harvard University Press, 1995).

66. *New Orleans Bee,* November 28 and 30, 1835; Isidore Lowenstern, *Les États-Unis et la Havane: Souvenirs d'un voyageur par Isidore Lowenstern* (Paris, 1842); Berquin-Duvallon, *Travels in Louisiana and the Floridas in the Year 1802,* 53.

NOTES TO CHAPTER 5

1. Although neither the petition nor the answer identifies Rousseau as either Hazaca's or Nicholas Mallet's son, the jury verdict references a judgment in a court in Les Cayes, St. Domingue, that recognized Rousseau as one of the heirs of his father, Nicholas Mallet.

2. Slavery had been abolished in St. Domingue by the French National Convention in 1794.

3. Mallet asked for $2,000 representing the value of three of the four slaves, Charles, Marie, and Rabelle; $2,640 for the services of the four slaves from March 7, 1805, until the date of the City Court suit; and $2,000 in punitive damages for fraud, for a total of $6,640.

4. See *Mallet v. Hazaca,* case no. 3420, October 13, 1812; and *Doute v. Mallet,* case no. 3434, September 21, 1812. Sannite Hazaca called herself Sannite Doute in the lawsuit she filed in September 1812.

5. Robin Blackburn, "Haiti, Slavery, and the Age of Democratic Revolution," *William and Mary Quarterly,* 3rd ser., 63 (2006): 650–51.

6. Edmund Morgan, "Slavery and Freedom: The American Paradox," *Journal of American History* 59 (1972): 9–10.

7. Blackburn, "Haiti, Slavery, and the Age of Democratic Revolution," 650.

8. Ibid., 650–51. As Blackburn states, "The American Declaration of Independence, one of the finest expressions of the patriot creed, famously described as 'self-evident' truths the claims that 'all men are created equal' and are 'endowed by their creator with certain inalienable rights,' among which are 'Life, Liberty, and the pursuit of Happiness.' This assertion was easier to reconcile with the enslavement of blacks than might be thought, since the rights it asserted could only be claimed by members of a people with their own properly organized government. Natural rights doctrines had traditionally declared that all men were born free but qualified this notion immediately by insisting that liberty could only be realized in specific communities organized by the law of peoples" (ibid., 649).

9. Ibid., 652.

10. James E. McClellan III, *Colonialism and Science: St. Domingue and the Old Regime* (Chicago: University of Chicago Press, 2010), 64.

11. Laurent Dubois, *Avengers of the New World: The Story of the Haitian Revolution* (Cambridge, MA: Harvard University Press, 2004), 64.

12. Ibid., 161. On pages 43–45, Dubois cites "Proclamation of Étienne Polverel," August 27, 1793, in Gabriel Debien, "Aux origines de l'abolition de l'esclavage," *Revue d'Histoire des Colonies* 36 (1949): 356–87.

13. Sue Peabody examines this issue in "'Free upon Higher Ground': Saint-Domingue Slaves' Suits for Freedom in U.S. Courts, 1792–1830," in David Patrick Geggus and Norman Fiering, eds., *The World of the Haitian Revolution* (Bloomington: Indiana University Press, 2009), 261–83.

14. Paul Lachance, "Repercussions of the Haitian Revolution in Louisiana," in David Geggus, ed., *The Impact of the Haitian Revolution in the Atlantic World* (Columbia: University of South Carolina Press, 2001), 209–30.
15. *Rey v. Lugois*, case no. 1867, September 27, 1809.
16. Book 2 of the *Civil Digest of 1808*, "Of Things and the Different Modifications of Property," defines the different types of property as well as the different types of rights to ownership and use of that property. Book 3, "Of the Different Manners of Acquiring Property and Things," mostly deals with successions, gifts, and contracts (including express contracts, implied and quasi contracts, and marriage contracts). It also deals with, among other things, loans, mortgages, and secured credit.
17. *Cuvillier and Kernion v. Rodriquez*, case no. 1415, October 28, 1808.
18. *Lartigue v. Godefroy*, case no. 3146, March 28, 1812.
19. Free people of color were involved in four boundary disputes.
20. *Vincent v. Portigo*, case no. 2972, December 20, 1811; *Mentsinger v. Portigo*, case no. 3015, March 7, 1812.
21. *Durand v. Dupuy*, case no. 1227, May 1808. There is no judgment in the case.
22. *Lalande, Peter Guillaumet, Garçon Nibert, Bethomme, and George Michael, Petitioners, v. Anfoux and Marigny*, case no. 107, 1812; *Marcellin Gilleau v. Anfoux and Marigny*, case no. 108, 1812.
23. *Duval and Boucher v. Ash*, case no. 1769; *Callender v. Ash*, case no. 1757, July 25, 1809; *Foley v. Ash*, case no. 1776; *Mayhew and Wells v. Ash*, case no. 2061, May 28, 1810; *Ash v. Mayhew*, case no. 2155, April 3, 1810; *Young v. Mayhew*, case no. 2318, July 21, 1810.
24. *Blanchard v. Marigny*, case no. 3279, June 9, 1812; *Bouqui v. Narcisse*, case no. 1974, December 7, 1809. The name Bouqui is spelled differently in the case title than in other records.
25. *St. Jean v. Goux*, case no. 2015, January 29, 1810; *Gabaroche v. Madour*, case no. 3436, October 21, 1812; *Daromaut v. Laporte*, case no. 2285, July 2, 1810; *Espagnette v. Schormberg*, case no. 1796, August 23, 1809; *Le Blond v. Solary and Daromant*, case no. 1946, November 9, 1809.
26. Although fraud is an intentional tort in the private law of modern common law jurisdictions, the *Civil Digest* dealt with fraud in book 3 in its articles dealing with contracts. The *Civil Digest of 1808*, tit. 3, ch. 2, art. 9, dealing with consent to contracts, states that it is "no valid consent that is given through error, or is extorted by violence or surprised by fraud." Article 16 states that "fraud is a cause of nullity in a contract, when the artifices practiced by one of the parties, are such that it is evident that but for these artifices, the other party would not have contracted. It is not presumed and must be proved."
27. There were three cases in which the perpetrator fraudulently obtained a deed to real estate and one in which the perpetrator mortgaged a piece of real estate he did not own. Three involved slaves. One was a false mortgage, and one was the sale of a slave under false pretenses.

28. *Bienvenu v. Andre*, case no. 1755, April 1809. The term "Hiboos" may have come from the African *Ebo*, but it is more likely a variation of the word "Hebrew." "King of the Hebrews" may have had religious importance for Bienvenu.

29. *Marie Lalande v. François Durand*, case no. 1247, May 1808; *Moraud v. Voisin*, case no. 2484, February 16, 1811.

30. *Masson v. Dobbs*, case no. 3379, September 4, 1812.

31. *Jean Pierre v. Noel*, case no. 2397, October 19, 1810.

32. These lawsuits did not involve "stealing" of slaves per se. In only one case did a party to a lawsuit use force to abduct the slave(s) in question, and he was a constable purporting to be acting in his official capacity. Moreover, while slave stealing was a crime, these cases were private lawsuits.

33. See, for example, *Convignes v. Foure*, case no. 2437, December 20, 1810.

34. *Phelippon and Yellies v. Clerge*, case no. 3488, December 11, 1812.

35. Most *gens de couleur* refugees were female, which helps to explain the numbers.

36. Dubois, *Avengers of the New World*, 70.

37. *St. Amant and Cuvillier v. Burel*, case no. 2030, April 17, 1811.

38. *St. Martin v. Gautier*, case no. 1811, August 30, 1809; see also *Rey v. Lugois*, case no. 1867, September 27, 1809.

39. *Convignes v. Foure*, case no. 2437, December 20, 1810.

40. The certificate stated the following: "It is certified that the négres des deux sexes named Savoir Geneviéve aged 56, Helene 35, Charlotte 25, Magrande 25, Desiree 26, Sanitte 20, Adelaide 30, Caroline 5, [illegible name] 14, Marie Joseph 30, Julien 5, Pascaline 5, Delores 3, Eduard 3, Isaac 3, Cherie 7, and Josephine two months old; all seventeen individuals were all introduced into the territory by Victoire Desriveaux, Mulatresse Libre, a passenger on the ship 'Two Brothers' arriving from the island of Cuba in August of 1809 and that the seventeen individuals were declared at the time by Victoire Desriveaux as her slaves for which she consequently furnished security to the territorial government."

41. *Vincent v. Laroche*, case no. 2934, October 17, 1811.

42. Most of the cases were tried by the judge without the aid of a jury. Hazaca was unusual in this sense.

43. *Poiney v. Durand*, case no. 2178, April 17, 1810.

44. *Floté v. Aubert*, case no. 2130, March 26, 1810; *Aubert v. Martineau*, case no. 2157, April 5, 1810.

45. *St. Amant and Cuvillier v. Burel*, case no. 2030, April 17, 1811. Walter Johnson has a brilliant analysis of slave agency in slave sale transactions in his book *Soul by Soul: Life inside the Antebellum Slave Market* (Cambridge, MA: Harvard University Press, 1999).

46. The "race" is known for forty-two of the slaves. There were thirty-nine Negroes, one griffe (a person who is one-fourth European and three-fourths of African descent), and one mulatto.

47. Dubois, *Avengers of the New World*, 5–6. See also John D. Garrigus, *Before Haiti: Race and Citizenship in French St. Domingue* (New York: Palgrave Macmillan,

2006); and Stewart King, *Blue Coat or Powdered Wig: Free People of Color in Pre-revolutionary St. Domingue* (Athens: University of Georgia Press, 2001).

48. Sue Peabody argues that *nègre* had become synonymous with "slave" by the mid-eighteenth century, if not earlier. See *"There Are No Slaves in France": The Political Culture of Race and Slavery in the Ancien Regime* (New York: Oxford University Press, 1996). In the view of the early American courts in New Orleans, however, *gen de couleur* was *not* synonymous with *nègre* and thus *not* synonymous with "slave."

NOTES TO CHAPTER 6

1. *Auger v. Beaurocher,* case no. 1846, September 16, 1809.

2. Preponderance of the evidence is defined as "the greater weight of the evidence: superior evidentiary weight that, though not sufficient to free the mind wholly from all reasonable doubt, is still sufficient to incline a fair and impartial mind to one side of the issue rather than the other." Brian A. Garner, ed., *Black's Law Dictionary,* 7th ed. (St. Paul, MN: West, 1999).

3. Inhabitants of early New Orleans used the terms "Negro" and "African" to refer to persons perceived to be entirely of African descent; they used the terms "mulatto" and "person of color" to refer to persons perceived to be of mixed African and European descent. "Quadroon" and "octoroon" were also used to describe someone who was of one-quarter or one-eighth African descent, respectively.

4. *Auger v. Beaurocher* and *Adele v. Beauregard,* 1 Mart. (o.s.) 183 (La. 1811) are the same case. The former is the caption recorded on the original records of the trial court, while the latter is the caption shown in the published Superior Court opinion. While impossible to know for sure, it is likely that the person recording the case in Martin's Reports mistakenly replaced the name Beaurocher with Beauregard.

5. John Parrish, *Remarks on the Slavery of Black People* (Philadelphia: Kimber and Conrad, 1806), 9.

6. Ulrich Bonn Phillips, *American Negro Slavery: A Survey of the Supply, Employment, and Control of Negro Labor, as Determined by the Plantation Regime* (1918; Baton Rouge: Louisiana State University Press, 1960), 443.

7. Two online databases contain the records of well over a thousand freedom suits in the antebellum South: the St. Louis Circuit Court Historical Records Project compiled at Washington University in St. Louis, and the Race and Slavery Petitions Project compiled at the University of North Carolina at Greensboro. Not all of these cases arose from allegations of kidnapping, but the majority of them did. Moreover, these databases are far from an exhaustive compilation of freedom suits. In the end, it is impossible to know with any certainty how many free blacks were kidnapped into slavery in the American South, but given the unequal power relationships, it is likely that the number of kidnapped free blacks far exceeded the number of slaves who escaped to freedom via the Underground Railroad.

8. Carol Wilson, *Freedom at Risk: The Kidnapping of Free Blacks in America, 1780–1865* (Lexington: University of Kentucky Press, 1994), 10.

9. *Chalon v. Drouin*, case no. 1793, August 3, 1809; *Lewis v. Perry*, case no. 1775, August 8, 1809.

10. Born free in Essex County, New York, in 1808, Northrup was tricked into traveling to Washington, DC, in 1841, where he was drugged, kidnapped, and sold to a slave trader. He was then shipped to New Orleans, where he was sold, again, to a Louisiana sugar planter. See David Fiske, Clifford W. Brown, and Rachel Seligman, *Solomon Northup: The Complete Story of the Author of Twelve Years a Slave* (Santa Barbara, CA: Praeger, 2013).

11. As Walter Johnson has masterfully shown in *Soul by Soul: Life inside the Antebellum Slave Market* (Cambridge, MA: Harvard University Press, 1999), the slave market represented the most horrifying aspects of antebellum slavery, the commodification of human beings. Johnson based his study on research of the slave markets in New Orleans for a reason.

12. See Wilson, *Freedom at Risk*, 11–12.

13. *Langlois v. Labatut*, case no. 2313, July 17, 1810; *Hervey des Romain v. Rodriquez*, case no. 1893, October 9, 1809.

14. *Lewis v. Perry*, case no. 1775, August 8, 1809; *Thereze v. Munier*, case no. 3537, February 8, 1813; *Caroline, by Jesse v. David*, case no. 3483, December 1, 1812; *Bovais v. McCarty*, case no. 3474, August 29, 1812; *Jones v. Kohn*, case no. 2224, May 22, 1810.

15. Wilson, *Freedom at Risk*, 9.

16. *Prigg v. Pennsylvania*, 41 U.S. 539 (1842).

17. Wilson, *Freedom at Risk*, 59–63; *Oxendine v. McFarland*, case no. 2992, January 9, 1812.

18. See Wilson, *Freedom at Risk*, 62–63. According to Thomas Buchanan in *Black Life on the Mississippi*, "In Louisiana in 1841, for example, the state legislature required that all free black rivermen and sailors be jailed when they came into New Orleans. In 1852, the law was amended so that out-of-state free blacks no longer had to be jailed but instead were required to obtain passes from the mayor's office when they were in port. In 1859, the old law was brought back" (24).

19. Wilson, *Freedom at Risk*, 31.

20. Ibid., 67–68; Judith Schafer, *Becoming Free, Remaining Free: Manumission and Enslavement in New Orleans, 1846–1862* (Baton Rouge: Louisiana State University Press, 2003), 116.

21. See Wilson, *Freedom at Risk*, 84–89.

22. This quotation is from a letter of May 26, 1826, from the attorney general of Mississippi, Richard Stockton, to Mayor Joseph Watson of Philadelphia. It can be found in the *African Observer*, May 1817, 41–42.

23. Wilson, *Freedom at Risk*, 25–30.

24. Garner, *Black's Law Dictionary*.

25. While it may be impossible to know how many free blacks were kidnapped during the antebellum period, historians have begun to get a sense of how many blacks initiated lawsuits for their freedom. The St. Louis Circuit Court database contains 301 freedom suits. The UNC Greensboro database includes 989 cases (even though it says 1,089), but 58 of these are petitions to the legislature, leaving 931 freedom suits. The breakdown according to jurisdictions is as follows: Alabama, 6; Arkansas, 2; Delaware, 188; DC, 59; Florida, 4; Georgia, 5; Kentucky, 111; Louisiana, 126; Maryland, 124; Mississippi, 3; Missouri, 212; North Carolina, 13; South Carolina, 1; Tennessee, 36; Texas, 1; Virginia, 40. All statistical analyses of freedom suits in this section are based on numbers from the UNC Greensboro database.

26. David Thomas Konig, "The Long Road to *Dred Scott*: Personhood and the Rule of Law in the Trial Court Records of St. Louis Slave Freedom Suits," *UMKC Law Review* 75 (2006): 53.

27. *Civil Digest of 1808*, bk. 1, tit. 6, ch. 3, art. 18.

28. In her study of freedom suits in Brazil, Keila Grinberg divides them into seven categories. See Keila Grinberg, "Manumission, Gender and the Law in Nineteenth-Century Brazil: Liberata's Legal Suit for Freedom" (paper presented at the Conference on Manumission in the Atlantic World, College of Charleston, South Carolina, October 4–7, 2000). However, the different legal systems of Brazil and Louisiana as well as the different purposes of her study and this one call for different categorizations.

29. See John C. Hurd, *The Law of Freedom and Bondage in the United States* (Ithaca, NY: Cornell University Press, 2009).

30. See *Marie v. Martel, Curator of the Succession of Algue*, case no. 1983, December 1809.

31. In her study of race and slavery in France under the ancien régime, Sue Peabody defines the "freedom principle" as "the notion that any slave who sets foot on French soil becomes free." See Sue Peabody, *There Are No Slaves in France: The Political Culture of Race and Slavery in the Ancien Régime* (New York: Oxford University Press, 1996), 3. England also adhered to the freedom principle. In the 1772 English case of *Somerset v. Stewart*, 98 Eng. Rep. 499–510, the King's Bench opined that slavery was contrary to natural law and could only exist through positive law. The court ruled that a black man and former slave in Jamaica named Somerset had gained his freedom by virtue of the time he spent on English soil, where slavery was not recognized. The Somerset principle set the precedent for hundreds of freedom suits brought by slaves in America throughout the antebellum period on the basis that their master had voluntarily taken them to states or territories where slavery was not permitted.

32. The infamous *Dred Scott* case was a freedom suit based on the freedom principle and invoking comity. It is noteworthy for, among other things, the

breakdown of comity between slave states and free states. See Paul Finkelman, *An Imperfect Union: Slavery, Federalism, and Comity* (Chapel Hill: University of North Carolina Press, 1981).

33. Sue Peabody, "'Free upon Higher Ground': Saint-Domingue Slaves' Suits for Freedom in U.S. Courts, 1792–1830," in David Patrick Geggus and Norman Fiering, eds., *The World of the Haitian Revolution* (Bloomington: University of Indiana Press, 2009), 265.

34. *Auger v. Beaurocher,* case no. 1846, September 16, 1809; *Jones v. Kohn,* case no. 2224, May 22, 1810.

35. Wilson, *Freedom at Risk,* 19.

36. Schafer, *Becoming Free, Remaining Free.*

37. See John C. Hurd, *The Law of Freedom and Bondage in the United States,* vol. 1 (Ithaca, NY: Cornell University Press, 2009).

38. These calculations are based on the Digital Library of American Slavery Database, compiled at the University of North Carolina at Greensboro. The New Orleans City Court heard just a small fraction of all freedom suits in New Orleans courts. See note 25 for all the numbers.

39. *Lafite v. Dufour,* case no. 3019, March 9, 1812. See also *Marie v. Martel, Curator of the Succession of Algue,* case no. 1983, December 1809.

40. The allegations in the petition are ambiguous. On the surface it appears as if she was purchasing herself out of slavery with this payment. However, as Rebecca Scott argues in *Paper Thin,* general emancipation in St. Domingue came with a condition that some former domestic slaves were to remain and provide "essential" services to their former master, such as caring for children or the elderly. According to Scott, "When Adelaide offered money to Charles Metayer in 1801, she was thus technically buying her way out of a labor obligation, not out of legal bondage." See Scott, *Paper Thin,* 1076–77.

41. Bk. 1, prelim., tit., ch. 4, art. 10 of the *Civil Digest of 1808* explicitly stated that when ruling on contract issues, the Louisiana courts were to apply the law of the place where the contract was executed.

42. This was done in the case *Metayer v. Noret,* case no. 2093, May 28, 1810. For a full discussion of all the cases involving Metayer and Noret, see Rebecca J. Scott, "'She . . . Refuses to Deliver Up Herself as the Slave of Your Petitioner': Émigrés, Enslavement, and the 1808 Louisiana Digest of the Civil Laws," *Tulane European and Civil Law Forum* 24 (2009): 115–36; and Scott, "Paper Thin: Freedom and Re-enslavement in the Diaspora of the Haitian Revolution," *Law and History Review* 29 (2011): 1061–87. *Metayer v. Noret* is also one of the cases analyzed by Peabody in "'Free upon Higher Ground.'"

43. *Marie Françoise v. Borie,* June 12, 1845, Fourth Judicial District Court, Iberville Parish, Louisiana. For a detailed discussion of Adelaide Durand's many court battles for her freedom, see Scott, "Paper Thin."

44. *Zephir v. Preval,* April 5, 1819, New Orleans Parish Court.

45. *Jean Baptiste v. Delaronde and Castillon,* case no. 2967, December 16, 1811; *Bouligny v. Arnould,* June 19, 1807.

46. The two cases for which there is no judgment are *Marie v. Martel,* case no. 1983, December 1809; and *Metyayer v. Noret,* case no. 2093, May 1810.

47. At common law, any individual who was unable to look after his or her own interests or manage his or her lawsuit, including minors, the mentally disabled, or the infirm, required a "next friend." In the early nineteenth century, a next friend represented a plaintiff, whereas a guardian ad litem represented a defendant, but this distinction has been removed in modern common law. A next friend is not a party to a lawsuit but an officer of the court. When the lawsuit is concluded, the next friend's duty ends. The next friend has no right to control the property of the person she or he represents or to assume custody of that person. These rights may be given to a person designated by a court as a minor's or incompetent person's guardian. See Garner, *Black's Law Dictionary.*

48. See City Court cases *Auger v. Beaurocher,* case no. 1846, September 16, 1809; *Thereze v. Munier,* case no. 3537, February 8, 1813; and *Caroline, by Jesse v. David,* case no. 3483, December 1, 1812.

49. *Augustin and Others v. the Estate of Marie Françoise de Magnan,* case no. 407, 1807. In this case, Augustin claimed his freedom by virtue of the will of Marie de Magnan. Lafontaine was a creditor of de Magnan's estate. He filed a successful action against Augustin in which he treated Augustin as a piece of property of which he was claiming ownership (this type of lawsuit in which the named defendant is effectively a piece of property is known as an action *in rem*). On appeal, the Supreme Court reversed on a procedural error, ruling that Lafontaine should have named the estate as the defendant, won a money judgment, and then satisfied the judgment by attaching the slave property of the estate.

50. "Pro bono" is a legal term meaning that the client is not expected to pay for legal representation and services. To be clear, there is no conclusive evidence that the lawyers did not take the cases pro bono.

51. *Lewis v. Perry,* case no. 1775, August 8, 1809; *Oxendine v. McFarland,* case no. 2992, January 9, 1812; *Jones v. Kohn,* case no. 2224, May 22, 1810.

52. He also offered the affidavit of Robert Randolph, who testified "that he knew in Pennsylvania William Jones, a black man, [to be] a free man [who] was hiring himself out and receiving his own wages." Finally, the statements of William Moore and Abraham Seldis verified that Jones was a free man in Orange County (formerly Crawford County), Pennsylvania. Kohn filed a general denial and submitted the affidavit of a Major Wellington, a resident New Orleans whose statement did not provide much support for the defendant's allegations that Jones was a slave. Wellington alleged only that Kohn had purchased a Negro named Bill, around twenty-two years old, from him in Maryland for $600.

53. Harry Oxendine's third-party support came indirectly. His mother had been freed in a Claiborne County, Mississippi, freedom suit. Charity Oxendine's

claims that she was free fell on deaf ears until Thomas and Anna Ard arrived there from North Carolina and recognized her. The Ards helped Charity escape Ingles's custody and hired a lawyer named William Bridges to sue for Charity's freedom. At trial, the Ards testified that Charity was born a free person in Bladen County North Carolina, that her mother, a free woman of color named June Oxendine, had resided at the house of Anna Ard's father, and that Charity's father had also been free. This Claiborne County testimony was made part of the record in Harry Oxendine's case.

54. *Langlois v. Labatut,* case no. 2313, July 1810.

55. *Chalon v. Drouin,* case no. 1793, August 3, 1809. Chalon was a woman of perceived mixed ancestry. But her case was decided before the Louisiana Supreme Court's opinion in *Adele,* so she did not receive the benefit of the precedent set in that opinion—that people of color were presumed to be free.

56. A general denial is an answer that "puts in issue all the material assertions of a complaint or a petition." Garner, *Black's Law Dictionary.* The general denial is the most common answer to any petition. By denying all the allegations, the defendant then forces the petitioner to meet his or her burden of proving them.

57. *Caroline, by Jesse v. David,* case no. 3483, December 1, 1812.

58. Barutteaut was a doctor in Cap Français, St. Domingue, and an officer in the city's militia. He died in 1793 during the sack of Le Cap. In 1793, Saloman left St. Domingue for Philadelphia, where she lived until coming to New Orleans in the summer of 1809. When she learned that Berton was living in the city as a free person, she filed suit in her capacity as executor of the estate of Barutteaut asserting ownership rights to the black woman.

59. *Saloman v. Berton,* case no. 1878, September 30, 1809. "Adverse possession" and "prescription" are legal terms that describe the acquirement of the title or right to something through its continued use or possession over a long period of time.

60. The end result for the people of color whose status was in question in both freedom suits and enslavement suits, therefore, was that sixteen people won their freedom and six people were ordered into slavery; the status of two others remained in limbo.

61. Due to his ties to Louverture's revolutionary government, many suspected Moreau-Lislet of radicalism. To be sure, the two men seemed to share a mutual respect. In November 1800, while in Port Republicain, Moreau-Lislet successfully petitioned Louverture for the return of properties he owned that had been sequestered. The *New York Herald* of August 18, 1809, picking up on a story of the *Baltimore Federal Republican,* claimed that Moreau-Lislet had been a secretary of Toussaint Louverture and "venerable" of a lodge the majority of whose members were men of color, though neither paper provided any proof for these assertions other than the unsupported claims of Louis Bonier de Clouet, an officer in the Spanish army and opponent of republican government. Alain A. Levasseur, *Louis Casimer Elizabeth Moreau-Lislet, Foster Father of Louisiana*

Civil Law (Baton Rouge: Louisiana State University, Law Center Publications Institute, 1996), 84, 104–5, 147; Gabriel Debien and René LeGardeur, "Les Colons de Saint-Domingue réfugiés à la Louisiane (1792–1804)," *Louisiana Review* 10 (1981): 98.

62. *Langlois v. Labatut.* The judgments (as well as the jury verdicts) in wrongful enslavement suits reflect a conservative approach. Hervey des Romain and William Jones, for example, asked the court for $1,000 and $2,000 in damages, respectively. But the court never granted monetary damages despite the prayer of most petitioners for such relief. At the most, judges required the defendant to pay costs of court. Furthermore, the language of the judgments did not claim to be "granting" freedom; rather, they "restored" the petitioners to their "former state of freedom."

63. Moreau-Lislet left the City Court in early 1813 to become a member of the Louisiana House of Representatives; he was replaced by Judge James Pitot, who presided over the only unsuccessful freedom suit, *Caroline, by Jesse v. David,* case no. 3483, December 1, 1812.

64. This is not to suggest that Moreau-Lislet was always friendly to freedom. As Rebecca Scott has demonstrated in "'She . . . Refuses to Deliver Up Herself as a Slave,'" the judge was emphatically unfriendly to the freedom of Durand. Indeed, after he left the City Court bench, he represented Durand's would-be slaveholder, Louis Noret, in a lawsuit in a different court.

65. *Fowler v. George,* case no. 1660, June 1809. Theodoseus Fowler's slave George could be better described as an indentured servant. Before George ran away to New Orleans, he had lived in New York, a state where slavery was being gradually phased out. In 1800, New York passed a law that all persons born of slave mothers after that date would acquire their freedom in fifteen years. Having been born in 1789, George did not directly benefit from this statute, but he did gain a little relief from the spirit of the times in the Empire State. In 1796, when George was seven years old, his then owner Stephen Steel sold him to Fowler under the condition that George was to become free in January 1815. George was not willing to wait this long, however, and in October 1806 he fled his "limited term slavery" in the "free state" of New York to live as a "free man" in the slave society of New Orleans. He passed as free for four years until he was seized by judicial order and returned to Fowler in November 1810.

66. *Saloman v. Berton,* case no. 1878, September 30, 1809.

67. *Bayle v. Fanny,* case no. 2472, February 2, 1811; *Fowler v. George,* case no. 1660, June 1809. There is some evidence that Lislet applied the *Adele* presumption of freedom for people of color in *Bayle v Fanny.* Fanny was described as a mulatto girl and had provided no proof of her freedom other than her own testimony. Since the plaintiff typically has the burden of proof, however, the *Adele* rule need never have been invoked in enslavement suits.

68. Scott, "Paper Thin," 1082.

69. See, for example, *Lewis v. Perry,* case no. 1775, August 8, 1809; *Chalon v. Drouin,* case no. 1793, August 3, 1809; and *Hervey des Romain v. Rodriquez,* case no. 1893, October 9, 1809.

70. "It must be assumed," Dwight Dumond has argued, "that anti-slavery societies or individuals initiated, provided the legal counsel for, and financed all cases involving the freedom of negroes." See Dwight Dumond, *Antislavery: The Crusade for Freedom in America* (Ann Arbor: University of Michigan Press, 1961). While this may have been true in the majority of freedom suits in the United States, it was decidedly not true in cases in the New Orleans City Court.

71. *Saloman v. Berton,* case no. 1878, September 30, 1809; *Caroline, by Jesse v. David,* case no. 3483, December 1, 1812.

72. *Pollock v. Canelle,* case no. 805, 1807; *Metayer v. Noret,* case no. 2093, May 28, 1810; *Metayer v.. Cenas,* case no. 2241, June 5, 1810; *Oxendine v. McFarland,* case no. 2992, January 9, 1812; *Marie Louise v. Saignal and Delinau,* case no. 2087, March 14, 1810; *Marie Louise v. Melanie,* case no. 972. Adelaide Durand filed the lawsuits to prevent the sale of herself and her children. Another court, believing that Durand was the slave of Charles Metayer's brother, Louis, ordered the sheriff of the parish to seize Durand and her children and auction them off to satisfy a judgment a Mr. Noret had obtained against Louis.

73. "An Act to Enable Persons Held in Slavery to Sue for Their Freedom," *Laws of the Territory of Louisiana, Chapter 35* (1807) Missouri State Archives. The decision in *Adele v. Beauregard* complicates the depiction in the scholarship that the law in slave states presumed all people of African descent to be slaves. See Finkelman, *Imperfect Union,* the introduction of which states that "the legal systems of the slave and free states diverged quite sharply on questions involving the status of Negroes. Most obviously, the South allowed slavery and *presumed that all blacks were slaves;* the North did not allow slavery and presumed that all people were free."

74. The Supreme Court of Louisiana held that a slave in Hispaniola at the time the general emancipation was declared there may reckon the period he enjoyed his liberty under that proclamation as part of the time of prescription.

75. *Langlois v. Labatut,* case no. 2313, July 17, 1810; *Delphine v. Deveze,* 2 Mart. (n.s.) 650 (1824).

76. Ironically, the rules regarding burden of proof in the Louisiana Territory, a common law jurisdiction, were set forth in a statute enacted by the territorial legislature.

77. "Beyond a reasonable doubt" is defined as the absence of any "doubt that prevents one from being firmly convinced of a defendant's guilt, or the belief that there is a real possibility that a defendant is not guilty." Garner, *Black's Law Dictionary.*

78. Scott, "Paper Thin," 1076 n. 38.

79. For a discussion of *calidad,* see Robert McCaa, "*Calidad, Clase,* and Marriage in Colonial Mexico: The Case of Parral, 1788–90," *Hispanic American Historical Review* 64 (1984): 477–502.

80. See chapter 4 for a discussion of the marriage laws and chapter 1 for a discussion of the recording of the immigration.

81. See Howard Bodenhorn, "The Mulatto Advantage: The Biological Consequences of Complexion in Rural Antebellum Virginia," *Journal in Interdisciplinary History* 33 (2002): 21–46, in which it is argued that lighter-skinned blacks were privileged in the Upper South, not just the Lower South as is commonly thought.

82. *State v. Cecil,* 2 Mart. (o.s.) 208 (La. 1812); *Hawkins v. Vanwickle,* 6 Mart. (n.s.) 418, La. 1828. "Dicta" is a legal term that refers to a part of the court's opinion that is not binding as precedent because it is not essential to the outcome of the case. In the *Adele* case, for example, the Superior Court's statement that a "negro" would "perhaps" be presumed to be a slave was not binding (and, therefore, not precedent) because it did not apply to the facts of the case at hand.

83. *Miller v. Belmonti,* 11 Rob. (La.) 339, no. 5623 (1845): 341–42. For a book-length discussion of this case, see John Bailly, *The Lost German Slave Girl: The Extraordinary True Story of Sally Miller and Her Fight for Freedom in Old New Orleans* (Sydney: Grove Press, 2003).

84. *State v. Harrison,* 11 La. Ann. 722 (1856). Of course the excepted rights are very significant.

85. These rights included the ability to bring civil actions against whites, equal protection of property rights, and full rights to make contracts and engage in all business transactions. See Laura Foner, "The Free People of Color in Louisiana and St. Domingue: A Comparative Portrait of Two Three-Caste Slave Societies," *Journal of Social History* 3 (1970): 406–30.

NOTES TO THE EPILOGUE

1. "Octoroon" was the term used to identify someone with one-eighth African ancestry and seven-eighths European ancestry. Although Plessy called himself an octoroon, both of his parents were so-called quadroons (one-fourth African ancestry), which would mean that he was also a quadroon.

2. The official name of the organization was the Citizens' Committee to Test the Constitutionality of the Separate Car Law.

3. *Plessy v. Ferguson,* 163 U.S. 537 (1896).

4. SLC Baptisms 34, p. 122; St. John the Baptist Church Baptisms, bk. 5, p. 130. Greg Osborn, at the New Orleans Public Library, has provided invaluable assistance in researching Homer Plessy's ancestry.

5. While some accounts say that Germain Plessy also spent some time in St. Domingue, there are no extant primary sources supporting this claim. In fact, Germain Plessy would have been fourteen at the time of the slave revolt on the northern plains of St. Domingue. It is unlikely that he would have immigrated to St. Domingue during the Haitian Revolution, and it is not likely that he would have migrated there as a young teenager or preteen.

6. New Orleans city directories of 1805, 1822, 1851; New Orleans Death Records, vol. 23, p. 552; U.S. census, 1860, www.census.gov.

7. U.S. census, 1860; marriage records for the Archdiocese of Orleans, St. Louis Cathedral.

8. The numbers of free people of color in New Orleans were growing in absolute terms but decreasing as a proportion of the city's total population.

9. For an excellent discussion of the legislative attempts to limit the growth and restrict the rights of Louisiana's free colored population, see Judith Schafer, *Becoming Free, Remaining Free: Manumission and Enslavement in New Orleans, 1846–1862* (Baton Rouge: Louisiana State University Press, 2003).

10. The quotation comes from Caryn Cosse Bell, *Revolution, Romanticism and the Afro-Creole Protest Tradition in Louisiana, 1718–1868* (Baton Rouge: Louisiana State University Press, 1997), 1. This book is one of the best available regarding the efforts of the *gens de couleur* to remake Louisiana in the wake of the Civil War.

ABOUT THE AUTHOR

Kenneth R. Aslakson is Associate Professor of History at Union College, Schenectady, New York. He grew up in Lake Jackson, Texas, named after the antebellum sugar plantation of Abner Jackson. He attended college at Southwestern University in Georgetown, Texas. He received both his law degree and his PhD in history at the University of Texas at Austin. In between the two, he practiced law for almost six years in Dallas, Texas.